CLASSIC HURLING MATCHES
1976–91

D0552248

CLASSIC HURLING MATCHES 1976–91

NORMAN FREEMAN

Gill & Macmillan

Published in Ireland by
Gill & Macmillan Ltd
Goldenbridge
Dublin 8
with associated companies throughout the world
© Norman Freeman 1993
0 7171 2142 9
Index compiled by Helen Litton
Print origination by
Seton Music Graphics Ltd, Bantry, Co. Cork
Printed by
ColourBooks Ltd, Dublin

A catalogue record is available for this book from the British Library.

1 3 5 4 2

To my wife Bernie,
for all her help and support

CONTENTS

ACKNOWLEDGMENTS

One of the great pleasures of writing these books has lain in meeting and talking to some of the men who played in these great games of hurling. They gave me the benefit of their time, their recollections, their insights into particular games and into hurling. The hurling community sees it not just as a sport but as an expression of skill, courage and endurance, something that strikes joyfully resounding chords deep within the human personality.

My thanks to those great exponents of the game. Invariably they were generous to their former opponents and modest about their own attributes — the characteristic of true sportsmen. They include John Henderson and Eddie Keher of Kilkenny and Diarmuid Healy who straddles both Kilkenny and Offaly; Damien Martin of Offaly; Jimmy Barry Murphy, Gerald McCarthy and Willie John Daly of Cork; Donie Nealon, Michael Keating and Nicholas English of Tipperary; Jimmy Gray and Larry Shannon of Dublin; Seumas Power of Waterford; Jimmy Smyth of Clare; Eamonn Cregan of Limerick; Ciaran Barr of Antrim; Joe McDonagh and Peter Finnerty of Galway; and Ned Wheeler, Billy Rackard, Ned Buggy and Phil Wilson of Wexford.

With so much detail in terms of names and events to be included and checked for accuracy, I was fortunate to get the help of Tom Ryall of Kilkenny, Tommy Barrett of Tipperary, Gerry Holohan of Cork, Seamus Grant and his colleagues in Waterford, Brendan Furlong of Wexford, John Murphy of Limerick and Michael Connolly of Offaly. Some fine journalists gave me sound advice and assistance and these included Seamus Hayes of the *Clare Champion*, Cormac Liddy of the *Limerick Leader*, Michael Dundon of the *Tipperary Star*, John Knox of Kilkenny and Sean Og O Ceallachain of RTE.

I owe a special word of thanks to the doyen of hurling writers, Paddy Downey of the *Irish Times*, for the benefit of his advice in identifying some of the outstanding games described in these volumes.

The fountainhead of hurling writing is Raymond Smith and during the course of work I turned to his many fine books about hurling, particularly the painstaking record book compiled by himself and Donal Keenan of the *Irish Independent*.

There were other people who gave me help and encouragement and these include Pat Quigley, former PRO at Croke Park and his successor Danny Lynch as well as Fionnbarr Breathnach of Cork and Dalkey and, not least, my colleague Pat Heneghan.

I want to thank Fergal Tobin of Gill & Macmillan for his guidance and support and his able assistants, Jillian Tynan and her successor, Clare Connolly, who did so much research work for these books. A special word of thanks has to go to Jonathan Williams, literary agent exemplaire, for his role in the commissioning and publication of these volumes.

Jim Connolly, the official GAA photographer, provided many of the photos for these books and was very helpful generally.

I willingly share any credit these books may engender with those mentioned above. At the same time I must take full responsibility for the content and the details.

My attitude to the players mentioned in these books is essentially one of gratitude for the great entertainment they gave to hurling lovers. They, and the great games of which they were part, provided marvellous material for a writer. I hope I have done them justice.

Cover Photograph

Munster hurling final 1987, Tipperary v Cork.

1976

Cork v. Wexford — **All-Ireland Final**

CLIMAX TO A GREAT HURLING YEAR

It was a memorable year for hurling. There had been a succession of thrilling, extraordinary games. Undoubtedly the crowning glory of that year was the final between Cork and Wexford. In its skill, speed, heroic endeavour and in its sportsmanship it evoked memories of the two great finals between these sides in the 1950s.

This game was so thrilling, so tense, so close, with fortunes changing and changing again as the game went on that it created a great glow of elation and pride in the 62,684 spectators who were lucky enough to be there that Sunday. When this enthralling encounter was over, the presentation speeches made and the teams gone to their dressing-rooms, people hung about Croke Park — out on the pitch itself, beneath the stands, in the forecourt outside — like a swarm of animated bees reluctant to disperse from a centre of sweet delight.

The last ten minutes of that game saw two fine sides reach deep down within themselves for the stamina and courage needed to get on top. It saw two of the best full forwards in the modern game, both captaining their sides, strive might and main to turn the game. It also saw astute tactics by the Cork mentors bear fruit. It revealed also how important it is to be able to keep going in those last, lung-pumping minutes on a warm, exhausting day in early September.

One of the most extraordinay sideshows of those hectic minutes was the sight of a bald, stocky man racing along the sideline as if to keep pace with a player on a solo run. This was the most famous and enigmatic hurling personality of the era, Christy Ring, who was now an influential figure in the Cork dugout.

Spectators that Sunday also saw, contesting its first All-Ireland, one of the best forward lines ever to play the game of hurling. These sharp-shooters were the spearhead of a Cork side that would win three All-Irelands in a row and give tremendous entertainment and delight to hurling followers everywhere. The attendance also saw a Wexford side that showed all that county's great battling heart. Wexford were the losers that day but they lost none of the respect and affection in which their hurlers were held since the early fifties.

Baulked by Kilkenny

This was the first Wexford team that had overcome the rampant Kilkenny side that had dominated Leinster and the All-Ireland scene for the previous five years. No matter how good Wexford were or how hard they tried they still could not overcome the Kilkenny of Keher, Delaney, Purcell, Henderson and the other great Noreside hurlers. They often came within an ace, a point, a minute of finally toppling their greatest rivals but were always on the losing side when the final whistle went.

Those years of defeat built up a head of steam and frustration within the county. They felt they could have won All-Irelands if it had not been that, year after year, they had to face the best team in the country in order to get out of Leinster and into the final.

At the start of the championship in 1976, Kilkenny were reigning All-Ireland champions. They had taken the crown two years in a row. And in the replayed final of the National League they had given one of their best displays of the decade when beating a fine Clare side by five goals.

Kilkenny Steamrolled

Once again, in the Leinster final against their arch-rivals Wexford, Kilkenny were hot favourites. They now seemed to have some strange power over the Slaneysiders. Even in Wexford people were saying that it would never be enough for their side to be better than Kilkenny — that they had to be much, much better if they had any chance of overcoming the astute sideline tacticians, the clever hurling, the sharpened skills of the Kilkenny side.

In the Leinster final of 1976 it was as if all the pent-up disappointment of successive defeats came boiling to the surface to give Wexford an astonishing power. They came out on the field of play loping about like famished, frustrated wolves. Even before the game began there was an urgency about them as they pucked the ball about with gritted teeth, gestured to one another with clenched fists, flexed their shoulder muscles.

Right from the throw-in Kilkenny were swept aside. Virtually the same side that had beaten Wexford year after year now succumbed to the power play of their rivals. All over the field they were out-run, out-manoeuvred, out-hurled. Only the brilliance of Noel Skehan in goal kept them in the game, with the half-time score of 1–11 to 1–5. Though playing with the breeze in the second half Kilkenny were, incredibly, able to add only one point to their total. The Wexford full forward and captain, Tony Doran, delivered the *coup de grace* only five minutes into the second half when he belted the ball into the net. The final score was 2–20 for Wexford against 1–6 for Kilkenny. After that game, which had sensationally overturned the form book, the men in purple and gold were mobbed for ten minutes by their delirious and grateful followers.

Upsurge of Spirit

There was a joyful upsurge of spirit in the county. They felt that at long last the perennial pretenders now had a real chance of regaining the All-Ireland title that they had last held in 1968. Hurling lovers in the county already began to make holiday arrangements to ensure they were free to attend the final in September. There was one very substantial stumbling block — a resurgent Galway team that had unexpectedly overcome Cork in the semi-final of the previous year and gone on to contest the final, unsuccessfully, against Kilkenny.

In Wexford they did not see Galway as a really serious threat. But in overcoming them they had to expend a great deal of energy and, of equal importance, fully reveal their strengths and weaknesses to the sharp-eyed Cork mentors.

The Cork Side

The Cork mentors that year included Christy Ring, now a mellowed personality, who was developing a respected and supportive rapport with the members of the Cork team. The side, well aware of its own potential, had been full of hope the previous year. It had been badly wounded by the semi-final defeat by Galway, a county that up to that year was regarded as one of the no-hopers of the championship.

'That Cork team had great heart. We were great battlers. We recovered from our beating by Galway and made up our minds that we were going to come out fighting in the championship', recalls Gerald McCarthy.

They needed all their combative qualities in the Munster semi-final against Tipperary. The intensity of the play bordered on the frightening. These counties with a long history of tribal rivalry would never give in to one another. The player who was seen to wilt in such searing encounters was taken off by the hard-faced men in the dug out; players were not meant to draw back from challenges even if they had a broken finger or loosened teeth.

There was nothing between the sides in this tough clash. It was the intro-duction of a tall, willowy forward that seemed to attract the ball to himself and be capable of scoring through a narrow slit, that helped turn the game Cork's way. This was Jimmy Barry Murphy's championship debut and he was to prove his worth at a crucial stage of the All-Ireland final.

There were other players that came to the fore in Cork's one-point win. Their goalkeeper, Martin Coleman, made two marvellous saves. Ray

Cummins, the lanky full forward, Charlie McCarthy, in the corner and Seanie O'Leary, the bulky opportunist from Youghal, had scored three fine goals. Yet Tipperary put up a great fight and Cork were regarded as some-what lucky to win.

However, Cork showed their quality in the manner that they demolished Limerick in the Munster final, which was played in the recently-built Pairc Ui Chaoimh.

Youth and Experience

'We were a mixture of young and experienced players', recalls Jimmy Barry Murphy. 'There were fellows like Gerald and Charlie McCarthy, that had been on the side since the All-Ireland win in 1966. Then there was Denis Coughlan, Ray Cummins and Pat McDonnell who had been playing since in '69 or '70. These fellows knew all about playing in and winning — and losing — All-Irelands. Then there were those like myself who had never been in a senior final before — Pat Moylan, Johnny Crowley among others. We blended together very well and there was a great camaraderie among us.'

One of the strengths of that side, Barry Murphy asserts, is that they had players who were good enough to turn a game, to have a major influence on the outcome.

'One of these players would have a great game one day and another have a great game the next day — there was always someone to carry the day for us', he says. The captain of the Cork team, Ray Cummins, had already won a football All-Ireland medal in 1973 as had Denis Coughlan, Brian Murphy and Jimmy Barry Murphy. The Cork side had a very good sideline team as well. The coach was Fr Bertie Troy and the mentors included Frank Murphy, Jimmy Brohan and Ring.

Galway-Wexford Saga

These men got a great opportunity to assess the team they were to meet in the final because the semi-final between Galway — the side that had beaten them the previous year — and the newly emergent Leinster champions, was played in Pairc Ui Chaoimh.

They and nearly all the players went along on a blazing hot Sunday of one of the warmest, sunniest summers on record, to watch the semi-final.

This game vibrated with excitement and thrills. There was great hurling and great endeavour as two evenly-matched sides fought it out. Some of the best players of the game were on view — John Connolly and Sean Silke of Galway, Mick Jacob and John Quigley of Wexford. This game was a semi-final on a par with the great game the year before when Galway met Cork. It ended, fittingly, in a draw.

The replay took place in the same venue a week later on another hot sunny day. Wexford went nine points in front after only thirteen minutes. It became part of the play pattern of that fine team that right from the throw-in they sought quick scores, especially goals from Tony Doran, to dishearten their opponents, put them under the pressure of seeing the game go away from them from early in the match. This Galway side, however, had no intention of being undermined by early scores. They fought their way back into the game. In that match they proved that they had the best half-back line in the country in Clarke, Silke and McDonagh. They hauled back Wexford's lead and had the match for the taking in the second half but they could not clinch it.

A matter of great anger and argument was the goal scored by John Quigley near the end of the game. As he came charging goalwards he was fouled. The referee had seemed to whistle for a free. Some of the Galway backs stopped in their tracks. But Quigley kept going and lashed the ball into the net. To the consternation of the Galway team and supporters the score was allowed.

Shrewd Mentors

The Cork mentors sat in a group in the stand, surveying the surges of play, the abilities of the players, watching the personal duels intently. They looked on with the wrinkled eyes of men who had learned about character, about skill, about stamina, about a player's capabilities, about players wilting under tension or tiredness. They leaned towards one another, heads nodding, speaking from the side of their mouths, making mental notes about the men their side would face in the final. Nobody was better than Ring to sum up a player, to devise strategies, to maximise strengths and minimise weaknesses.

This was one of the factors that helped counties like Cork, Kilkenny and Tipperary to keep on the top: they had men who could analyse the opposition. They knew how a player could be marked out of a game and knew who was the best player on their own side to fulfil such a task.

For all that, everybody in Cork was impressed by the spirited hurling of the Wexford side, the way they had battled so determinedly against the great challenge of equally resolute opponents. And there was a feeling that Wexford would have benefited greatly from these two thrilling games on the sun-baked ground of Pairc Ui Chaoimh.

Team Preparations

When the two teams went into training neither of them was made firm favourites to take the title, although many of the commentators felt that the delicate balance of power lay with the Slaneysiders.

Their last meeting in a final, in 1970, had seen a decisive victory for the Cork side. Due to illness and injury some of Wexford's star players were unable to play — Wilson, Buggy, Keogh, and Willie Murphy. In that game Pat McDonnell had got the better of Tony Doran. That had been a crucial duel and it was now to be renewed on the first Sunday in September in 1976.

Most of the players were not strange to one another. They had played a number of indifferent games in the league but several had met at All-Ireland level when Cork and Wexford contested the under-21 finals of '69, '70 and '71. On all occasions Cork had come out on top.

Both captains were at full forward. Ray Cummins was aiming to be the first player from Blackrock to lead a Cork team to victory since 1931 when Eudie Coughlan was captain. Coughlan and Jim O'Regan were now the only survivors of the Cork team that had won the All-Ireland in 1926 against Kilkenny. The two men were to be guests of the Cork county board at the final.

Tom Neville in Charge

As Wexford got down to training in Enniscorthy under the direction of Tom Neville, a familiar figure was missing from the scene for the first time in decades. Nick Rackard, the man who had inspired and led the county to hurling greatness had died of cancer in April of that year. The preparations for the All-Ireland evoked many memories of the big man. His photograph and even laudatory poems appeared in the local newspapers.

This Wexford side was expected to restore the county's pride by winning the senior final. It was not that hurling was not as strong as ever in the county but there was now a feeling that it was high time a title was won. Not since 1968, when both senior and minor titles were claimed, could the county cheer a winner. They needed the boost that comes from winning.

When the teams were announced and the media commentators began to examine the merits of both sides and to pinpoint what they saw as the pivotal areas on which the game might turn they highlighted the centre back positions.

Centre Backs

Wexford, after trying out Colm Doran for a while, now put Mick Jacob there. He was slighter than the normal centre back but he was a great catcher of the ball. He was a neat hurler and sent long clearances away.

Jacob's opponent would be Brendan Cummins, brother of the captain, who could be expected to keep the ball moving, to keep it out of the clutching hand of the Wexfordman. Cummins was well capable of doing that, as he had proved in the Munster and county championships.

Cork had not had a permanent centre back since Seamus Looney departed the scene but they now nominated a young player from Bishopstown, Johnny Crowley. He had the size and the power for a centre back but he would need to be on his mettle in the final where his opponent was one of the powerhouses of the Wexford side, Martin Quigley. Big and strong, Quigley had great thrust in his play and had performed well in the previous matches.

Full Forwards and Backs

There was a lot of attention on the two full forwards and the two full backs marking them. Without any doubt the two best full forwards in the game would be on display in the final.

Ray Cummins was 6 ft 3 ins tall and when he jumped for the ball coming high into the square and reached a long arm upwards he was able to catch them well above the heads and hurleys of opponents. He forced his opponent to stay behind him in case he turned and in two long-legged strides was on the goal-line to palm the ball to the net; this meant that he was free to race out and swivel to send points over the bar. Most of all however, Cummins was a team player who who flicked and scooped and hand-passed the ball to his colleagues, particularly O'Leary and Charlie McCarthy.

Cummins' marker would be the fair-haired Willie Murphy from the Faythe Harriers club. He had been an outstanding wing back who had frustrated the best forwards in the business, including Eddie Keher and Michael Keating. The question was whether his open, quick-striking style of play could contain his opponent.

At the other end of the field the battle would be between Pat McDonnell and Tony Doran. McDonnell had given great displays of full back play in the past, fast to the ball, confident in the way he struck the ball on the ground to get it well out of the danger area, covering and blocking with speed and alacrity. His prowess had earned him the Hurler of the Year accolade some years before.

Tony Doran's capacity to catch balls coming into the goalmouth and to score by the handpass or the hurley had been a key factor in Wexford winning their last All-Ireland in 1968. He had the strength, weight and determination to fight for and win the ball, especially those coming in high, because he could hold his ground and hold off his opponent until he had got possession of the ball. Then he was lethal with the hand-pass in front of goal. There was no fitter player on the field — he was out and about his farm from dawn to dusk and was in top physical condition.

There was one disadvantage. Wexford had come to rely on him a great deal and at every opportunity sent in the ball to him. Their forward play had become predictable and allowed the opposition to work out ways and means of effectively countering it.

Wexford Midfield

There was a question mark over the Wexford centrefield. The mentors had tried a variety of players and combinations there and had now taken Ned Buggy out of the half back line to partner Billy Rowsome. Both of these players were neat strikers of the ball and Buggy, especially, revelled in the open play at midfield. But they were both comparatively light men and many in Wexford felt that there was need of a strong, sturdy, hard-running, long striking centrefield man to match the kind of power likely to be generated by Gerald McCarthy. There was such a player but he was not included in the panel: Phil Wilson.

His omission from the Wexford side of 1976 was much discussed in the county. He was certainly in the veteran stage but he was one of the fittest hurlers playing the game and was outstanding for Raparees in the county championship games. There was some dark muttering that his dismissal by the referee in that torrid epic, the 1974 Leinster final against Kilkenny, was held against him by some of the selectors.

Injuries

Another talking point was the toe injury that was hampering the training of Christy Keogh, the 33-year-old veteran of the side. The big corner forward was expected to take some of the pressure off Doran when the ball came into the square.

This injury was not seen in the same light as the cartilage trouble in the left knee of the Cork left full forward, Sean O'Leary. He was a goal-poacher supreme, always lurking about the goal area, ready to pounce on a half chance. 'Don't make any mistakes when the tubby fellow is around', once warned a coach from a Munster county to the men in the full back line; backs who fumbled a ball were apt to find it whipped into the net by O'Leary.

He was going to be marked by a small, tenacious player, a terrier who would snap at his heels, give him little freedom — Teddie O'Connor. This hard tackling player from Rathnure had marked Eddie Keher well when the sides had met in recent games and he could be relied upon to concentrate on O'Leary all the time. O'Connor himself was recovering from an injury but was passed fit a few days before the game.

Jimmy Prendergast of Wexford was also recovering from injury. He was the man who had the job of marking Charlie McCarthy, Cork's quick striking predator on the other side of Ray Cummins. The Oulart player had been carrying an injured knee for some time but it had responded well to treatment. He would need to be fully mobile to keep up with his small but lightning-fast opponent, so adept at pulling with the incoming ball.

Some of the hardest body contact and toughest play was going to be between two uncompromising players: Mick Malone of Cork and his marker Colm Doran. The bearded Malone played a swashbuckling game, running hard all over the forward line in search of the ball, collecting it and tearing in goalwards, all the time challenging the backs in his vicinity. His marker, Doran, from the Buffer's Alley club, revelled in the bodily clashes, never drawing back from flailing hurleys and charging shoulders. He was fast and nimble footed and would be able to keep pace with his opponent.

'When you are trying to predict how a game will go, who the key players may be, the likely outcome of the important duels, it is dead easy to forget that there are thirty players on the field. Some may be quiet, low-profile fellows but they all have a job to do and many do it in an unobtrusive way', says Jimmy Barry Murphy, who was to see little of the ball for most of that game. 'And very often the star of the match may be some fellow whose name is not mentioned at all in the media summing up.'

Unlike their last meeting, in 1970, these two teams were training for a seventy-minute final. The eighty minute experiment had been found to be most unsuitable for one of the fastest, most demanding field games in the world.

'It is not just that players became so physically exhausted. It is the mental exhaustion as well', says Donie Nealon of Tipperary, who has had a long career as team trainer and mentor. 'All the good players are good because they read the game right from the puck in, watch the ball intently even when it is furthest away from them, watch how their own fellows are shaping up, watch how their near opponents are playing. You have to concentrate, see the pattern of play, estimate how the ball is going to break, see the changes that come about in a game, how the momentum is gained and lost. There is a huge mental as well as physical effort if you are going to play to your best. And to do that for eighty minutes in a game as fast as hurling was to ask too much from amateur players', he says.

Sunday 5 September 1976 was a warm sunny day. In the stands and terraces there seemed an equal amount of support for the teams.

The teams as they lined out were:

CORK

Martin Coleman
(Ballinhassig)

| Brian Murphy | Pat McDonnell | Martin O'Doherty |
| (Nemo Rangers) | (Inniscarra) | (Glen Rovers) |

| Pat Barry | Johnny Crowley | Denis Coughlan |
| (Glen Rovers) | (Bishopstown) | (Glen Rovers) |

| Gerald McCarthy | | Pat Moylan |
| (St Finbarr's) | | (Blackrock) |

| Mick Malone | Brendan Cummins | Jimmy Barry Murphy |
| (Eire Og) | (Blackrock) | (St Finbarr's) |

| Charlie McCarthy | Ray Cummins, capt | Sean O'Leary |
| (St Finbarr's) | (Blackrock) | (Youghal) |

Substitutes: Eamon O'Donoghue (Blackrock); John Horgan (Blackrock); Bertie Og Murphy (Sarsfields); Michael O'Connor (Erin's Own); John Allen (Ahabullogue). *Coach*: Fr Bertie Troy (Newtownshandrum). *Trainer*: Kevin Kehily (Newcestown). *Selectors*: Denis Murphy (St Finbarr's); Christy Ring (Glen Rovers); Jimmy Brohan (Blackrock); Frank Murphy, county secretary; Denis Hurley (Sarsfields). *Team doctor*: Dr Con Murphy (UCC). *Masseur*: John 'Kid' Cronin (Glen Rovers).

WEXFORD

John Nolan
(Geraldine O'Hanrahans)

Teddie O'Connor	Willie Murphy	Jim Prendergast
(Rathnure)	(Faythe Harriers)	(Oulart)

Liam Bennett	Mick Jacob	Colm Doran
(Faythe Harriers)	(Oulart)	(Buffer's Alley)

Ned Buggy   Billy Rowsome
(Faythe Harriers)   (Monageer)

Johnny Murphy	Martin Quigley	John Quigley
(Ballymurn)	(Rathnure)	(Rathnure)

Mick Butler	Tony Doran, capt	Christy Keogh
(Buffer's Alley)	(Buffer's Alley)	(Raparees)

Substitutes: Declan Rowsome (Monageer); Martin Casey, Henry Butler, Paddy Kavanagh (Buffer's Alley); Tom Byrne (Oulart); Tom Walsh (Cloughbawn); Andy Doyle (Ramsgrange); Martin Furlong (Cloughbawn); John Conran (Rathnure). *Coach*: Tom Neville. *Trainer*: Ned Power. *Selectors/mentors*: Syl Barron (Rathnure); Pat Murphy (Faythe Harriers); Mick Hanlon (Horeswood); Pat Nolan (Oylegate). *Masseur*: John O'Brien. *Team doctor*: Dr Bob Bowe.

The referee was Paddy Johnston of Kilkenny. There was little or no wind on a warm sunny day. The ground was firm and the grass dry. Wexford were to play into the railway goal in the first half.

Game Under Way

As the national anthem was played — at the end of protracted ceremonials — the flags over the stands were drooping. When the anthem ended 10,000 flags flowered vigorously all about the stadium. In the minds of many were memories of the epic finals played between these two counties in the 1950s.

When the ball was thrown in there was an indecisive scramble for a few moments. The players were tense and the marking so tight that there were no clean strokes. Then, to a great cheer from the Wexford followers the white ball was sent flying into the Cork goal area. Thousands of eyes were glued on McDonnell and Doran as they pranced shoulder to shoulder in front of goal.

However, in the tussling between backs and forwards Martin Quigley was fouled. This was a scorable free. Out came the stocky Mick Butler in his familiar green helmet. He had been entrusted with the crucial job of free-taker and this was his first. He rose the ball well and sent it over the bar. A good start for Wexford and the team's free-taker.

Martin Coleman hopped the ball on his stick and then belted it away down the field. Ned Buggy and Gerald McCarthy went for it together but Buggy caught it, dodged away to one side, ran forward a few yards and from 70 yards hit the ball with force and accuracy. It sailed over the bar for another point for Wexford.

'Come on Cork, wake up out of that', shouted several voices in unison from among the red and white brigade as Coleman got ready to take his second puck out.

The ball flew about so fast, the hurleys clipped it so quickly, that it was impossible for any one player to get clean possession. But the fierce competition was enthralling to watch and already the spectators sensed that this was going to be a real cracker of a match.

Great Wexford Start

Then, in the fifth minute there came a thunderous roar as the ball came down into the Cork goalmouth and Doran grabbed it to the right of the goal. McDonnell shoved hard against him to see to it that he did not find a way to the goal and kept him from striking it. Suddenly the red-haired man palmed the ball over his shoulder and it flew high across the goal area. There, just to the left, the tall Martin Quigley met it overhead and crashed it into the net for a great goal.

A huge, delighted cheer went up from the armies of purple and gold all round the stadium. This was a stunning start for Wexford. Right from the beginning they had gone onto full power. And the cheers seemed to spur them on even further. Almost from the puck out the ball came back into the Cork goalmouth. Again the muscular Doran caught it, despite McDonnell's best efforts. Doran managed to get a shot in but the white-garbed goalkeeper, in a split second reaction, parried the ball with his wide-bossed hurley. Martin Quigley, running into the goalmouth, met the dribbling ball with a ground stroke and whipped it into the net for another goal.

In the stands the Wexford followers jumped to their feet in joy. The Cork supporters shook their heads in dismay. Some may have been remembering the semi-final of the year before when Galway got off to a similar bewildering start and then managed to keep ahead to the end.

Few teams could have asked for a better start than Wexford. With six minutes gone the score was 2–2 to no score.

'It was hard not to say to ourselves, "We're halfway home already"', recalls Ned Buggy. His immediate midfield opponent, with whom he fought a great battle, Gerald McCarthy, remembers that tumultuous start to the game.

'We were rocked. No question about it. But we were a team of battlers. And they had hit us hard early enough to give us time to get back', he says.

Cork Fight Back

McCarthy, one of the few players on either side who could double accurately and consistently on the moving ball, was himself fouled a minute later. The Cork free-taker was his midfield partner, and club opponent, the dark-haired Pat Moylan. Moylan was a slim player who had excelled for Blackrock as a free-taker. This one was 65 yards from the Wexford goal. Moylan struck it well and the ball soared between the uprights.

A minute later the ball came in once more to the Cork goal. Almost inevitably it ended in the big right hand of Doran and he was fouled. Mick Butler put the free over the bar.

At that moment it seemed as if Wexford were going to be able to hold on to the lead built up in those devastating first minutes, exchanging scores with Cork as the game went on. This is not what happened. About this time Cork got a rhythm going. Their plan was to counter Wexford's lift and strike style with first-time pulling, keeping the ball moving at all costs, not allowing their opponents to settle on it.

Rhythm of Cork

Cork began to set up attacks, to get the ball into the dangerous full forwards. In one of these forays, Jimmy Barry Murphy managed to elude Liam Bennett and ran in to get a shot at goal. The ball was grabbed by the aggressive Malone in front of goal. For a second it seemed as if he had the goal at his mercy but he took the safe option and palmed it over the bar.

Running out, Malone gave a clenched fist signal to his colleagues in the red jerseys. John Nolan's puck out never got much further than the Cork half back line. There the tall, well-built Denis Coughlan had a clear advantage over the small, slight Johnny Murphy. In addition, Murphy had only recovered from a series of injuries, including a fractured jaw; he was a deft and skilled ball player but a lot of ball was high. Coughlan kept reaching up to his full height, bending backwards and catching the ball at full stretch behind his head.

Cork set up one raid after another. Brendan Cummins kept pulling first time on the ball and Mick Jacob got few opportunities to take it in the hand and clear it away. Brendan's brother, Ray, pounded out and took possession. With Willie Murphy right behind him he did not try to turn but suddenly sent a ball into open space for Charlie McCarthy to run to. There was a gasp from the spectators to see this compact, controlled player race on to the ball in front of goal. He whipped on it fast and it skimmed over the bar, when it might just as easily have gone under it.

Dangerous Cummins

Ray Cummins got the ball again in the next attack. He was fouled by Willie Murphy inside the large square. Moylan ran forward to take it. Many wondered if he was going to try for a goal. He hit the ball with great force but sent it several feet over the bar. It was clear that the Cork captain was so dangerous that fouling him had to be an option to prevent goals going in. Two minutes later he was fouled again. The free was close in and this one was taken by Charlie McCarthy. He had such a neat way of placing, rising and hitting the ball that nobody doubted that he would send it over, and he did.

Despite the best effort of Buggy and Rowsome, the Cork pair were getting the better of matters at centrefield. And the Cork backs were quick to break up any attacks mounted by the Wexford forwards. After the nerve-shattering start of his man scoring two goals, Johnny Crowley had settled down and was more than holding his own with Martin Quigley. Pat Barry and John Quigley were cancelling one another out. But the upshot of the battle of the half back line was that less ball was going into the Wexford forward line.

At this stage John Nolan was having a lot to do in the Wexford goal with all the goalmouth scrambles going on. Fast and lithe, he several times ran out and took possession of momentarily loose balls in front of the goal and cleared them away. But in one desperate scuffle he picked the ball off the ground and a free was awarded which Moylan pointed.

Ray Cummins got his first point from play when he latched onto a hard-hit centre from Gerald McCarthy, leapt away from his marker and sent the ball over the bar.

A minute later Gerald McCarthy himself was fouled in a bout of midfield play. This free was a good distance out, 80 yards. Moylan came over and struck it beautifully and the ball went over for yet another Cork point. This was six points in a row without reply.

Wexford Reply

This sequence was broken when at last Wexford mounted another serious attack. Doran was fouled with the ball and Mick Butler sent the free over the bar. Cork scored again. This was Moylan's first point from play. He took a hand-pass from Gerald McCarthy at midfield, swivelled about, steadied himself and sent the ball on a long high journey between the distant uprights.

Wexford went on the attack again. The Cork corner backs — Murphy and O'Doherty — were doing all they could to aid their Doran-minding colleague as well as minding their own men and they came into the picture in repelling this assault. But a 70 was conceded. The long distance frees had been entrusted to Buggy, who had a very good stroke on the ball. He pointed it. Just after that Martin Quigley got free and was heading goal-wards, to the roars of the Wexford supporters, when he was fouled. Buggy pointed this also to leave his side three points ahead.

Cork Goal

Wexford's lead was wiped out a minute later. Martin Coleman was pucking out the ball enormous distances and the ball was landing among his half forwards. On one of the rare occasions Barry Murphy got free of Liam Bennett he sent the ball towards the Wexford goal. His shot was blocked down but came to Ray Cummins, who, having lost his hurley, put his footballing skills to use in kicking the ball into the net for Cork's first goal.

This goal was a tremendous boost for Cork who were now level after a great burst of determined and skilful play. The Cork supporters showed how heartened they were by prolonged cheering and flag-waving. This was the great come back and it had required a lot of courage and effort.

To add to Cork's joy they took the lead just after that. Teddie O'Connor had marked O'Leary very well but on this occasion O'Leary blocked down his clearance, and whipped the ball over the bar. At that stage O'Leary was limping; his damaged ligament had given way near the end of the first quarter; he would not reappear after half time.

Cork went further ahead when Charlie McCarthy ran from his line to take a Malone pass and sent over a point. Only the excellent goalkeeping of John Nolan, which he maintained for the duration of the game, saved a goal going in at this time.

Wexford Surge

Now Wexford made a great effort to regain the initiative. All during the first half the ball had gone fast over the dry grass, the play had crackled with excitement as every ball was contested with tremendous urgency. Now the excitement rose again as the men in purple and gold fought to get the ball into the hand and send it on its way.

At this stage John Quigley swapped places with the injury-slowed Christy Keogh — a move for which few could see any justification. In the next Wexford attack Martin Quigley, never ceasing to forage and run, was fouled. Ned Buggy took the free and sent it over.

The last point of the game came from John Quigley, who had less impact in the corner. This was his first score of the half and it put his side level. Then Paddy Johnston blew the whistle on a momentous first half, with the score at 1–11 for Cork to 2–8 for Wexford.

Dramatic Restart

During the half-time discussions several questions dominated conversation. Had Cork expended too much energy in hurling their way back from eight points behind? Would Doran and Cummins escape their markers enough to make crucial scores? Would Murphy and McDonnell have to keep giving away frees? Would John Quigley and Jimmy Barry Murphy come more into the picture in the second half? Would Cork continue to control midfield?

The second half opened as dramatically as the first. And Tony Doran was the star performer. John Quigley got the ball and lobbed it into the square. Once again the burly red-headed Doran bustled his way beneath it and caught it. He then side-stepped Pat McDonnell to shoot a smashing goal. Croke Park erupted with the excited cheers of the huge Wexford contingent.

Coleman sent a long puck out and after a flurry at midfield Malone got it and went running with it. He was stopped by a foul. Pat Moylan sent it unerringly over the bar.

Great McCarthy Goal

It was in the third minute of the second half that the most delightful goal of the game was scored. Brendan Cummins sent the ball towards the Wexford goals. It went over the heads of the half backs and half forwards. Then Charlie McCarthy came racing across from the right corner. He was already swinging the hurley as the ball hit the ground. With impeccable timing, in the split second as the ball hopped upwards, McCarthy met it on the half volley and sent it flying into the net. Croke Park erupted again with sound and a frenzied flowering of red and white flags.

Cork were now a point ahead. Wexford came back and the scores were levelled by a Martin Quigley point. Three minutes later Cork were ahead again when Moylan sent over a free from 40 yards.

Battle of Mentors

At this stage the battle of wits and judgment between the mentors was evident. The Cork sideline men took off Pat Barry, who was tiring, and sent in the tall blond-haired John Horgan. He was normally a left corner back with a capacity to make long clearances; under harrassment he could turn towards his own goal and then strike the ball away by hitting it back over his shoulder. The Cork mentors sent him to centre half back, despite the fact that Crowley was now playing well. However this was the first part of a rearrangement of the back division that was to have an important bearing on the outcome.

The Wexford mentors replaced the limping Christy Keogh with Declan Rowsome, and replaced his brother Billy by sending in the hard-working Martin Casey. Casey, from the Buffer's Alley club, was used to playing with Doran. The sideline men also put Johnny Murphy to midfield where he and Buggy began to get the upper hand for a time. For a while Tony Doran was at centre forward and Martin Quigley at full but this did not work for either player and was reversed — but in the meantime some scoring chances went abegging.

Jimmy Barry Murphy, who had shifted about the half forward line without fulfilling his potential, now put his side two points ahead after a shot by Moylan had come back off the upright.

Another Wexford Goal

Then came a score that began a period when Wexford went onto full power in a great burst of energetic hurling. Ned Buggy, a fine striker of the dead ball, sent a sideline cut right into the Cork goalmouth. Butler, playing very well, slipped his marker and took the ball in front of goal to send in an unstoppable shot for his side's fourth goal. It put his side a point ahead once again.

It was at this stage that Mick Jacob began to give a memorable exhibition at centre back. He could read the play well, was fast and agile to get beneath the ball and, most of all, he had the courage and capacity to catch the ball amid a maelstrom of clashing hurleys, thumping elbows and arms. When he caught it he side-stepped nimbly to send the ball right into the Cork goalmouth.

Cork had changed about the forward line and several went to mark Jacob but for 15 minutes of this game the ginger-haired Oulart man was unbeatable. With Colm Doran and Liam Bennett playing very soundly this trio acted as a barrier to the Cork attacks. Little good ball went into the forward line while dangerous lobbing balls were sent floating into the Cork goalmouth. And this came at a time when the Leeside defence was in some disarray.

Wexford were now in control of the game and the crowd at Croke Park rose in successive cheers as Jacob caught and cleared and Tony Doran bustled to position himself under the dropping ball. He caught several. The Cork backs kept behind him to stop him charging into the goal. In doing so however they left their men free for a few hurried seconds. Doran, though badly harassed, managed to get several handpasses across the goal to his colleagues. Two of these came to Mick Butler, the only one of the forwards who seemed capable of giving the full forward any real support at this crucial stage. Unfortunately for him and for Wexford these chances were lost in the frantic set-to's in front of the goal.

Cork Seal Gaps

Wave after wave of Wexford attacks ended in frustration and missed chances. The Cork mentors by that stage had made several adroit moves. Brian Murphy had been moved over to full back to try to cope better with Doran. Martin O'Doherty went to centre back and John Horgan went into his familiar left corner. These three now began to seal off the holes in the defence. Their colleagues, Coughlan, who had not been as prominent as in the first half, Crowley and McDonnell started to come more into the game. This new Cork defence played well and Wexford had lost their chance to finish off the opposition.

And after eight minutes of scoreless play — the time of missed chances for Wexford — it was Cork who scored when Moylan pointed another free to level the scores again.

Wexford, however, shook off their frustration and with great heart and spirit set up several more attacks. They missed more chances for goals. Johnny Murphy took a blow of a hurley as he went racing into the goal. His side were awarded a free which Mick Butler put over.

A goal at this stage could have won it for the Slaneysiders. In the next attack five forwards combined to get the ball near the goalmouth where it ended up with Mick Butler who scored a good point.

Cork's Vital Switch

It was at this point, when the game seemed to be going Wexford's way, despite their wastefulness in front of goal, that Cork made what was perhaps the most telling tactic of all. They moved Jimmy Barry Murphy to centre forward, on Mick Jacob. It was one of these moves which may have seemed foolish at the time, because Barry Murphy had hit few balls in the entire game. Yet it worked. Here was a player tall enough and skilful enough and fast enough to get to the ball first, take it and then jink and weave his way goalwards. Jacob, after the great effort he had made for total dominance of the half back line, was now running out of steam.

With ten minutes to go and two points ahead Wexford mounted another attack. Tony Doran was pulled and dragged and a free was given almost opposite the right post. Mick Butler came over to take it. To the dismay of the Wexford supporters he failed to rise the ball properly and mis-hit it. Instead of being three points ahead the ball was cleared away, Cork went on the attack, were awarded a free which Moylan duly pointed.

'It's easy to hit frees over the bar when you are seated in the stands', said a former player afterwards, referring to Butler's miss which was seen as one of the turning points of the game.

When Butler went to take the free his chest was heaving with exertion. He was covered in sweat. At that stage of the game he had given and taken a succession of bone-shaking challenges.

Levelling Score

Barry Murphy got the equalising score for Cork, a beautifully struck point from far out which brought a great appreciative cheer from the spectators. As it sailed between the uprights, white in the sunlight of a hot afternoon, it signalled a great upsurge in Cork's hurling power. Now it was the turn of the men in red and white, coming into their own in the crucial last eight minutes of the game.

It was Barry Murphy who got the point that put Cork ahead when he picked up a Moylan free and clipped a smart ball over the bar. The St Finbarr's player, who was to grace the hurling scene in the subsequent years, added a new thrust to the Cork attack at a time when Jim Prendergast had subdued Charlie McCarthy and the two other Wexford full backs were also playing well.

Then five minutes from time, Ray Cummins, playing a captain's part, dodged several despairing tackles in front of goal, and used his skilled boot to kick the ball over the bar.

With their supporters roaring them on and McCarthy and Moylan getting back a measure of control at centrefield Cork kept up the pressure. Several balls that fell into the Cork left corner were gathered by Horgan and sent soaring back down the field. Barry Murphy, able to elude and race past Jacob, took a pin-point pass from Ray Cummins and swung stylishly on it to send it high between the posts.

At this pivotal juncture one thing was obvious. Cork were physically in better shape than their opponents, faster to the ball, lasting the pace better in the warm, energy-sapping conditions.

'Looking back with the benefit of hindsight I think that those two hectic games against Galway in the heat of Pairc Ui Chaoimh took a lot more out of us than we realised at the time', says Ned Buggy. 'In the All-Ireland we began to wilt in those last ten minutes.'

Wexford's Last Chance

With Cork three points ahead and thundering towards the finishing post Wexford had one final chance to at least force a draw. In one desperate last assault the ball came in to the lion-hearted Doran on the edge of the square. Despite hurleys and shoulders his magnet-like right hand closed round the ball and he turned to go for goal. Brian Murphy had his arms around the Wexford captain and hauled him to the ground. Most of the spectators and the players expected a penalty to be awarded. A great buzz of expectation rose from the crowd. However the referee, Paddy Johnston, awarded a slap-ball, judging Doran to have been barging with ball in hand.

This was a bitterly contested decision in the aftermath of the game. The RTE television coverage was scrutinised again and again. Doran's bustling, charging style in front of goal was hard to counter without a great deal of pushing and shoving and grappling. Most observers felt that Wexford should have got a penalty.

It was not to be. From Coleman's next long puck out the Cork side went on the attack. In a frantic effort to stop it and to try to get a Wexford attack going Colm Doran pulled hard on the ball. The referee pulled him up for what was judged to be dangerous play. Pat Moylan, whose unerring skill and calm temperament with the placed ball was largely responsible for keeping Cork in the game at difficult times, now took his last free for his side. Over it went to leave his side four points ahead as the hands of the stopwatches showed that 35 minutes of the second half had been played. When the ball was pucked out Paddy Johnston blew the whistle.

One of Best

At the presentation, the President of the GAA, Con Murphy, who himself had played at full back for Cork in the '40s, said that this was one of the best finals ever seen. He remarked also on the sporting way this tough and competitive game had been played. There was another warming aspect of this final: the great sense of camaraderie and goodwill among the rival followers.

The most delighted spectator, if such he could be called, was Christy Ring. He was aglow with pride and joy, thrusting out his own battle scarred hand to congratulate the players. He was essentially a shy man but in the steamy noise of the Cork dressing-room he even joined in some celebratory singing.

This 22nd All-Ireland title was one of Cork's finest victories. Few finals were so hard to win. They had met a great Wexford side and had been almost overwhelmed at times during the game. But with great courage and endurance they had hung on and in the end their skill and physical fitness had won the day for them. One of the rewards for their victory was a trip to San Francisco to play an exhibition game.

Wexford Regrets

The Wexford team and followers felt that this was a game that could and should have been won. This is what made this defeat so hard to bear. There was criticism of some players, most of it unfair. There was criticism of the mentors, made with the benefit of hindsight. A strong forward like Tom Byrne had been left in the dugout while speedy forwards like the Kinsella brothers of Gorey and Phil Wilson were not even on the panel. Selectors and mentors are easy targets of frustration and ire.

'Let's hope we meet Cork again — we won't let it slip next time', said many in Wexford. They did meet again in the final of the following year. Virtually the same sides were in opposition. Yet this time the game was flat and disappointing. It showed how much rain and wind can utterly spoil a game of hurling. It showed too how much Cork had improved and Wexford remained static. This time Cork were clearly the superior side, even though their winning margin was only three points.

This was the best Cork side since the three-in-a-row side of the early 1950s. They provided game after game of delightful entertainment and skill and won the All-Ireland again in 1978.

Few in Wexford could have foreseen the decline into which the county's hurling fortunes would fall. After the second failure in a row, in 1977, the county side have not since contested, let alone won, an All-Ireland final. Nor, up to the present time, have the side in purple and gold won the Leinster title, though they have managed to get to the final on a number of occasions.

The great final of 1976 was the start of a glittering parade by Cork. It marked the beginning of the end for Wexford as a major hurling power. Those who saw this match, in Croke Park or on television, will always wish that the men in purple and gold will some day return to Croke Park on the first Sunday in September and that their opponents will be the gritty, skilful hurlers from the Leeside.

1978

Cork v. Clare

Munster Final

THE PRESSURE OF GREAT EXPECTATIONS

A high-definition surveillance satellite would have noted a population movement in the Munster area at the time of the last Sunday in July 1978. The Munster hurling final that year in Thurles between Cork and Clare drew a massive crowd of 54,000 to Semple Stadium. The gates were pushed shut half an hour before the game began and some 3,000 to 4,000 fans were excluded.

The most visible movement of people, in cars, buses and trains was from the county of Clare. It began as early as Thursday and Friday. By Sunday morning it seemed like an invasion force crossing the Shannon and converging on the flat plain of the Suir in the hurling heartland of Tipperary.

Men, women and children set out from the far west of the county, where the land on the northern shore of the Shannon Estuary narrows into a spear-point to meet the sea at Loop Head. 'They're from as far back as Carrigaholt and further', said a man in Sixmilebridge, surveying the great army of followers streaming past on the way to Thurles. They set out from lone houses and little hamlets near the strange bare mountain land of the Burren, from Ballyvaughan and Bell Harbour and Lisdoonvarna.

The bulk of the Clare forces came from the eastern part of the county where hurling is part of the weft and weave of everyday life and conversation. In those parts the game has been played for centuries and legends of feats and heroism have become part of the folklore. From Crusheen, in the northern part of the county near the Galway border down to Cratloe on the edge of the Shannon came people with blue and gold flags, streamers, paper hats and badges.

Folklore of Hurling

It was said that hurling thrived on those areas east of a line from Ennis northward because there was enough flat land for playing fields and enough ash growing in groves and in hedges for the hurleys. There are playing pitches in villages and townlands and in lonesome countryside near the slopes of Slieve Bernagh where the folk-memory of great games hangs over the old, spindly goalposts and boot-worn patches in front of goal. Ballads and poems were composed about by-gone heroes. One of the best-known commemorates the goalkeeper on the 1932 team which contested the All-Ireland, Tommy Daly, whose grave on the 'wind swept Hill of Tulla' looks down on a famous hurling field.

For all their great hurling tradition Clare won the All-Ireland only once, way back in 1914. That team had many big men, famed for the art of doubling on the high ball. Amby Power the captain was 6 ft 4 ins tall. They had a great full forward in Tom McGrath from O'Callaghan's Mills. Willie Considine — known as the Dodger — was a strong and courageous man. His brother Brendan, still a pupil at St Flannan's college in Ennis at the time, was on the side. Now, white haired and venerable, he was among the throngs packing into the stadium that day in 1978, one of the few survivors of All-Ireland glory.

Some of the 1932 side which last won a Munster championship were still alive, hoping that Clare's hour had come. John Joe 'Goggles' Doyle, who captained the team, expressed his confidence that the men who had performed so well in the National League final could now win the Munster crown.

In the days coming up to the Munster final the county was abuzz with expectation. It seemed as if the county's agonisingly long wait had every chance of being ended. In the homes, streets and pubs of Clarecastle, Sixmilebridge, Feakle and Newmarket it was the dominant topic of conversation.

Unhappy Memories of 1977 Final

The previous year, before a huge crowd, Clare had lost to Cork by five points, 4–15 to 4–10. That game had been completely ruined as a contest by the sending off of the Clare full back, Jim Power, after an incident involving the tall and talented Cork full forward Ray Cummins. It happened just before half-time. The saddest thing about this clash of heads and bodies is that both players were good sportsmen with reputations for fair play.

On that unhappy occasion the tension generated by the Clare followers, aching to win, urging their men on to a do-or-die effort from the throw-in, cascaded onto the pitch. It affected some of the Clare players who played below their best. Many judges of the game said that Cork would probably have won even if Power were playing. But one could never be sure. Clare were upset and handicapped by the loss of a stalwart player. Even neutral spectators felt they had been deprived of what might have been a rip-roaring game by this unfortunate happening. This re-match between the same sides promised to be a much better encounter.

Buoyed by League Victory

The huge army of Clare supporters dominated the streets of Thurles, crowded into the perspiring pubs, stood outside the fast-food shops. As they streamed along the crowded streets which crackled with excitement and expectation towards Semple Stadium many of them recalled the scene only three months before. For the third year in a row Clare had confronted one of the game's dominant counties, Kilkenny, in the final of the National League.

Before a crowd of 25,000 the two sides gave a thrilling display of hurling. By this time these two teams had developed a tough rivalry. They had met in the previous two finals, Kilkenny winning after a replay in 1976 and Clare winning the following year.

The Clare followers, long deprived of the exultation of winning, had come in droves that day in April. Their display of colour and the great repetitive chant, 'Clare, Clare, Clare', had helped to sweep their side forward powerfully to grind down the opposition and win decisively by 3–10 to 0–9.

Now they were back again, going to the stadium early to find their seats without any last-minute fuss or claim good vantage points on the terraces. There had been great annoyance in the county over the decision to make the game an all-ticket one. The feeling was that the faithful followers, often living miles away from centres of GAA influence, would have little chance of getting a ticket.

Faithful Followers

These were the people who followed the team in the barren years of constant championship defeat and disappointment. They were used to seeing the victorious jubilation of the rival followers. When they saw the broad smiles of the faces of the winning team they felt sad for their own downcast players, felt sad for one another, sharing disappointment with a wry shake of the head and a long exhalation of breath.

'Clare has the best supporters in the country. But when people have no experience of winning, of victory at championship, at All-Ireland level, they find it difficult to weigh up their own team objectively and the opposition team also', says Jimmy Smyth, to whom Clare hurling has been a religion. 'When that Clare team had won two national leagues, winning game after game, many people took it for granted that they were going to beat Cork in the Munster final. This kind of expectation puts terrible pressure on the players in the days leading up to the game.'

Need for Self-Belief

One of the big failings of fine Clare teams in the past was lack of self-belief. Some players felt that the honour of wearing the gold and blue jersey was enough in itself and that if the team gave a good account of itself in a key championship game the hurling tradition of the county had been maintained, even if they didn't actually win.

'Christy Ring once said to me that if a player is not convinced that he will win a 50/50 ball then he won't have the resolve and confidence to win it', recalls Jimmy Smyth. 'Many Clare players were worn down by the burden of past defeats and it was hard to get into the right frame of mind.'

One man who had striven might and main to induce self-belief was the Clare manager, Fr Harry Bohan. He was a great protagonist of the self-sufficiency of communities, of harnessing local energies and ingenuity to get things done — houses built, industries set up. Bohan was an energetic man, bristling with determination. He was the power behind the side's success in the National League and was now determined to bring a well-deserved All-Ireland trophy to the county.

Cork Vibrant

The Cork side had no problems about self-belief. 'The strong counties like Cork, Kilkenny and Tipperary are never far away from winning year after year', says Gerald McCarthy, who played in that game. 'It must have been difficult for the Clare fellows — they were under great pressure to produce the goods at long last. They had a fine team and they were good enough to go all the way. But the sort of pressure they were under from their own supporters was bound to have an effect on them.'

Great Side

There was another reality. This was one of the best Cork teams ever to wear the red jerseys. They were now going for their fourth Munster championship in a row, something that had not been achieved by the county since 1926–29 and by any other county in the province since Limerick were kingpins in 1933–36.

After the semi-final defeat at the hands of Galway in 1975 the side had come back with great resilience and resolve, a combination of game-wise veterans and exceptionally talented newcomers. In one of the great finals of the seventies they had beaten a fine Wexford side in 1976, repeating that win the following year. Now they were poised for three-in-a-row.

'The great strength of that team was in the forwards. We had good backs and centrefield but any one of the forwards was a match-winner on his day', recalls Gerald McCarthy.

All players were well used to the big occasion, each knowing the capabilities of their team mates. They passed deftly to one another, backed one another up, supported the man having a difficult time with an opponent. They were well managed and motivated by an astute team of mentors, who were quick to know when to change players, to put a fresh man on in place of a tiring or injury-slowed one.

Colourful Cork Supporters

Their followers too came trooping to Thurles, ebullient and flamboyant. The clusters of shouting supporters around huge flags radiated humour, delight and confidence as they walked in the middle of the streets of Thurles, marching down from the railway station and doing a turn around the Square before heading up towards Semple Stadium to claim a special place beneath the scoreboard at the town end.

Mentors Worried

The Cork mentors, however, were anything but easy. The team was seriously depleted. Sean O'Leary, the brilliant left full forward from Youghal, was taken ill in training and hospitalised. There was no question of him playing. This was a big loss to Cork. O'Leary, a low-slung player who often seemed deceptively overweight, was fast and sharp. The merest half chance, left or right, and the ball came off his stick going fast. Another of the team's fine players, Brian Murphy, had a serious hamstring injury and was unlikely to play. He was one of the sheet anchors of the defence, calm, methodical and totally reliable.

The selectors drafted in Mick Malone to fill the gap left by O'Leary. Denis Burns replaced Murphy as corner back. The other two on that line were Martin O'Doherty and the fair haired John Horgan. There would be no easy scores from these two. O'Doherty was a fast-moving, quick-striking full back, while Horgan was very hard to beat in his corner. When he got the ball he made huge clearances down the field. He was renowned for his accuracy from long-distance frees.

Half Backs and Centrefield

Both Dermot McCurtain and Johnny Crowley in the half back line had been plagued by injuries and were not fully fit but the Cork selectors, headed by the county secretary, Frank Murphy, could not afford to leave these two stalwarts off the depleted team. Someone of Crowley's weight and determination was going to be needed to counter the physical power of Clare's Noel Casey while it was going to need an astute and sharp striker like McCurtain to counter a player of Colm Honan's virtuosity. The elegant, ever reliable Denis Coughlan held the left half back berth. His height and ability to reach up for high balls were considered to give him some advantage over his smaller opponent, Jimmy McNamara.

Tom Cashman and Tim Crowley were at centrefield. They complemented one another. Crowley was a strong forager, always in the thick of the tussles round the centre of the field, hitting long balls with a wide swing of a big hurley. Cashman was the stick artist, neat and fast and energetic. He rarely failed to strike the ball with the sweep spot on the boss of his hurley and could send it spearing away with a smart, sharp stroke. How they would match up to Moroney and Callinan was a matter of much speculation.

Cork Attackers

The Cork half forward line of Gerald McCarthy, Jimmy Barry Murphy and Pat Moylan was one of the best in the country. It had played a big role in winning the last two All-Irelands. All three were very skilful players, who could race on to the moving ball, tip it up and send it accurately in towards goal or over the bar. Moylan's stickwork in the All-Ireland of 1976 earned him the Man of the Match accolade. Jimmy Barry Murphy was one of the great forwards of the game. He always seemed to know where the ball was going to be and he was always there, so sharp in his striking that danger threatened whenever he was near goal.

McCarthy, his hands and wrists toughened by his calling as a stone-mason, was immensely skilled. He could double on the ball accurately, keep it moving without touching it with the hand. He often met it at waist height and sent it on into the right corner where his St Finbarr's team-mate, Charlie McCarthy, the captain of the side, was expecting it. Cork's full forward. the tall and gangly Ray Cummins, was lethal when high balls came in, flicking them goalwards. How Jim Power was going to handle him after the unfortunate incident of the previous year was a talking point. The hard-running, tough battler, Mick Malone was in the other corner. He was carrying a knee injury but he had not let it bother him in training.

Hoping for Clare Win

Most of the hurling lovers from other counties in the bubbling rivers of spectators converging on Semple Stadium were hoping for a Clare win. Many had seen some of the great hurlers from that county who had graced the scene but had never played in an All-Ireland final — Larry Blake, the McInerneys and Greenes, Matt Nugent, Donal O'Grady and perhaps the longest-playing and most admired player, Jimmy Smyth from Ruan.

The pressure to win on the Clare team had been growing since their memorable triumph in the National League final. 'It's now or never', said a banner headline in the *Clare Champion*. They had one of the finest goalkeepers in Seamus Durack, an inspirational player who sometimes sallied out of goal to send the forwards into the attack with long clearances. In front of him the full back line of Jackie O'Gorman, Jim Power and Johnny MacMahon had performed well in the league campaigns of the previous years.

Clare's Half Back Line

It was the Clare half back line which inspired so much hope and confidence in the side. Ger Loughnane, Sean Hehir and Sean Stack were among the top echelon of hurlers in the country. In game after game they proved utterly reliable. Stack, the captain of the team, played with great style and verve, striking the ball beautifully left or right, flicking the ball away from opponents, gaining possession constantly from dropping balls. The men on either side of him were rarely bested by any opponent. They both set attacks going by well weighted balls to the forwards.

The centrefield pair of Michael Moroney and Johnny Callinan were two vigorous, able hurlers. Moroney, a ruddy-faced farmer from Crusheen, who held the hurley in the left-hand-upper grip, had perfected the art of the sideline cut. When he went over to take one the crowd buzzed in anticipation; as often as not the ball went soaring goalwards, sometimes over the bar or dangerously into the square. Callinan was a forager who often ran hard with the ball, towards the opposition goal, forcing the backs to challenge him and leave a forward unmarked.

In the centre of the half-forward line was the big, strong man, Noel Casey, who bustled and tussled for every ball. On the wings were Jimmy McNamara, famous for scores from all angles off his left side and the reliable free-taker Colm Honan. The O'Connor brothers, Pat and Enda, from Tubber were in the corners with Martin McKeogh at full forward. These three players and their colleagues in the outside line had got many fine scores in the league campaigns. Their mettle had been severely tested in a thrilling semi-final against a very strong Limerick team only four weeks before. Casey had given the fine Pat Hartigan a difficult time and the three full forwards had each scored a goal.

Clare Favourites

Because of the team's consistently good form and Cork's injury problems many neutrals and most of the media commentators favoured Clare to win. No team likes to go into a game as favourites. It adds to the pressures on players as they go about their daily lives, in their workplaces, with families and friends. This was at its height in Clare. None of the players could go outside the door of their houses or walk down a street or a roadway without being greeted in terms of the game. Behind the 'best of luck' remarks, the smiles of encouragement and the handshakes was the unspoken wish: 'Don't let us down on Sunday. This is the best Clare team in a long while and this is your best chance to end our years of disappointment.'

Now, with the stadium packed to overcapacity and the sun shining, all that remained was for referee John Moloney of Tipperary to throw in the ball. The expectations of a titanic struggle were high. The expectations of the Clare followers, who seemed to constitute about two-thirds of the attendance, were expressed in the great roar that went up at the end of the playing of the national anthem. Sean Stack had won the toss for Clare and elected to play into the wind blowing strongly from the Killinan end.

Game Gets Under Way

The game got under way. One of the most significant things was the way Tom Cashman got neat possession almost from the throw-in. This slight player, shirt outside knicks, smacked the ball smartly into the Clare half of the field with a quick, effortless swing of the hurley.

The teams as they lined out were:

CORK

Martin Coleman
(Ballinhassig)

Denis Burns	Martin O'Doherty	John Horgan
(St Finbarr's)	(Glen Rovers)	(Blackrock)
Dermot McCurtain	Johnny Crowley	Denis Coughlan
(Blackrock)	(Bishopstown)	(Glen Rovers)

Tom Cashman   Tim Crowley
(Blackrock)   (Newcestown)

Gerald McCarthy	Jimmy Barry Murphy	Pat Moylan
(St Finbarr's)	(St Finbarr's)	(Blackrock)
Charlie McCarthy, capt	Ray Cummins	Mick Malone
(St Finbarr's)	(Blackrock)	(Eire Og)

Substitutes: Eamon O'Donoghue (Glen Rovers); Pat Horgan (Glen Rovers); Donal O'Grady (St Finbarr's); Jerry Cronin (UCC); Pat McDonnell (Inniscarra); John Buckley (Newtownshandrum). *Coach*: Fr Bertie Troy (Newtownshandrum). *Trainer*: Kevin Kehily (Newcestown and Cork RTC). *Selectors*: Christy Ring (Glen Rovers); Frank Murphy, county secretary; Tim O'Mullane (St Finbarr's); Jimmy Brohan (Blackrock); Denis Murphy (St Finbarr's). *Medical advisor*: Dr Con Murphy. *Masseur*: John 'Kid' Cronin (Glen Rovers).

CLARE

Seamus Durack
(Feakle)

Jackie O'Gorman	Jim Power	Johnny McMahon
(Cratloe)	(Tulla)	(Newmarket)
Ger Loughnane	Sean Hehir	Sean Stack, capt
(Feakle)	(O'Callaghan's Mills)	(Sixmilebridge)

Michael Moroney   Johnny Callinan
(Crusheen)   (Clarecastle)

Jimmy McNamara	Noel Casey	Colm Honan
(Newmarket)	(Sixmilebridge)	(Clonlara)
Pat O'Connor	Martin McKeogh	Enda O'Connor
(Tubber)	(Kilkishen)	(Tubber)

Substitutes: Brendan Gilligan (Eire Og); Barry Smythe (Banner); Leo Quinlan (Sixmilebridge); Gerry Nugent (Scariff); Tommy Keane (Kilmaley); Tom Glynne (Eire Og); Michael Murphy (Clooney); Tom Crowe (Clonlara). *Manager*: Fr Harry Bohan. *Coach*: Justin McCarthy. *Trainer*: Colum Flynn. *Mentors/selectors*: Matt Nugent, Gerry Browne, Jim Woods, Noel O'Driscoll, Michael McTigue, Flan Hynes. *Team physician*: Dr Tom McGrath.

The referee was John Moloney of Tipperary.

But, surprisingly, it was nine minutes before a score was recorded. This was a tense, tight-marking game, with defences well on top and little time for forwards to get sight of goal. There was a good deal of nervous, scrambling play. Forwards had to strike quickly before they were bottled up and Cork began to have a succession of wides.

'We had the very strong wind behind us but that is not always an advantage', says Gerald McCarthy. 'You can see a lot of ball with a strong wind but it can be the wrong kind. When high balls are coming in it is easy to predict where they are going to land — you get four or five players bunching under it and the backs have the advantage.'

Then Cork were awarded a free nearly 90 metres from the Clare goal. John Horgan trundled up from the corner position to take it. This player had a great technique with such frees, lifting the ball forward and then coming behind it with a mighty swing which always connected in the dead centre of the boss. The ball, helped by the wind, went soaring between the posts to a huge roar from the beflagged Cork contingent on the terraces behind.

A minute later it was the turn of the massed Clare contingent to cheer. Clare were awarded a sideline ball 30 metres out from the Cork goal and the specialist, Michael Moroney, chopped down on the ball and sent it over the bar.

Seamus Durack made the first of many fine saves and clearances, catching a long incoming ball from John Horgan. When it came floating in nobody among the Clare followers doubted that he would put up that reliable left hand. But there was a scramble in the goalmouth and Durack lost his hurley. His handpass out went over the sideline. Tom Cashman came up and sent the sideline ball high into the goalmouth. The beanpole figure of Ray Cummins reached up for it, higher than anyone, and, protecting his catching hand with his hurley, grabbed the ball. He quickly spun inside Jim Power. The Tulla man, determined to prevent what looked like a certain goal, held his opponent. John Moloney came loping up and awarded a penalty.

Cork Penalty

Durack was flanked by Jim Power and Ger Loughnane as Tim Crowley, one of the strong strikers on the Cork team, placed the ball. He held the hurley with the right hand under grip and, like all such players, looked awkward when he came running in to scoop up the ball and twist his body slightly as he swung. But he always had a mighty stroke and a goal at this stage would have been a key event. This time Crowley's powerful shot went in low but the alert Durack got his hurley to it. In the ensuing tussle Jim Power put the ball over the end line for a 65.

Again Horgan came up. This was another long, high and very accurate puck and it sailed way past the uprights and onto the terraces behind.

It was dour hurling for much of the time and no prospect of an open rip-roaring Munster final so beloved of hurling fans. Twenty-one minutes elapsed before the first score from play. Then Tom Cashman, who kept getting the ball wherever he ran, scored a beautiful long-distance point. His performance was one of the delights of a dull battle of attrition between these evenly matched sides.

The two big beefy men, Noel Casey and Johnny Crowley, shouldered one another heavily but Crowley prevented his opponent from making his typical bursts down the middle. The Clare mentors, helped by the former Cork player, Justin McCarthy, brought out Enda O'Connor in a switch with Casey. Not long after, Clare got their first score from play when Colm Honan got possession and sent the ball over carefully. The Cork forwards, well policed by the efficient Clare backs, sent several balls wide.

The next score came again from Cork's corner back, Horgan. It was seventy metres out but even before he bent to lift it people felt he was going to put it over.

'Those were great points for Cork. After the Clare backs holding their men so well, here were these balls coming from so far out, everybody looking up at them, not being able to do a thing as they went over the bar', says Jimmy Smyth. 'It must have been a bit disheartening for our fellows.'

Almost immediately Colm Honan managed for once to escape Dermot McCurtain who was playing very soundly. He got the ball through to Noel Casey who, despite the attentions of Martin O'Doherty, pulled hard on the ball. It went zipping just over the bar. There was now a feeling that Clare would need a goal to allow them to shrug off the inhibiting tensions that seemed to affect them more than Cork. At least Cork were shooting at goal far more often, sending the ball towards the posts even if it went to the wrong side of them far too often for the comfort of the Cork followers. The Cork goalkeeper, the reliable Martin Coleman, had little to do, so few were the Clare attacks that posed real danger.

The last score of the first half was another long-range free from Horgan, his fourth in the half. This was one of the most memorable feats of long-range shooting for a long time. It had kept Cork in contention when their vaunted forwards were unable to come to grips with the game. It left the score 5 points to 3 in the champions' favour as the referee blew the whistle.

Looking Good for Clare

As the teams walked off the field there was an exultant roar from the Clare crowd and shouts of, 'Take them out now lads in the second half. Ye have them now.'

It seemed to augur well for Clare. They had been beaten at midfield and their forwards had been well mastered. But the much-feared Cork attack had not got a single score. They would have the wind at their backs in the second half. They were only two points behind when an accurate Cork attack might have doubled their scoreline. It seemed that, at long last, they were going to emerge triumphant at the end of the game.

The prospect of a Clare win gave a fillip to neutrals who knew that tension had made this into a moderate Munster final, although not the disappointing anti-climax of the previous year. Semple Stadium was abuzz with excitement, mostly from the faithful Clare followers, so happy to have made the journey on what now seemed to be a momentous occasion for the county. Their shouts of exhortation and expectation as the team members made their way to the dressing-rooms undoubtedly put additional pressure on many players still trying to shake off the tensions of a Munster hurling final before a huge crowd.

Cork Fired Up

It was this prospect of defeat that stung the Cork team in the dressing-room. The ferociously proud Christy Ring, one of the selectors, prowled about, big fists clenched. Gerald McCarthy later recalled that every member of the team was fired by a determination not to go under without giving it their all.

'We decided that we had no intention of surrendering our Munster title without a fierce fight and that we had every intention of keeping it', he said.

The Cork mentors decided on a second-half strategy. The players were told to play the ball first time, to keep it low on the ground against the wind. To help achieve that objective they made switches. The neat-striking Pat Moylan was sent to midfield and Tim Crowley to right half forward. Jimmy Barry Murphy, who had gone into the full forward line for part of the first half, having made little headway against Sean Hehir, was restored to centre forward. Gerald McCarthy went to left half forward where he was being marked by the very competent Ger Loughnane.

While Cork had a certain carefree determination about them as they emerged onto the field the Clare players had a frowning intensity. If they could only make things happen in the second half the long-denied Munster title could be theirs. With the wind behind them they would surely be able to get a goal or maybe two, as they had done against Kilkenny in the league final. It was now or never.

Second Half Opens

Cork opened the scoring of this half when the captain, Charlie McCarthy, to whom short distance frees were assigned, put a 20 metre free over the bar. This darting, accurate player was being well marked by Johnny McMahon but, like Barry Murphy and Cummins, he now carried a far greater threat than any of the Clare forwards.

Shortly afterwards it seemed as if the Clare attack was at last going to get into gear. Enda O'Connor, timing his run perfectly under an incoming ball, rose up to field spectacularly and shot over a good point.

But the expected Clare wind-assisted dominance was not materialising. The Cork half back line, playing into the breeze, were getting on top, with the small-statured McCurtain always able to gain possession and clear well. They kept the ball low on the ground while the half forwards pulled first time to keep it moving just over the grass towards the full forward line.

Mick Malone's leg injury was slowing him up and he was replaced by the tall Eamon O'Donoghue. This player, racing in along the end line or the sideline, sometimes beating Jackie O'Gorman for pace, made a significant impact on the Cork attack. Cork supporters wondered why he had not been in from the very start.

Tim Crowley, who had played second fiddle to Johnny Callinan at midfield, now opened his shoulders in the forward line and foraged vigorously. Sean Hehir was finding him difficult to curb.

Cork Points

The dash and spirit of the Cork side contrasted with the burdened efforts of the men in blue and gold. The Leeside forwards began to sweep into the Clare goal area. The Clare backs had recourse to fouling to prevent a goal. From two of these frees Charlie McCarthy put over two points. Then, in a long-legged race to the sideline, Ray Cummins outpaced Jim Power and collected the ball. He twisted and turned to get clear and then shot one of the best scores of the game, a point from a narrow angle.

Clare, struggling as they were in the forward line, made desperate efforts. They strove hard for a goal that would give them the lift that they badly needed but in their anxiety the forwards tended to bunch down the centre. However, the Cork backs conceded a number of frees and Colm Honan put two over to reduce the Cork lead to three points with twenty minutes remaining.

From each puck out he took, Martin Coleman managed to send the ball soaring well down the field, even now against the wind. The length of these puck outs were a significant factor in tilting the game Cork's way. Cashman, playing so well in the centre, collected many of them and sent them on. As well as that the Cork full back line was giving little away and Denis Burns was providing a very adequate substitute for Brian Murphy.

Durack, at the other end, had far more dangerous shots to save and clear than Coleman. But he did it with great fire and verve, often running far out to send a long puck to his forwards.

A free for each side and McCarthy and Honan exchanged points.

Clare Substitution

Now Clare introduced Brendan Gilligan at full forward for Martin McKeogh, who had made little headway against the full back, O'Doherty. But Cork continued to dominate and they restored their five point lead with a point from Tim Crowley and another great acute angle effort from Ray Cummins.

Only ten minutes remained and it seemed a certainty now that Clare were not able to open their shoulders to match the dash of the men in red. But Honan put a point over to reduce the gap. Right after that the game might have been finished if Durack had not brilliantly saved a piledriver from Tim Crowley.

At this stage Cork replaced Pat Moylan with Pat Horgan. Moylan was playing well and many of the spectators were puzzled by the decision.

There was disappointment on the dark-haired Moylan's face as he walked towards the sideline.

With six minutes remaining Johnny Callinan from Clarecastle, who was playing his heart out, raced through for a point which raised Clare's hopes.

Three Points Behind

Now, with three minutes remaining, there was only a goal between the sides and the tension rose in the massed stands and terraces. The Clare supporters roared in unison to try to lift their men. A great buzz of excitement went round the ground when Clare were awarded a free. Colm Honan ran over to take it. 'Come on now Honan — in around the house' people shouted, expecting him to land it in the square in the hope that it might be tipped to the net. He looked towards the sideline before he bent, lifted and struck the ball over the bar.

Durack Runs Down Field

From the puck out Tom Cashman gathered the ball and, still full of running, raced towards the Clare goal. Jackie O'Gorman hounded him desperately and the referee awarded a free. Charlie McCarthy trotted over and struck it neatly over the bar. Time was running out when Cork attacked again. The ball came flying in towards goal. Once again Durack saved, gathered the ball and, to a despairing cheer from the Clare followers, raced frantically outfield on a last-gasp solo run. Very few goalkeepers had the speed to tear along the turf like him. At centrefield he saw the unmarked Ger Loughnane and passed the ball to him.

Last Effort

With time almost up the only thing Loughnane could do was to land the ball in the goalmouth and hope that someone would get a hurl to it. The Feakle star sent in a high ball which began to drop down as backs and forwards jostled for position. But the wind carried the ball over the bar. Cork were two points ahead. With the puck out came the final whistle.

Cork Delight

The Cork team and supporters danced for joy. They had shown great grit in adversity, had displayed tremendous spirit after half time when the dice seemed to be heavily loaded against them. Pride and tradition and hurling skill had propelled them to victory, their fourth Munster title in a row in a game in which there were no goals and most of the scores came from placed balls.

When the whistle sounded Ger Loughnane had fallen to his knees and slapped his hurley against the sod in anguish and frustration. His team mates were numbed with shock and despondency. They came trailing across the field, oblivious to the words of comfort that some offered to them.

The faithful Clare fans, so bitterly disappointed, drifted away. Had Clare won their voices would have echoed round the square in Thurles for hours and hours. Some may have dreamed of celebrating with song and cheer into the small hours. Many now drifted away sadly silent, got into their cars and buses and trains and headed for home.

There was a feeling that this was the swan-song of the team that had brought two National League titles to Clare, that had now contested two successive Munster finals. They had given great value to their followers. Players like Stack, Callinan, Loughnane would have found a place on any team. The Clare followers had had many happy and entertaining days with this team and now that era seemed over. The championship title they deserved had eluded them.

The verdict was that the longing for victory, both by team and followers put a terrible strain on these fine players, shackled them with nervous tension.

'They can play better than that', a follower said and he was right. But they had not played to their best at the crucial time.

Love Not Lessened

This heartrending defeat did nothing at all to lessen the love of hurling in Clare. The county could claim to have the most faithful army of followers in the country. All of the three major counties — Cork, Tipperary and Kilkenny — had a marked drop in support during their lean years, only holding on to a phalanx of die-hard followers on the days of defeat. For Clare every year was a lean year in terms of Munster or All-Ireland honours but their supporters still came in droves.

On the evening of the game in 1978, a few bedraggled men came walking unsteadily to the railway station. They were singing 'Spancel Hill' in sorry fits and starts. The station was almost deserted.

The second of the excursion trains to Ennis had long since disappeared down the line into the hedges and fields of the Tipperary countryside. 'We missed the boat this afternoon and now we've missed the train as well', said one.

'That was a great Clare team. At another time they would have won an All-Ireland. But they emerged in Munster at a stage when Cork had a great team also', is the verdict of Gerald McCarthy. Clare were beaten that day but the team and their faithful followers had nothing to be ashamed about.

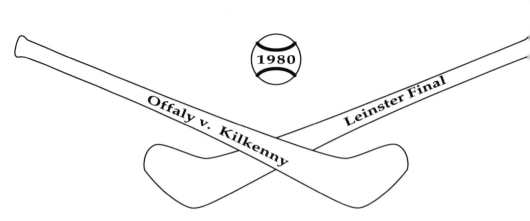

THE GREAT
BREAKTHROUGH

A mere 9,500 people waited for the teams to come out. This was the lowest attendance at a Leinster final since the '40s. The reason was understandable. Very few hurling followers believed that Offaly, who had never won a Leinster senior championship, would beat Kilkenny who were now going for their fiftieth Leinster title. Few could have sensed that one of the most heartening events in the history of hurling was about to take place.

There was a feeling that the game would not be a good one, would have none of the full-blooded competitiveness, the thrills and spills that characterised clashes between Kilkenny and Wexford. These two fierce rivals had been meeting every year since 1970 and had provided some of the best matches ever seen at Croke Park or elsewhere.

Open Draw

It was Offaly who had proposed that there be an open draw in 1980 and there was some resentment against the county because the traditional colour and expectation of a Kilkenny-Wexford final was missing. There seemed a certainty that Offaly could not win and that it might end up a lack-lustre one-sided match. Some of the hidebound traditionalists felt Offaly had spoiled the occasion by being there at all. But their ever-hopeful followers were there in force.

There was no more than a small contingent of Kilkenny supporters scattered about Croke Park that day. They expected their team to win rather easily. It was seen as no more that an outing for them, another step on the road to another All-Ireland final. They were the reigning All-Ireland champions, a team laden with All-Ireland medals, senior and minor, and with great hurlers like Frank Cummins, Ger Henderson and Joe Hennessy in its ranks.

Many of the Kilkenny players felt the same as their followers and the media commentators.

'They had never beaten us in a championship game and I suppose it was difficult not to feel that they would not last the pace', said John Henderson, who played at right corner back that day. 'No matter how much those in charge of a team warn you that this may be a difficult game, it is hard not to be affected by the attitude of people you meet in the highways and byways and streets. They tell you that it is a foregone conclusion. And most important of all, we had a very strong and experienced team.'

The previous year Kilkenny had met a fine Galway team in the All-Ireland. By clever deployment of their forces, shrewd power play and the snuffing out of some of the key Galway players, allied to an amount of luck, they had emerged comfortable winners in a poor final, spoiled by rain and wind.

Now, in 1980, they had already got over the first major hurdle when they beat a good Wexford side in a thrilling semi-final which was part of a two-game programme, with Offaly playing Laois in the other match. Most hurling followers felt that the game between the old rivals was the real final.

As the scattered spectators waited for the Offaly and Kilkenny teams to emerge there was little of the buzz of excitement and anticipation that characterised Kilkenny-Wexford encounters.

'Look — you can say what you like but this is a thoroughbred versus a dray horse', said one grizzled follower.

Offaly Determined

The one place where all these views of the game were being challenged was in the Offaly dressing-room, beneath the Hogan stand. Diarmuid Healy, their Kilkenny-born coach, stood about watchfully in the tense moments as the team prepared to go out, tightened and re-tightened bootlaces, exchanged strained banter, pursed their lips, frowned with the intensity of motivation, gripped their hurleys for comfort.

As the players stood up, ready to set forth from the haven of the dressing-room and along the passage way to the wide open field of combat, Healy called for attention. Beside him stood Andy Gallagher, the trainer and former county goalkeeper as well as the team captain, Padraig Horan from St Rynagh's hurling club by the banks of the Shannon.

'Have no doubts at all — you can take this Kilkenny team. You can do it', Healy said, his square jaw hard with conviction. 'Give it everything you have but hurl cleverly. And keep your concentration all the time.'

Horan spoke a few words of determination and encouragement. What earned him the unqualified respect of his colleagues was his courage, his lion-hearted spirit which burned with an enlivening flame through every game.

He and the other players were resolute in their aim to win recognition for their county in an environment which was slow and sometimes reluctant to welcome new colours from outside the counties that had monopolised the All-Ireland championship.

Offaly Hurling

There had always been hurling in the southern part of the relatively small county of Offaly. On the farmlands and the boggy country between the Slieve Bloom and the Shannon, where the county bordered on Tipperary and south Galway, hurling was always part of the local tradition.

It was played in a small area, with only six or seven senior clubs, no more than 100 senior players and usually less than 20 of inter-county standard or aspiration. It was said that if you climbed half way up a good sized tree somewhere near Birr, you could see the entire hurling area of the county. Not alone that but a section of this small territory, the Moneygall/Dunkerrin area, was traditionally affiliated with Co. Tipperary for GAA purposes and its hurlers played in the Tipperary county championship.

Intense Club Rivalry

As elsewhere, hurling was more than just a form of recreation in Offaly. It was seen as an expression of the courage, skill and endurance of the menfolk of a district or parish.

It was an outlet for the competitive spirit. Unfortunately this sometimes degenerated into rivalries which engendered deep-seated dislike between people in rural areas. The club games developed a reputation for the toughest hurling to be seen anywhere, with players charging at one another, wild swinging and dangerous pulling.

The spleen generated by such intense rivalry was exacerbated by the fact that the same teams and players from the same small pool kept meeting one another each year in the championship and the county final. For years the two leading sides were from two country areas, Drumcullen and Coolderry, with the towns, Birr and Tullamore, making the occasional challenge.

There were players on the county sides who were hardly on speaking terms with one another. They met only on the morning of the championship game and, after being ritually beaten, scattered to the comfort of their own clubs.

The 1920s

Only in the 1920s did the county overcome this internal rivalry to put together a very good side that won the junior All-Ireland championship in 1923 and again in 1929. In that era they got to the Leinster senior final on three occasions — 1924, 1926 and 1928. They were beaten by Dublin and by Kilkenny in those games.

Always Beaten

That team left a legacy of pride and prowess that at least helped sustain the game during the following bleak decades. Year after year the county side was beaten, usually in the first round, by teams like Wexford, Dublin, Laois, Westmeath or the Leinster king-pins, Kilkenny.

They were often humiliated in these games, beaten by ten or even twenty points. They were regarded as sorely lacking in refined hurling skills as well as the astuteness needed to play to their own strengths, to size up opponents and work out a winning strategy.

All of this was a source of annoyance to the many in the county and outside it who wanted Offaly to make a better showing in the senior championship. But it needed leadership, the will to come together to develop the skills, to break away from the introverted club attitudes. The county team had rarely got together for team talks or any serious kind of collective training. Most importantly there was little sense of the teamwork and camaraderie that characterised the success of the Big Three of hurling.

New Dawn

Then came the 1960s and a new dawn for Offaly hurling. There were social and cultural reasons such as the advent of television, the comparative growth in prosperity which brought about greater mobility through motor cars, the questioning of old verities and old attitudes. This certainly helped to diminish some of the narrow-mindedness which put parish above all else.

A key factor in Offaly was the presence of the Presentation College in Birr, the town at the centre of the hurling area. Here the game was encouraged. Teams from the college began to give serious challenge in all the schools competitions. One of the most enthusiastic lovers of the game was Brother Denis, a native of Co. Cork. He got to know all the people involved in hurling in the county. He was a man of vision who saw that the game would benefit from success at national level.

As an outsider he may have had a clearer view of what was preventing the county team making an impact at All-Ireland championship level. Brother Denis began to influence the culture of the county team. He brought them together for training sessions, emphasised the value of team-work and skills training. He placed great importance on the players — and club rivals — sitting down together after training for tea and sandwiches and friendly chats.

Brother Denis encouraged free discussions on games and tactics. A spirit of companionship began to develop. His influence on senior Offaly hurling was immeasurable and remained so, even when he turned his attention fully to the school and minor teams. There could be hard games of club hurling but the county players now met one another as sporting friends.

Rise of Other Clubs

There was another important development which had a bearing on the strength of the county team. The monopoly of the three or four strong clubs was challenged by the appearance of revitalised or new teams from such areas as Kinnity, on the slopes of the Slieve Bloom, and Banagher on the banks of the Shannon. It opened up the championship, gave encouragement to clubs from Clareen, Lusmagh, Shinrone and other parishes to try to put good teams together. This produced new players and brought them to the forefront. Some were to prove exceptionally able.

Of the new teams which emerged the most influential in the 1960s was St Rynagh's of Banagher. This side began winning the county championship regularly. When they contested the county final they always insisted on a referee from outside the county, men who would not tolerate rough or dangerous play. This undoubtedly put the emphasis on skill and fair play.

To the surprise of many, St Rynagh's began making a great bid for the All-Ireland club championship, contesting the final on two occasions. They were unsuccessful but their presence and performance gave a boost to Offaly hurling and they were supported in these finals by followers from all the clubs in the county. Their players were also getting a taste of the big occasion.

1969 Leinster Final

It was in 1969 that all the new influences on Offaly hurling came to fruition. They put together a very good team for the championship. They reached the Leinster final for the first time since 1928. There they met an outstanding Kilkenny team, with top calibre players like Eddie Keher, Pat Delaney, Pat Henderson, Martin Coogan and Ted Carroll.

The unknown Offaly side showed amazing dash and enthusiasm. The teams were level at half-time in a thrilling encounter. With seven minutes to go Offaly led by two points. Then Paddy Delaney of Johnstown Fenians scored another goal to put Kilkenny ahead. But the midlanders would not give in. They fought fiercely for every ball for every second of the game until, at the final whistle, they found themselves two points behind the team that went on the win the All-Ireland.

This close run thing was a source of encouragement to the county team. They took the championship seriously each year and the league too. By the end of the 1970s the Offaly team had emerged as a challenger-in-waiting to the major sides. In the championships of that decade they ran both Kilkenny and Wexford close on several occasions.

The team management, in which Andy Gallagher had a key role, and the players got together and made a firm decision to get into the top division of the National League so that they could match their worth with the top hurling teams. Gallagher, who had played for fourteen years with the county team, was at the helm when they first gained promotion to division one in 1976–77.

In the league campaign of 1979/80 they played well, winning most of their games, including one against Kilkenny at Nowlan Park, one of the few times they ever beat the Noresiders in a league or challenge game. They found themselves in the final stages. They contested the quarter final against Wexford and, to the surprise of many, won the game. They were beaten by Clare in the semi-final but they were pleased to have done so well.

Lack of Self-Belief

The Offaly team was now fired by determination to make the breakthrough. The members of the team were well aware of their own worth. But they were also aware that they lacked a certain self-belief, a confidence which was needed to sustain them at crucial times in big games, usually in the last five minutes of neck-and-neck races to the line.

'When a team hasn't got a deep belief in itself then it is very hard to keep calm when the pressure really comes on in the last minutes of a tight game', explains Damien Martin, the veteran goalkeeper who was a survivor of the 1969 side. 'Players begin to hit the ball anywhere just to clear it. They give away unnecessary frees. And any mistake — a score missed or a point given away — is magnified out of all proportion so that players get frustrated or downhearted, feeling that they have thrown it away, instead of keeping cool.'

There was a feeling that no matter how good their own mentors might be they needed outside help. Martin and the St Rynagh's club proposed that they look for a coach from outside the county, ideally a person who could add that extra dimension that was the difference between winning and losing. They were talking about someone who not alone knew the game of hurling, but knew how to handle players and had experience of winning teams.

Diarmuid Healy

Offaly were lucky to find a journalist from Kilkenny called Diarmuid Healy. He was an astute reader of the game and had trained Kilkenny minor teams for All-Ireland honours. He understood personality and character and motivation. More than anything else he understood the virtues of top-class hurling as played by Kilkenny — keeping cool under difficulty, flicking the ball out to a colleague who had run into position to receive it, being adept at getting out of tight corners by well-rehearsed side-stepping, pretending to hit from the left and then suddenly switching to the right, having a well-developed sense of where the breaking ball would go.

Healy very soon recognised that these were good players. They had the potential to benefit greatly from more skills training and adapting the kind of clever play that had served Kilkenny teams so well in the past.

'He had a conviction that once a team really believes in itself, believes that it is as good if not better than any opponents, then that team will never give up', says Martin. 'He knew also that when you have this inner certainty you are able to hurl better, to be confident in all you do and thereby do it better.'

Preparations

The team began to prepare for the 1980 championship. With Andy Gallagher as trainer Healy put the team through skills training sessions, building up self-confidence, strengthening teamwork. He emphasised the value of the quick flick to get the ball away from an opponent as against the heavy pull which often did no more than break a hurley. He told players that it was better to make space, pass the ball back to a colleague than waste energy trying to go forward by bulldozing through a wall of opponents.

'When I went up there from Kilkenny I took a pile of light Neary hurleys to replace the heavy ones some of the players were using', recalls Healy. 'I emphasised that if you hit the ball right you don't need a heavy hurley to send it far and fast.'

New Style of Play

The team members adapted quickly to the new regime. They discarded some of the Offaly hurling tradition in front of goal where players who got the ball wanted to blast it out through the net — more often than not being hooked or hustled off the ball while they tried to set themselves up for a cannonball shot. The value of a quick, deft flick of the ball at the right split second was emphasised.

Offaly met Dublin in the first semi-final of the double-header in Croke Park and won on a scoreline of 0–18 to 0–10. It was the first time since 1909 that they had beaten the metropolitans in the championship. The team felt pleased with themselves. When they came out of the dressing-room they went out onto the Hogan Stand to watch the Kilkenny-Wexford game. It was a thrilling match. Most spectators could not see Offaly standing up to the winners. But the Offaly team, sizing up their opponents, thought that they were capable of taking the stars in the black and amber.

Inside Knowledge

One of the key factors in Offaly having Diarmuid Healy on their side was that he knew the form of each of the Kilkenny players. He watched them play each week in club matches in Kilkenny. He had trained some of them at under-age level. He knew how good they were.

Noel Skehan was one of the great goalkeepers, with amazing reflexes, had a radar-like monitoring of the outfield play and seemed to know exactly how each ball would come to him.

It could fairly be said of the outfield players that they had all the skills associated with Kilkenny hurling — quick, wristy stickwork, the ability to flick the ball accurately to a colleague or into the net. They had the ability to hit the ball on the 'sweet spot' of the hurley and in doing so to send over points from long range.

In front of Skehan were three experienced stalwarts in John Henderson, Brian Cody and Dick O'Hara. Many claimed that this was the best full back line that year. Henderson, from the Johnstown Fenians club which had become a big force in Kilkenny hurling, was a tight, undemonstrative marker. He used a light hurley to tip the ball away from forwards and out of harm's way. He had got the better of his duel with Galway's razor-sharp forward, P.J. Molloy, in the previous year's All-Ireland.

Cody was a big strong player who raced well out to meet the ball and didn't hesitate to go in front of his man. He could solo out far and then make a long delivery into the forwards. In the other corner was the heavily-bearded Dick O'Hara from Thomastown. He was a hard battler and it was not easy to pass him. When he got the ball he often came thundering out along the left touchline, his feet only inches from the white-washed line on the grass. Pursuing opponents had no option but to keep outside him. O'Hara would then shorten the grip on his hurley and hit the ball so close to his body on his left hand side that he was almost impossible to hook as he cleared the ball downfield.

Half Back Line

The Kilkenny half back line had the captain, Ritchie Reid, at right half back. Fast and reliable, he had been one of the players who had brought the Ballyhale Shamrocks to the forefront of Kilkenny hurling.

In the centre, wearing his familiar light-brown helmet was Ger Henderson, who had followed his brother Pat into the centre back berth and created a unique family succession for this position in senior hurling. This tough, left-handed player had an astounding ability to catch the ball amidst swinging hurleys, flailing arms and elbows and come bursting out with it to make telling clearances. He had great courage and a never-say-die spirit and his play was inspirational for the whole team.

On the left was the stocky, broad-shouldered Nicky Brennan, who played with a relentless determination. He had many of the clever touches typical of the Kilkenny half back tradition stretching from Paddy Phelan to Paddy Buggy to Seamus Cleere. In the second half of the All-Ireland of the previous year he had given an outstanding display.

Centrefield

At centrefield were two of the best hurlers Kilkenny ever produced — Frank Cummins and Joe Hennessy. The thrusting, barrel-chested Cummins used his considerable weight legitimately but very effectively. He shouldered opponents out of the way and then went on charging solo runs, his heavy muscular legs pumping fast.

He often got well ahead of his pursuers and then spectators saw him swing back the hurley, swish it forward in a big semi-circle to meet the ball and produce one of the hardest left-handed shots seen at any time. He had played exceptionally well on Galway's John Connolly the year before.

His partner was the slightly built but immensely skilful Joe Hennessy. Sometimes he was referred to as 'Gentleman Joe' because he was one of the most good-natured, sporting players from any county. He had an uncanny instinct for where the ball was going to be and how it was going to break, so much so that he often seemed to have nobody marking him. Fast and agile, he went on jaunty solo runs which ended in rousing points.

Half Forwards

The two Fennelly brothers, Ger and Kevin were on the right and left half forward positions respectively. They were members of the hurling family that had played a major role in making Ballyhale one of the most vibrant centres of Kilkenny hurling. They were sinewy, rangy players, side-steppers and opportunists, weaving and racing along the wings. They were both clean strikers of the ball and could send over points from far out. Where they were most dangerous was where the ball was bobbing about near the goal — out of nowhere one or other of them was liable to lose their marker before running in and whipping the loose ball to the net.

Joe Wall, from one of the oldest and most famed clubs in south Kilkenny, Mooncoin, had been a minor and under-21 star. In the Kilkenny club championship he had given outstanding performances and kept his side in the running. He was a good distributor of the ball, kept it moving, had a good first touch, had a lot of skills in the close encounters.

Strong Full Forward Line

Kilkenny's full forward line was one of the reasons that commentators and hurling judges had made the Noresiders hot favourites. Mick 'Cloney' Brennan from Castlecomer was one of the most effective right corner forwards of modern times. He was tigerish in his efforts to get possession. He had a fast, accurate stroke on the ball, usually off his left hand side. He was sometimes referred to as the 'Master of the Narrow Angle' for the way he could slot points from the corner or out on the sideline. He was famous also for his bursts along the end line into the goalmouth. He had been chosen as an All Star in the right corner in '75, '76 and '79.

Full forward was the tall, quick-striking Billy Fitzpatrick from Johnstown, equally accurate left or right. He could lift the ball effortlessly into his hand at full speed and snap it over the bar without stopping to look goalwards. In the other corner was a grey haired player from Bally-ragget, Matt Ruth. He was one of the great opportunists of the game who scored goals out of the merest chance. He was extremely difficult to mark because he moved about constantly, snapping up loose balls and either racing into the square or striking them over the bar.

The team was under the joint control of Pat Henderson and Eddie Keher, two of the great Kilkenny luminaries of the recent past.

Henderson Warning

Henderson, in an interview with the *Kilkenny People,* warned that this would be no walkover. 'Offaly will be approaching this game as if it is an All-Ireland. For them to win a Leinster championship is like Kilkenny winning an All-Ireland.'

He said that it could be difficult for the players to get into the right frame of mind after reaching such a height in beating Wexford. Henderson also recalled the fact that Offaly had beaten Kilkenny in the league match at Nowlan Park earlier in the year.

For all that, the mood among the players was one of confidence. The feeling was that Offaly might stay the pace for three quarters of the game but then Kilkenny power and experience would draw them inexorably ahead.

In the Offaly camp Healy had called the players together for a long session some days before the game. He spoke about each member of the Kilkenny team, the kind of players they were, how they would need to be handled. He explained the kind of ploys that could be expected from the sideline. Very few teams taking the field were so well briefed on the character and playing pattern of their opponents.

Unknown Offaly

The same could not be said of the Kilkenny side. John Henderson recalls: 'We knew something about them but I suppose we were not that interested in the kind of players they were. Maybe in our confident approach we did not feel we needed to concentrate on who or what they were.'

This lack of knowledge about the Offaly players extended to most of the neutral spectators and indeed to many of those there wearing or waving the green, white and orange colours.

The goalkeeper, Damien Martin was one of the best known. He was now in his seventeenth season with the senior team, a record not often equalled in any county. For his superb anticipation and solid play he was chosen on the very first All-Star team in 1971, when these major awards were initiated by Pat Heneghan, then director of public relations with the Carroll tobacco company, together with a group of leading GAA journalists.

Not a great deal was known about the full back line of Pat Moloughney, Mick Kennedy and Pat Fleury. All three were seen as solid performers without having the style or stature of their opposite numbers. Fleury had come to some prominence when hurling with one of the best Fitzgibbon Cup teams that UCG had ever produced. In the game against Dublin he proved to be very strong under the high ball. One thing that was known to the attendance — all three were going to be fully tested by the men they were marking.

Right half back was one of those who had brought St Rynagh's to the forefront of Offaly hurling, Aidan Fogarty. He was proving a rock of reliability, very hard to beat for the incoming ball. In the centre was a tall, rangy player, with tousled blond hair, from the slopes of Slieve Bloom, Pat Delaney of Kinnity. His duel with Joe Wall was seen as one of the key factors by some commentators. On his left was one of the smallest men who ever hurled at senior level, Ger Coughlan, also of Kinnity. Even before this major trial he had shown that he could turn on a sixpence, could pull confidently on oncoming balls, block and hook, could ride the heaviest tackle.

Centrefield Battle

Few could see the centrefield pair, Joachim Kelly and Brendan Keeshan, making any fist of Cummins and Hennessy. The judgment of many was that Kilkenny's victory would be launched from the middle of the pitch. The left-handed Kelly was a PT instructor at the Garda depot in Templemore and was always in peak physical condition. Keeshan was a small, compact player who had shown many deft skills in the game against Dublin. Mark Corrigan, on the right wing of the Offaly attack, was showing himself exceptionally adept at grabbing the breaking ball and sending over points. Whether he would do so against a player of the calibre of Nicky Brennan was a matter of some doubt. In the centre was Brendan Birmingham, already known as someone who kept the ball moving goalwards, pulling first time on it in the air and on the ground. He was going to have to do just that if he were to prevent Ger Henderson from commanding the half line, as he was accustomed to do.

The red-haired Pat Carroll was on the right wing. Even at this early stage of Offaly's emergence the stories of his dedication to hurling and training were spreading. A dairy farmer from Coolderry, he milked the cows an hour earlier than customary in the evenings so that he could get away for training. He was an indomitable battler for every ball that came his way.

Paddy Kirwan, the sole representative of the Ballyskenach club, had a very strong and accurate pull on the ball. He had the longest puck of anyone on the team but how he would fare against O'Hara cooped up in the corner was another matter.

Offaly's full forward, Padraig Horan, was the best known player on the team. This strong, steel-willed player had started out as a back and had given such outstanding performances during the years of Offaly frustration that he was selected several times for the provincial team. Usually the sole Offaly representative on the Leinster side, he won Railway Cup medals in 1973, '74 and '75. If any player was going to inspire the team it was going to be the captain. Diarmuid Healy had appointed him to take close-in frees.

'We needed someone who had the character and temperament to take frees under pressure without wilting', says Healy.

The small, stocky man in the left corner was a veteran of the 1969 side, Johnny Flaherty of Kinnity. After that game he had gone to the US and had not returned to live in Ireland for nearly ten years.

The teams as they lined out were:

KILKENNY

Noel Skehan
(Bennettsbridge)

John Henderson	Brian Cody	Dick O'Hara
(Fenians)	(James Stephens)	(Thomastown)

Ritchie Reid, capt	Ger Henderson	Nicky Brennan
(Shamrocks)	(Fenians)	(Conahy)

Frank Cummins	Joe Hennessy
(Blackrock, Cork)	(James Stephens)

Ger Fennelly	Joe Wall	Kevin Fennelly
(Shamrocks)	(Mooncoin)	(Shamrocks)

Mick Brennan	Billy Fitzpatrick	Matt Ruth
(Erin's Own)	(Fenians)	(St Patrick's)

Substitutes: Liam O'Brien (James Stephens); Mick Crotty (James Stephens); Murty Kennedy (St Lachtain's); Maurice Mason (Shamrocks); Michael Meagher (John Locke's); Tom McCormack (James Stephens); Tommy Malone (Rower-Inistioge); Frank Holohan (Shamrocks); Paudie Lannon (Thomastown); Liam Fennelly (Shamrocks). *Coaches:* Pat Henderson; Eddie Keher. *Team doctor:* Dr Kieran Cuddihy.

OFFALY

Damien Martin
(St Rynagh's)

Pat Moloughney	Mick Kennedy	Pat Fleury
(Coolderry)	(Birr)	(Drumcullen)

Aidan Fogarty	Pat Delaney	Ger Coughlan
(St Rynagh's)	(Kinnity)	(Kinnity)

Brendan Keeshan	Joachim Kelly
(Shinrone)	(Lusmagh)

Mark Corrigan	Brendan Birmingham	Pat Carroll
(Kinnity)	(Lusmagh)	(Coolderry)

Paddy Kirwan	Padraig Horan, capt	Johnny Flaherty
(Ballyskenach)	(St Rynagh's)	(Kinnity)

Substitutes: Eugene Coughlan (Seir Kieran); Martin Cashin (Birr); Danny Owens (Killoughey); Christy King (Killavilla). *Coach:* Diarmuid Healy. *Trainer:* Andy Gallagher. *Mentors/selectors:* Tom Errity (Coolderry); Charlie Daly (Na Piarsaigh); Andy Gallagher (Tullamore); Mick Spain (Drumcullen); Padge Mulhaire (St Rynagh's); Tony Murphy (Seir Kieran). *Team physician:* Dr Brendan White. *Masseur:* Ossie Bennett.

The referee was Noel O'Donoghue from the Cuala club in Dalkey, Co Dublin. He called the captains together on the centre line. Richie Reid won the toss and elected to play into the Railway end.

After the national anthem had been played and the bandsmen marched off the field the referee threw in the ball to a cheer from the big Offaly contingent in the small attendance.

Offaly Tear Into Game

Right from the very start Offaly tore into the game, full of a resolution that could be felt in the farthest and most deserted corner of the stadium.

The first tense moment of the game came when Joe Hennessy cut in a fine line ball that just went wide, with the Offaly backs glued to their opponents.

Damien Martin pucked out the ball. It soared over the halfway line and dropped down on the right. Corrigan was fast onto it, got it in his hand, steadied himself and sent over the first point of the game. Kilkenny replied almost immediately. After a fierce tussle in the left corner Kevin Fennelly flicked the ball Kilkenny-style out to Ruth who put it neatly over the bar.

Opportunist Goal

Then came the encouraging score that Offaly needed. From Martin's puck out the ball once again went to the right and once again Corrigan was fast onto it, despite the attentions of Nicky Brennan. He sent another shot goalwards. It seemed as if it would make it over the bar but Noel Skehan, ever confident of his own ability and the competence of the backs before him, reached up his hurley high and blocked it down. Waiting like a prowling wolf was Flaherty. He grabbed the ball and struck it fast and hard into the net, his feet leaving the ground with the effort. A huge echoing roar came from the faithful followers of the underdogs.

This was a great start for the outsiders. Horan, who was going to run far out to pull Cody with him during the game, was on the 45 metre line when Joachim Kelly got the better of a tussle with Frank Cummins and sent the ball in. Horan caught it and struck it in his characteristic style, close to his body. The ball went over the bar.

A minute later the ball fell between Reid and Carroll. Reid got it but the dogged Carroll, who never gave up, chased and dispossessed his marker and sent it across the square. Paddy Kirwan caught it and lashed it towards goal. Only for Dick O'Hara's hurley this would have been a goal. The ball was deflected over the bar.

All Afire

Offaly were pounding along with great fire while Kilkenny seemed taken aback by the zeal of their opponents. And the midlanders were showing style as well. Brendan Birmingham, graceful as a ballet dancer, collected a clearance on his own 65 metre line, turned and swung his hurley in one movement and sent the ball on a long trajectory until it began to fall to earth behind and between the tall white wooden uprights at the far end of the field. There was a delighted burst of applause for one of the great scores of the game from the hurling-lovers, including those from Kilkenny.

Offaly's first five scores had come from different players, auguring well for the performance of their underrated forward division. Kilkenny came back into the picture when they were awarded a 40 metre free. The moustachioed Billy Fitzpatrick bent, lifted and struck the ball elegantly and accurately over the bar.

Once again the puck out by Martin went past the battling midfielders on to the right hand side of the Offaly attack. It seemed like a deliberate plan to keep the ball out of the magnetic grasp of Ger Henderson in the centre. Once again Mark Corrigan got hold of it and from 45 metres struck the ball over.

Shortly afterwards a free was awarded to Offaly from 65 metres out, on the right hand side of the field looking towards the Kilkenny goal at the canal end. Pat Delaney came loping up. This was one of his special skills — long range points. In the years to come he would often keep Offaly in the hunt, even on occasions when he himself was having a difficult game, by his long-distance accuracy. He straddled the ball, bent down, briefly raised his head to get another look at the posts, raised the ball carefully and swung confidently. It took off and four seconds later the umpire raised the white flag.

Kilkenny Goal

Offaly were going at a searing pace, keeping the pressure on each and every one of their opponents. Then, in the fourteenth minute, some of the steam was taken out of their efforts by a Kilkenny goal which came against the run of play. It came about when Ger Henderson won a ball in an aerial battle and sent a long clearance down the field.

Matt Ruth, in the left corner of the Kilkenny attack, tried to grab the ball but, under harrassment from Pat Moloughney, dropped it. But it bounced luckily back into his hand and he soloed goalwards from 22 metres out, with Moloughney breathing down his neck. He ran into a maelstrom of tussling backs and forwards, lost his footing and dropped the ball. His momentum carried him into the back of the net while the ball dribbled over the line, despite the effort of Damien Martin.

When the green flag was waved there was a feeling among the spectators that this untidy goal would take some of the fire out of Offaly. One fumbled effort had negatived all their point-scoring endeavours. There was also great admiration for the opportunism of Ruth. Indeed this was to be for him one of those games that all players dream about — when they can do nothing wrong, when balls roll up on their hurleys or come into their hands, when opponents are unable to match their wiles.

Before the Kilkenny cheers had died down Offaly's response was to mount another attack. The Noresiders conceded a free. Padraig Horan trotted out to the 50-metre mark. Since his appointment as free-taker he had practised diligently. The work stood to him well. He put this one over the bar confidently. He was to miss no frees this day.

Kilkenny Come Into Game More

At this stage Kilkenny had shaken off some of the shock of Offaly's whirlwind start and were beginning to win more of the play. The ball was sent fast into the right corner for the dashing Mick Brennan. He broke away from Pat Fleury for the only time in the match and raced goalwards. His fast shot was deflected over the line by an Offaly hurley.

Joe Hennessy came over to take the 65. He and Brendan Keeshan were just about breaking even at centrefield but Kelly was winning the battle against Cummins. Hennessy had a lovely clean stroke of ball and he had no problem, on this day of little breeze, in sending the sliotar over the bar. Yet, in a pattern which was to become characteristic of Offaly, they counter-attacked. A free was awarded from 35 metres out. Once again Horan, with an air of nonchalance, sent it over.

Ruth Again

It was now halfway through the first half and Offaly were leading by 1–8 to 1–3. Richie Reid and Nicky Brennan were coming more into the game and a long ball from their line of defence whistled into the Offaly goal-mouth. The grey head of Matt Ruth rose above the ruck of players and he grabbed possession of the ball. There was no way the Offaly backs were going to allow him to palm or strike the ball into the goal.

The referee decided that they had fouled him. He awarded a penalty. Billy Fitzpatrick placed the ball and looked towards the goal. There stood three players, hunched with concentration, eyes laser-beamed on the ball sitting on the grass. On either side of Martin, with his wide bossed hurley, were Coughlan and Fleury. They knew that Fitzpatrick had taken thousands of penalties and could place the ball where he liked, at whatever height he wanted. Fitzpatrick rose the ball and sent in a blurred bullet at shoulder height. Martin's hurley almost got to it but the ball cracked into the netting. The Offaly followers shook their heads in dismay.

Yet the way Offaly came back from this blow was heartening. The men in the tricoloured jerseys raced into another attack. The ball went off a Kilkenny hurley 50 metres out on the right. Offaly's line ball expert, Brendan Keeshan, stood back from the ball, raised his stick, advanced slowly and cut the ball upwards with the heel of his hurley. It went floating in goalwards to a murmur of admiration from the crowd. As the backs and forwards jostled for position before the ball dropped in the square Noel O'Donoghue blew his whistle. He awarded a penalty for holding against Kilkenny.

This was Offaly's chance to reply in kind. Horan stood over the ball. On either side of Skehan was Cody and John Henderson. The St Rynagh's player hit the ball shoulder-height, not unlike Fitzpatrick's effort a minute earlier. But the lightning-fast hurleys of Skehan and Cody stopped the flight of the missile and the Kilkenny backs cleared it away.

This lost chance caused some dismay among the Offaly following. They were alarmed when their rivals went on a dangerous attack and Joe Wall, evading Pat Delaney, got the ball in the net. To Offaly's relief the referee disallowed the score and gave a free out for an infringement inside the square. A few seconds later Ger Fennelly, for once getting free of the fast, limpet-like Coughlan, took the ball on his hurley near the half-way mark and sprinted along the sideline for nearly fifty metres before slotting over a great point. This reduced Offaly's lead to a single point.

At this juncture there were wides from both sides. The corner forwards kept moving out to get possession, often leaving spaces at the top, and several balls hopped harmlessly over the end line.

Changes Being Made

With ten minutes of the first half to go Pat Moloughney was moved out to the half back line while Aidan Fogarty came into the corner to watch Ruth. Tight a marker and strong a player as Fogarty was, he had the unenviable job of trying to curb a player who was right on song in everything he did.

A few minutes later the Kilkenny mentors tried to repair their creaking midfield. They moved Frank Cummins to right half forward in a straight switch with Ger Fennelly, the former captain of the team. Spectators watched the barrel-chested Cummins, one of the heaviest men on the field, go over to take his place beside the diminutive Coughlan. It looked an uneven match. But the frail-looking Kinnity player was the master of the quick flick to take the ball away from opponents. He was difficult to shoulder because he was so small and light. He could duck in under an opponent's arms and race away. As it transpired there was to be no real David and Goliath battle that day as Cummins was replaced at half time.

With less than five minutes to go to half time Brendan Birmingham escaped the clutches of Ger Henderson and sent over a point from near the goal. This was replied to by his opposite number, Joe Wall, who did likewise at the far end. Paddy Kirwan and Dick O'Hara were engaging in a relentless duel in the corner but Kirwan kept racing out to collect balls. He did so about 50 metres out near the sideline, turned his marker and went flying in before striking the ball from 20 metres out to put Offaly further ahead.

Another Ruth Goal

There were two minutes to go to half time when, against the run of play, Ruth struck again. The ball came flying into the right corner of the Kilkenny attack. All eyes were on the fierce tussle between Brennan and Fleury. Then Ruth ran across from the left and gathered the loose ball. He spun round and, despite being jostled and baulked by hurtful hurleys, pulled on the ball. It went hopping across the line for another unexpected goal. This had to be a dispiriting experience for Offaly. It seemed to demonstrate that no matter how hard they tried to get ahead they could always be hauled back to reality by scrappy goals.

In a typical Kilkenny thrust to demoralise the opposition, Ger Fennelly got hold of the ball from the puck out and from 65 metres out struck a neat point to make the score 3–6 to 1–10 in Kilkenny's favour at the break.

As the teams left the field the small attendance gave them a spontaneous ovation. This was one of the best 35 minutes hurling seen anywhere in a long time. There was, however, a feeling that the second half could not be as good, that Offaly would gradually succumb to the superior skill and experience of the All-Ireland champions.

'Look at that — Offaly hurled them out of it all over the field and yet Kilkenny are going in two points up. If Kilkenny get into their stride that will be the end of it', said one of the neutral spectators.

In the Offaly dressing-room Andy Gallagher and Diarmuid Healy told their charges to keep up the way they were playing and not to lose any composure, especially coming up to the end of game. There was some talk about putting Joachim Kelly back to mark Frank Cummins in case he opened up in the second half and Coughlan was unable to handle him. They need not have worried. The Kilkenny mentors, Henderson and Keher, decided to replace the flu-diminished Cummins by Liam 'Chunky' O'Brien for the second half.

O'Brien's appearance, with his bushy hair and lively gait, raised a cheer among the Kilkenny supporters. They knew well his ability to take long-range scores at crucial times in games as he had done against Galway in the All-Ireland of the previous year.

Skehan Saves

Right from the throw in Offaly went charging into the attack, as they had done in the first half. Two cracking shots were sent at the Kilkenny goal but Skehan made two fine saves. There were moans of disappointment from the followers from the midlands. And worse again, from one of the clearances Billy Fitzpatrick got possession and struck the ball over the bar to put Kilkenny three points in front.

There was a feeling in the stadium that from here on it might be downhill all the way for Offaly. On the contrary, this was when they showed their real mettle. They roared back into the game and attacked again. Corrigan and Kirwan were proving extremely hard to curb on the right side of the Offaly attack. From the sideline Paddy Kirwan floated a long ball over the bar.

With their followers and many neutrals now cheering their grit the Offaly men set up another attack which ended with a free being awarded to them from a narrow angle on the left. It was a difficult assignment for Horan but he was imperturbable as he lifted the ball and sent it between the posts for a heartening score.

Kilkenny Make Changes

Billy Fitzpatrick sent over another point but at this stage the Kilkenny mentors seemed to acknowledge that they had caught a tartar. They set about making wholesale changes. Mick Crotty was introduced as a sub for Kevin Fennelly. Billy Fitzpatrick, who had been playing at centre half forward for a short while, moved to his well-established position at left half forward. Joe Wall, who had been at full forward, went back to the centre forward berth. The Kilkenny forward lines were now somewhat unsettled.

When the ball was sent along Offaly's left wing of attack, Pat Carroll whipped it forward along the ground. Johnny Flaherty, with John Henderson on his heels came racing out, got the ball in his hand and sent a fast, accurate ball across the field to Paddy Kirwan who clipped it over the bar from 30 metres out.

Offaly Level

From a Kilkenny wide Damien Martin once more landed the ball on the right-hand side and once again Mark Corrigan got it. He usually struck the ball from the right although he held the hurl in the left-handed grip but it made no difference to his accuracy. As the ball went soaring over the bar a great cheer of encouragement echoed about half-deserted terraces and stands. The sides were level.

Yet Kilkenny went ahead again when they were awarded a 45-metre free which the immaculate Fitzpatrick sent over the bar. At this stage Aidan Fogarty, who had suffered an injury, was replaced in the corner by the tall Eugene Coughlan from Clareen, who was at the start of a career as one of the great full backs.

In a mad scramble in the Kilkenny goalmouth Brian Cody, who along with the other full backs was having to endure endless pressure, fell to the ground and tried to hand pass the ball away. The referee said he had thrown it and awarded a free. Padraig Horan, with his dogged blocking and tough hustling, was making it difficult for Cody and the other backs to make any real clearances from in front of goal. The St Rynagh's man now took the free and put the ball over the bar.

Clever Play

Halfway into the second half the ball once again came down the right wing of the Offaly attack. Corrigan sent it in to Kirwan. But Dick O'Hara was on to him like a dark-haired hound and almost dispossessed him. Kirwan then did precisely what Healy and Gallagher had been telling the whole team to do — take the clever option. He passed the ball back out to Corrigan who had room to palm the ball over the bar. Offaly were back in the lead again.

Richie Reid and Nicky Brennan swapped positions in an attempt to curb the Offaly attack. It had taken the resourceful Reid all his time to hold the red-haired battler Carroll; whether he could now handle Corrigan any better than Brennan remained to be seen. However, at this crucial juncture Kilkenny's spirits were raised by another goal. The lanky Crotty took a neat pass from Joe Wall and flying on long legs into the square on the left whipped in a low ball across the face of the goal and into the far corner. Martin had little chance.

Looking Like End of Offaly

This seemed like the *coup de grace* for the gallant challengers. No matter how well they played it seemed that Kilkenny could always get goals. Offaly would work hard for three points and then in one fell swoop the men in black and amber would cancel it all out. Many in the attendance felt that Offaly's game would now go on the wane and the champions would run out fairly comfortable winners. This view was reinforced when Kilkenny were awarded a free 30 metres out and Fitzpatrick put it comfortably over the bar to give his side a three point lead.

This was the moment when Offaly showed the grit and indomitable will to keep going that was to characterise their team in the years to follow. Instead of dropping their heads they again took the game to the champions and mounted more attacks. The forays were never easily repelled because each of their forwards fought for each ball relentlessly. If they did not get it they blocked and hooked effectively, stopped it being cleared. Only the astonishing alacrity of Skehan saved a certain goal from Birmingham.

Then, two minutes later, Birmingham, who was fighting a great duel with Ger Henderson, again came thundering in towards the square with the ball. He was upended by two Kilkenny backs and the referee awarded a penalty. Once again Horan faced the same three guardians of the net, Skehan, Henderson and O'Hara. He rose the ball and sent in a cracker, also at shoulder height. There was a roar of delight from the Kilkenny followers when the ball was blocked. But the roar was stifled when Birmingham, following the penalty, got the rebound and kicked the ball into the net to level the scores.

The crowd were in a frenzy and hurling followers listening to the vivid radio commentary of Micheal O Muircheartaigh realised that not alone was one of the most exciting games being played but that it might be an historic occasion. There were many listeners in Kilkenny who regretted they had been put off setting out for Croke Park that morning by a spell of rain. Their team badly needed all the encouragement they could get.

Kilkenny however were a team who understood that the rhythm of games can change, that the momentum can be lost by one team and gained by another in a matter of minutes. The greatest example had been their astounding comeback from seeming defeat in the All-Ireland of 1972. The lithe men in black and amber struck at the Offaly goal and Mick Crotty whipped a fast ball goalwards. Damien Martin saved but only at the expense of a 65.

Backs and forwards waited for the ball to be struck. It did not go over the bar but fell short. Martin reached up and grabbed it under the crossbar.

'In the old days my inclination at this stage would be to lash it away anywhere down the field', recalls Damien Martin. 'But we were playing intelligent hurling at this stage. I saw Brendan Keeshan running out to the sideline towards the centre of the field.'

Martin's stroke was well directed and went straight to Keeshan. He sent in a long ball towards the Kilkenny goal. Horan and Cody came tearing out for it shoulder to shoulder as they had been doing all during the match. It broke loose between them. This time the big James Stephen's man got the better of the duel and grabbed the ball. Horan, however, would not give up and hustled the full back so that he missed his puck and the ball fell into Horan's hand. The full forward lobbed it into the square where Johnny Flaherty caught it, rounded John Henderson and palmed the ball to the net.

A tumultuous cheer greeted this score which put Offaly ahead. It was the kind of vital goal that the veteran corner forward would score in key games. This was the first championship occasion that John Henderson had the task of marking this mercurial player from Kinnity.

'He was never easy to mark. He was very deceptive. He would give you the impression that you were in command in the corner because he would wander away. Sometimes he left the field of play and squatted down behind the end line, chewing blades of grass as if he was just a spectator. Next thing the a high ball would come sailing in and if you didn't watch out, Flaherty would be behind your back, would reach over your shoulder and grab the ball, turn fast as a top and hit it or palm it into the net', said Henderson.

In subsequent years Henderson made a policy of never letting Flaherty out of his sight, staying beside him even when, on one occasion he wandered round the back of the goals in the middle of a game where he delivered New York-honed one-liners to the press photographers. If Flaherty had gone to the refreshment counter under the terrace for a paper cup of tea he would have found Henderson behind him in the queue.

Flaherty never stopped yelling advice and encouragement to his colleagues in a high-pitched voice that could be heard half way down the field.

Kelly Injury

As Flaherty's goal was being acclaimed by the delighted Offaly followers Joachim Kelly was lying on the flat of his back with a nasty head wound. There was dismay when the St John's Ambulance squad brought on a stretcher and carried Kelly away. This courageous player had tipped the scales in favour of Offaly at centrefield. It looked a serious setback for the team. Flaherty moved out to the middle and the substitute Martin Cashin took his place in the corner. As it transpired, Kelly's departure had little effect on the team's momentum. They kept up the relentless pace all over the field. Mick Brennan, less than his normal self because of the after effects of the 'flu, was replaced by Murty Kennedy at this stage.

Scoreless Period

For seven minutes the play swept back and forward without a score for either side. With only a few minutes to go, and the Offaly followers shouting themselves hoarse, the midlanders were awarded a free from about 44 metres out. Horan came out in his own good time, settled the ball, then lifted, struck it and sent his fifth free over the bar to put his team ahead by four points. It seemed that new ground was about to be broken with the underdogs creating the upset of the decade in dethroning the All-Ireland champions, beating them for the first time and becoming Leinster title holders for the first time.

Kilkenny Last Gasp Tradition

Kilkenny, however, were far from finished. Part of their great tradition was coming from behind in the very last minute of the game and snatching it with a late score from under the noses of opponents already beginning to celebrate victory. Everybody looking at the game or listening to it knew that the Noresiders were bound to make one all-out effort before the curtain came down on this pulsating game.

Throwing all caution to the wind they hurled like men inspired as the clock moved to full time. Offaly, aware of the danger, threw themselves into every tackle with abandon. But they kept their composure, did not give away needless frees, played the ball with careful desperation. Pat Fleury was playing a forceful game in the corner and repelled two dangerous attacks. In front of the goal Mick Kennedy blocked swinging hurleys with his arms and legs in the mad scuffles. The tension in Croke Park was electric, with the mentors and substitutes of both sides standing up and yelling encouragement to their players. Offaly were four points ahead.

With a minute to go Kilkenny swept the ball into the Offaly goalmouth. There was a nailbiting scramble, with flailing hurleys and jostling bodies in front of the goal. The ball skittered here and there and then went off an Offaly back out over the end line. The umpire raised his arm for a 65.

Another Ruth Goal

Press photographers scrambled to get in position behind the goal. There John Dowling, the Offaly county secretary, as well as bottle-carriers and bagmen from both sides paced about agitatedly, shouting encouragement as Ger Henderson came forward to take the 65. He struck it well and it soared goalwards. All eyes were beamed on it. Near the end of its flight it began to veer to one side. Some of the Offaly supporters behind the goal were already about to wave it wide when it struck the upright. The ball fell down onto the cross bar and hopped down again into the hand of Matt Ruth who slammed it into the net. Kilkenny were only a point behind as the game went into injury time.

Desperate Last Minutes

For the next three minutes there was one of the most frantic passages of hurling ever seen in Croke Park. Every ball was fought for with frightening abandon. Players blocked not only with hurleys but with limbs, uncaring of red weals and raw knuckles.

Joe Hennessy sent a fast ball towards the Offaly goal. It was met by an implosion of bodies and hurleys. Then, to the dismay of the Offaly supporters, the ever dangerous Ruth broke loose on the left. He was under great pressure as two Offaly backs lunged at him. The Ballyragget man had no less than a split second to get his stroke in for the equalising point. As the ball left his stick nine and a half thousand people held their breath in Croke Park. There was a huge collective sigh of relief from the Offaly supporters when the ball just went wide of the uprights.

Offaly Hold Out

Damien Martin, face full of fierce intent, struck the puck out as far as he could. As the ball came down there was an upward thrust of hurleys and arms, like hungry fishes jumping for the same fly. Players could only lash at the ball as it bobbed here and there along the grass. But the tension only served to hone the razor skills of Ger Fennelly and Billy Fitzpatrick and the other Kilkenny forwards and the ball kept zipping along the ground towards the Offaly goal.

In those last seconds the grit and skill of Ger Coughlan came to the fore and the calm and strength of his namesake, Eugene, was seen for the first time in a crucial championship game. No one could blame the Kilkenny forwards for not scoring in such a close scramble when the very able backs closed in on them. The players were cheek by jowl, elbow to elbow in those last hectic seconds and it was impossible to get in any kind of a clean stroke. Then, from the ruck in front of the Offaly goal the redoubtable Johnny Flaherty, expert at rising the ball into his hand with hurley and right foot, got possession and came racing out to clear the ball downfield. At that moment Noel O'Donoghue blew the long final whistle and the game was over.

The scenes which followed were full of exhilaration and uninhibited joy on the part of the winning team and their faithful supporters. The players of the dethroned champions shook hands with their victorious opponents and wished them well. Even in the moments of defeat Kilkenny players acknowledged the unflinching will to win of the Offaly men. They knew there was no shame in being beaten by a team of great triers who were growing in stature and skill with each year.

Emotion

The Offaly followers flooded onto the field like a tidal wave — club mates of the players, former players, families and children, shouting and hand-shaking and congratulating. They leapt into the arms of the players, hugging and kissing and backslapping. Each player was surrounded by a buzzing swarm of admirers.

There were big weighty men who worked on the bogs for Bord na Mona, with red, weathered faces and toil-thickened fingers, who shed tears of joy and of sadness. For former players and long-time followers this was a time of great emotion. They had known years of effort and hope and disappointment. This was an occasion they only imagined in fantasy. Now that it had come about many were speechless. One man walked endlessly about the field, head bent, talking to nobody, as if savouring every puck of the match from the bootmarks on the grass.

Padraig Horan went up the steps of the Hogan stand and was presented with the huge O'Keeffe Cup by the President of the Leinster Council, Paddy Buggy, one of the great Kilkenny hurlers of his era. There was a cheering army of supporters, waving the standards of long-sought victory, on the field below him as the joyful captain hoisted the cup over his head. He did not know at the time that the pulsating, blood-tingling game had claimed someone near to him; his own father, Tom, had been listening to the game at his home in Ballivor, near Banagher, when he died of a heart attack.

Celebration

That evening there were bonfires on the river meadows of the Shannon. One or two twinkled on the long slopes of the Slieve Blooms, and some on the brown bog plains. The biggest of all was in the square of Birr, the focal point of Offaly hurling. The team came there after a tumultuous welcome in Tullamore, Kinnity and the crossroads and byways in between.

This victory for persistence and the never-say-die spirit raised the morale of the county. It was a time of great pride when their team had beaten the unbeatable and shown great character and spirit in doing so. There was victorious singing in pubs and hotels and hostelries for many nights.

For a county like Offaly this was as good as winning the All-Ireland. It gave the team added confidence and determination to go further. This victory was no false dawn for the team. However, they found it hard to overcome the effects of the endless celebrations in order to wind themselves up for their first All-Ireland semi-final some weeks later. They met a fine Galway side who, like themselves, had to fight hard to overcome years of adversity. The westerners were on their way to winning their first All-Ireland in 57 years.

First Semi-Final

There was no question that Galway brushed their midland neighbours aside easily. Having been dominated for much of the game Offaly showed the kind of dogged spirit that was to be their hallmark and came back into the game in the last quarter. They were beaten by only two points and many judged that if the game had gone on another five minutes they might have won it. The game indicated the shape of the encounter the following year when Offaly, again underdogs, took on Galway, then the reigning champions, in the All-Ireland final.

Having held on to their Leinster championship crown the following year Offaly were to go on to contest every Leinster final in the 1980s, winning some, losing some. They became accepted as a formidable team which could never again be written off. This team and its successors brought a refreshing, vigorous presence to the hurling scene and enriched it greatly. Many of its members became household names and were awarded with well deserved accolades by the All-Star selection committees.

Kilkenny Generous in Defeat

The hurling lovers in Kilkenny acknowledged that they had been beaten fairly and squarely and that the emergence of a new force could only be good for the game. In the post mortems of the match there was some criticism of the mentors for taking off Frank Cummins, despite the fact that he was below his best. There was also criticism voiced about the wholesale changes made during the match. It was said, fairly or unfairly, that the selectors and mentors, like the players, had been unprepared for a real battle.

The Offaly side provided a heartening lesson to anyone who cared to learn. No matter how small or disadvantaged a county or a team might be, they could still attain great heights as long as they had fighting spirit, were willing to learn and to develop and had the courage to keep trying.

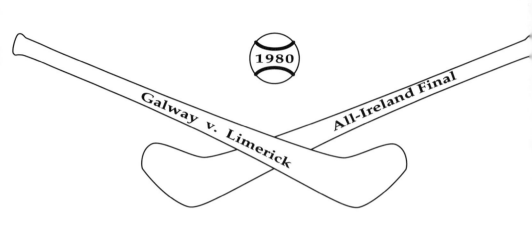

EXHILARATING TRIUMPH AFTER YEARS OF DISAPPOINTMENT

When the television coverage of the game ended, with the credits rolling over massed scenes of delirium and joy at Croke Park, a man in late middle age left the sitting-room of his bungalow in east Co. Galway. He told his wife and some neighbours who had come to watch the game that he was going down the fields to look at the sheep.

This man, lithe in his hurling days but now bulky, made his way over the closely cropped olive-green fields. He held his hands behind his back as he walked by the neat stone walls that divided his fields. Some of his fingers were gnarled from old hurling wounds and his hands were arthritic, partly because of the many blows they had taken during his years of playing for Galway.

Alone in the furthest field, under the wide evening sky over the plains of Galway, this tough man cried. He cried for joy that Galway had at last won the All-Ireland senior hurling title. He cried for all the years of disappointment and frustration when the team, of which he was a part, somehow could not win the title, no matter how good they were. He remembered all the hopes that he and all his family and all the neighbours and people about had reposed in the hurling team and all the times they came home crestfallen.

Like thousands of other Galway people and thousands who wanted to see the perennial underdogs break the circle of failure and thwarted hopes, winning the All-Ireland had, over the years, become a kind of wishful fantasy. He had imagined it many times, usually in spring, before the championship began.

Years of Disappointment

During his twelve years of playing for the senior team in the '40s and early '50s he had given his all, trained hard, honed his hurling skills diligently, been part of a fine team that just could not make it. They missed victory often by a whisker, by a single hop of the ball. Sometimes, in neck and neck races to the finish, they blamed a linesman or an umpire or a referee for a decision that made all the difference between winning and losing. Sometimes they blamed themslves for having lost their composure in the crucial last quarter of the game or for having needlessly wasted chances. But all the time they lost.

After he had retired from the game he had followed the team faithfully. He went to league games in the middle of winter, standing on muddy embankments in boots, with the collar of his grey coat turned up against the raw wind.

Before the championship began his spirits and hopes always rose and the date of the semi-final was in his mind for weeks in advance. He always put the teams down on a piece of paper so that he would know who would be marking who and carried it about with him like a personal programme.

At the game he would bellow and shout encouragement to the men in maroon and white, willing them on to win, directing all his energies and mental power onto the field of play like a laser beam. After each defeat he was always silent on the way home by car or excursion train. He would be downcast for days afterwards. 'Oh I don't know if we'll ever win it ', he used say to his wife when he arrived to his home near Oranmore.

High Hopes Dashed

The hopes of winning had been raised high after the winning of the National League in 1975 and the subsequent defeat of a great Cork team in a thrilling semi-final. In the final, however, the Galway team, in their first All-Ireland since 1958, were assailed by nerves and unease. The game went wrong for them from the start. And they were up against one of the great Kilkenny teams, full of stars whose names were part of hurling legend. That fact at least made the defeat easier to bear.

But the All-Ireland of 1979, when Galway had everything going for them and yet could do everything but win, had been the most galling of all for this faithful follower. It seemed on that day that Galway had a hidden fear of winning, a kind of paralysis of will which seized them whenever they had a game for the taking. After that he decided that he had enough of failure and disillusion and that he was not going to any of the big games again. He had borne enough.

Alone among the flat fields this man also cried because he had not been in Croke Park that Sunday in September 1980. That day, at long last, Galway's hour of triumph had been won in a great victory over a great Limerick team in a great game. As he made his way back to his house in the fading light he could see a tiny flicker of flame somewhere near the main Galway-Dublin road, two miles away. This was the first of the many celebratory bonfires that would be lit that night and the following night for a victory that opening the floodgates of what Joe McDonagh, one of the team stalwarts, described as 'the passion that is Galway hurling'.

Galway's Hurling Passion

That passion was displayed in Croke Park in a way which caught the imagination of all who were there, who watched the game on television, who heard it on radio, who read about it next day. As the game went into the final minute and it was clear that Limerick's vigorous effort to pull the game out of the fire was unavailing, Galway supporters began to climb over the wire all around the perimeter of the pitch. These were not just young people waving flags but the middle aged and the elderly.

The sounds of victory began to grow and grow, like a rising torrent starting to carry all before it, as the seconds ticked away. Even before the referee blew his whistle, one or two frenzied supporters were unable to restrain themselves and raced on to the field, to be ushered back by stewards.

The referee's full-time whistle not alone ended a marvellous game of hurling between two splendid teams but was the signal for a frenzied charge of thousands of flag-waving Galway supporters from all along the side and end lines of the field of play. Thousands converged on the players, delirious with joy.

People of all ages laughed in uninhibited delight and a mixture of emotions. There were tears of sadness too as people thought back to the fine players over the years who had been deprived of such a victorious scene as this.

Limerick Sadness

The Limerick players, many crestfallen, trudged off the field. It was hard at that moment for any one to tell them that they had made a truly enthralling game of it. They had come within the length of a hurley of pulling it off in the dying minutes of the game. They too could have claimed that luck was against them in a match where the bounce of the ball was the difference between victory and defeat.

Limerick had been the favourites that day with many commentators and followers because they had beaten Cork in a thunderous Munster final. There was also a firm impression abroad that Galway would never be able to rise to the big occasion against a team of Limerick's quality and vigour.

Most neutral hurling lovers wanted Galway to win but they had mixed feelings about it. They would have wanted Galway to win at the expense of one of the Big Three rather than against a Limerick team that was emerging as one of the great entertainers of the era with their flamboyant style of play but one which, so far, had little to show for it in terms of trophies won.

Victory Speech

Nobody understood this better than the Galway team and supporters now milling round the front of the Hogan stand. They knew what it was like to have little or no reward for great effort. When the Galway captain, Joe Connolly, in his celebrated victory speech in everyday Irish, praised the Limerick side and commiserated with them in defeat, the sincerity rang through his voice. He knew what he was talking about.

He spoke eloquently, in an Irish that all could understand, about hurling and its place in the lives of the people of the hurling part of Galway, about how it had survived the years of defeat in the championship.

When he had finished, his colleague, Joe McDonagh, took the microphone and led the singing of 'The West's Awake'. This had become an anthem of defiance against the adversity, poverty, emigration and deprivation that had engendered pessimism and defeatism in part of the public mind, especially along the western seaboard. This feeling had extended to the game of hurling as well. Many people felt — and some in Galway accepted — that they were always destined to be perennial losers.

The long-awaited victory of Galway was more than a sporting triumph. It was like a beacon of encouragement for the team and the hurling supporters and for all those who had struggled against disadvantage and who had often lost faith in themselves but who kept on nevertheless. So this anthem of defiance and hope was sung with fervour and feeling by the jam-packed crowds in front of the Hogan stand.

Even when the ceremonies were over and the team pushed their way to the corner of the stand through a swarm of handshakes and backslaps, the celebrations on the field continued. A band over at the Cusack stand side was playing 'When the saints go marching in', and huge circles of arm-linked supporters moved like gyrating wheels.

Hardest Triers

Nothing like this was ever seen in Croke Park before and is not likely to be seen again. This is because no team tried so hard over so long a period and came so near to victory on so many occasions without actually winning. Battling gamely but unavailingly became part of the Galway hurling legend. It endeared the county far more to outsiders than did the jaunty confidence of the Big Three of hurling. And Galway followers were faithful. They had come home from the US and Canada and Britain for the finals of '75 and '79.

The weekend of the All-Ireland of 1980 had seen Dublin airport full of returning supporters, buoyed up with hope once again. The incoming ferry boats at Dun Laoghaire discharged long rows of middle-aged men with weather-beaten faces and old-fashioned coats and jumpers — the generations of the '50s and '60s that had been forced to emigrate to the neighbouring island and take what work they could find on building sites, in public transport, in catering, anywhere that gave them a niche and a pay packet. There were Limerick followers there too but the Galway supporters seemed the most visible.

That weekend the hotels and guesthouses and pubs and restaurants were full of hurling lovers who had come from near and far. Many turned up at the Gresham hotel to view the fascinating hurling museum of Sam Melbourne from Horse and Jockey in Co. Tipperary.

Unusual Pairing

This was an unusual pairing of two of the counties that had a great playing tradition but had been pushed to one side by the dominance of the Big Three. The guttural accents of Limerick city and county could be heard. They were used to seeing Cork and Tipperary followers travelling along the roadways to the Gaelic Grounds on the Ennis road to engage in great contests while they themselves were spectators. Now this was their time and they intended to enjoy it.

For some of the Galway followers getting to Galway city itself was a major part of the journey before setting out for Dublin. They came from the remote headlands and stony landscapes of Connemara, from the Aran islands, speaking in their own tongue, in accents barely understood by others.

When the game was over it took a long time for the Galway supporters to disperse from the wide green field of Croke Park. It was as if they wanted to savour every precious drop of this unique occasion.

One and Only

Galway's first and only All-Ireland had been won in 1924. The game, coincidentally against Limerick, was for the 1923 title which had been deferred because of the widespread disturbance engendered by the Civil War. The sole survivor of the Limerick side was the captain, Paddy McInerney, who had gone to America in 1925 and was now living in the hot, dry climate of New Mexico in the American southwest, a far cry from the moist green fields of Limerick with its lush growth of bushes and trees along ditches and hedges.

In an article in the *Limerick Leader* he recalled how teams in that era got together for a full fortnight of training and preparation. For that particular final they had been closeted in a country mansion in Castleconnell. Their regular team trainer understood the capabilities and temperament of each player and knew how to get them on song for a game. Unfortunately he fell ill and the training regime at Castleconnell was severe and debilitating, according to McInerney, making no distinction between big heavy players and small light ones. His recollections highlighted the importance of the trainer in getting teams to the height of physical preparation without going over the invisible borderline into weariness. Galway won that game on a scoreline of 7–3 to 4–5.

There were four survivors of the winning Galway side alive in 1980. Jim Power and Packie Dervan still living in their native Tynagh and Stephen

Garvey was in America. The fourth was the most renowned Galway hurler of that era, Mick Gill. He has gone down in hurling history as one of the all-time great midfielders. A barrel-chested, square-shouldered man, he was in Croke Park that day. At 81 years of age his eyesight was failing, so he had a companion sit beside him to help him follow the flight and movement of the ball.

Different Fortunes

Since the 1923 All-Ireland the fortunes of Galway and Limerick had been quite different. Nine years after that defeat the Shannonsiders began to put together a truly great team of teak-tough highly-skilled hurlers. They were powered by players from the Ahane club near Castleconnell, most notably by the most flamboyantly resolute superstar of the era, Mick Mackey.

By 1933 they were in the All-Ireland again, beaten by Kilkenny. They were back the following year to reverse that decision. Limerick were now the dominant force in Munster and they steamrolled their way through the province the following two years, their players becoming legendary in the history of the game: John Mackey, Jackie Power, Timmy Ryan, Paddy Clohossey among others. They met Kilkenny in the finals of 1935 and '36, losing the first and winning the latter.

The team was beginning to age in 1940 but they burst their way out of Munster once more and beat Dublin in the final. They were narrowly beaten by Cork in a replay in 1944 and by Tipperary the following year. They still had great vigour and drive and were the most respected team because of their great dominance of the scene over the previous dozen years. But thereafter their fortunes went into decline. After the retirement of Mackey and the stars of that era the Limerick side went into a slump and were no longer the force they once had been.

It was 1955 before a speedy team, trained by Mick Mackey, again won the Munster crown. In the semi-final they came up against one of the really outstanding and memorable sides of all time, Wexford. They proved to be no match for the powerful Rackard-led side. But the same speedsters were back the following year in the Munster final against Cork and seemed to have the game wrapped up when Christy Ring, who had been well held up to then, suddenly broke loose and scored three famous goals in the last ten minutes.

After that defeat the Limerick side went into a period of obscurity. They were invariably beaten in the first round of the championship and their prestige as a hurling county began to wane, to be more and more based on fond memories of the Mackey years. Hurling lovers wanted the men in green and white to liven the stagnant scene once again but it was 1971 before they contested a Munster final and two years later before they once again emerged as provincial champions and went on to beat Kilkenny in a rain-soaked final. The following year Kilkenny beat Limerick in a return match.

They had their barren years and disappointments but never to the same extent as the westerners. In the 1980 final they were setting out to win their eighth All-Ireland while Galway had not won for 57 years. So tradition, so prevalent on the hurling scene, reflecting a somewhat narrow county feeling, decreed that they must be favourites.

Team Building

The most realistic reason for their favouritism was that they had put together a really fine team which built upon the talented survivors of the 1973–74 years and combined them with strong newcomers who had emerged from the county championship. By 1979 they had reached the Munster final. They were well beaten by their bogey team, Cork. But they grew in strength and in the league of 1979–80 they played the kind of exciting hurling that drew followers from all over the hurling areas. They played Cork in the final of the league, drew with them and were beaten in the replay. Those were two tremendous games and hurling followers expected them to meet in the Munster final of 1980. They did, on a memorable day in Thurles.

This game restored the fading reputation of the Munster final as a boiling, pulsating occasion which aroused the deepest feelings of primitive competitiveness among players and spectators. A great Cork team had been so dominant since 1975 that there was no team to really offer them a match in Munster. One year followed another and ever hopeful followers made their way to the final, usually in Semple Stadium, Thurles. Even the unique atmosphere in that venue could do little to rescue one-sided games. The Munster finals of those years suffered badly by comparison with the mighty contests in Croke Park for the Leinster title between Wexford and Kilkenny.

Now the new pretenders to the Munster crown, the eager Limerick side, met a Cork team full of fine hurlers who were going for their sixth Munster championship title in a row — the first time any team had attempted such a feat.

Great Win

The Shannonside followers were not disappointed. They saw a thrilling game that was searing in its urgency and in the battle for dominance. Limerick used their physical strength as well as their skill to overcome the wiles and vast experience of their rivals. Limerick showed pace and showed grit too. There were bone-crunching tackles and heavy shoul-derings that were legitimate and helped reinforce the fact that physical contact had a role to play in winning games.

Apart from a panel of good players Limerick had a good sideline team. Noel Drumgoole, the manager, was an astute, forceful individual who radiated determination to his players. He had won five senior club championship medals in Dublin with the St Vincent's club and had played at full back in the All-Ireland of 1961, which Dublin lost by the merest shave. The trainer, Tim Crowe of Sixmilebridge in Co. Clare, was an experienced athlete and a physical education graduate of Thomond College. In selectors Vincent Byrnes of South Liberties, Timmy Horgan of Tournafulla, Tony O'Brien of Patrickswell and J.P. Ryan of Garryspillane, Limerick had men who understood the importance of care and support for the players as well as motivation.

O'Connor and Flanagan

The Munster final provided one of the great moments for a small, speedy and exceptionally skilled corner forward, Ollie O'Connor from the Ballybrown club, who complemented the great veterans Cregan and McKenna in the full forward line. In the second half the ball broke about 30 metres from the end line on the right wing of the Limerick attack. So anxious were the Cork backs to block O'Connor's path that two of them, Martin O'Doherty and John Horgan, collided with one another. To a great gasp from the huge crowd O'Connor ran on to the ball behind the fallen players, lifted it at full speed, raced goalwards and gave the keeper no chance for a goal that was crucial for Limerick.

Another star that day was a bustling, battling farmer from Feohanagh, John Flanagan. He was the ideal centre forward, all the time contesting the ball down the middle, breaking it out to the wings, doing all the heavy work in whipping it along to the full forward line. He also made it difficult for centre backs to get in any sweeping clearances because he blocked and harried when he could not get the ball himself.

That Munster final victory, the first over Cork since 1940, was essentially a team effort. Their whole side played well against vastly experienced and skilful opponents. Their full back line of Donal Murray, Leonard Enright and Dom Punch made a great job of curbing the dangerous Cork forwards. Enright in particular shackled one of the greatest full forwards the game has ever known, Ray Cummins. And the goalkeeper, Tommy Quaid, had played well. Son of Jack, who had been on the '55 side, he had made the goalkeeping position his own after some outstanding games in 1976.

Limerick were a side that believed in making the ball do the work. They often whipped first time, fast along the ground, often across the field as they opened the game up with fast-running forwards reminiscent of the Waterford side of 1957–63. They favoured low, quick balls in to the forwards instead of the high balls that come soaring slowly in while backs get in position to catch and clear them. However, one of the unique facets of this Limerick team was that they had a full forward who was almost unbeatable under the high dropping ball.

Joe McKenna

Joe McKenna stood 6 ft 4 ins and weighed 14 stone. He stood like a colossus on the edge of the square. When a high ball came in he went under it and held his ground. Protecting his catching hand with the hurley he reached into the sky high over the milling backs below and let the incoming ball come into his large hand.

He seemed slow because of his size but he could whip the ball like lightening once he had it. More often than not he dropped the ball and hit it off his right ankle bone with a powerful swing. He was able to do this even when his back was to the goal. The most amazing thing was that full backs who got to know his style of play were still unable to stop him. He scored goal after goal in the same way, game after game — catch, drop and smack into the net.

This left-hander from Shinrone in Co. Offaly had played in 1973 and challenged Ray Cummins each year for the title 'Most dangerous full forward in the game'.

Eamonn Cregan

In the right corner forward position for Limerick was one of the most skilled and resourceful hurlers the county ever produced, Eamonn Cregan. At 35 he was the veteran of the side, had been playing with the senior team for all of sixteen years. He had played a major role in bringing the title to Limerick in 1973, scoring two marvellous goals in the Munster final against Tipperary and in the final playing at centre back where he effectively curbed Kilkenny's thrusting forward, Paddy Delaney of Johnstown. He was a consummate opportunist who went for half-chances like a cougar leaping on a prey. He had killed off teams by scoring spectacular goals — demoralising goals — at key moments in games.

Half Forwards

On either side of Flanagan in the half forward line were two brothers, both priests, from the Killeedy club in the west of the county. Paudie Fitzmaurice, now thirty, had been there in 1973 and shared in the great surge of joy when the county emerged triumphant after a wait of thirty-three years. Willie, a year older, had missed out on that experience. Both of them exemplified the importance of the hurling club. Together with another brother they had helped Killeedy attain great pride and prominence on the hurling scene in West Limerick. They gave the club a good deal of their time and inalienable loyalty. A big crowd of people came to Dublin from this rural district to see their kith and kin give their all for the county. Both of them were strong, forceful hurlers. They were not easily knocked off the ball and they kept going from start to finish.

Centrefield

At centrefield for Limerick was Jimmy Carroll and David Punch. They complemented one another. Carroll, who played football for the county as well, had a great style about him, running hard all over the midfield area, sometimes coming into the forwards. One of his attributes was the capacity to reach up his hurley and cushion and trap a moving ball, done at full gallop. His partner was David Punch, one of the key players on the Patrickswell championship team and brother of Dom. He was small, light and a neat hurler. He had played exceptionally well in the Munster campaign, hitting low fast balls to the wing and into the corner.

Half Backs

Limerick's half back line had the captain, Sean Foley, on the left. This was one of the most forceful hurlers on the side, full of drive and courage. He usually lifted and struck the ball in one flowing action, without handling it. He tackled with vigour. He had an inspirational way of charging out of the ruck with ball on stick and clearing it way up-field. His second-half performance in the Munster final of 1973, when he took over the centre-half back berth and played a storming game, made him one of the heros of that era.

Mossie Carroll of Garryspillane was a centre half back who played some outstanding games. When he was on song he had a finely tuned sense of where the ball was going to be and he cleared it with style. He had a great capacity to take a ball out of the air, to catch it among duelling hurleys. Some days he played brilliant hurling. Sometimes too much was expected of him and when he failed to deliver people said he was temperamental.

On his right was the pint-sized but lion-hearted Liam O'Donoghue of Mungret. He was an indomitable battler whom the crowd loved for his spirit and bravery. He was tenacious and never gave in and had been a key part of the Limerick side in 1973–74. He cleared the ball away with fast strokes from left or right. There was always a sense of safety about him, that he was going to do the right thing when the ball came his way.

The Limerick substitutes, all of whom were part of a panel of dedicated hurlers, included Eamonn Grimes, captain in '73, and his brother Mike, Brian Carroll, brother of Mossie, Pa Foley, brother of Sean, Seamus O'Sullivan of Tournafulla, Paddy Kelly, the national sprint champion, Ger Mulcahy of Dromin-Athlacca, Con O'Keeffe of Ballingarry, and the only representative of the famous Ahane club, Pat Herbert.

All-Ireland Inexperience

There was one disadvantage that Limerick laboured under. Only five of their fifteen had played in an All-Ireland and knew what a nerve wracking experience it could prove to be. Cregan, McKenna, Foley, O'Donoghue and Paudie Fitzmaurice were the old-stagers. They knew how a player's legs could turn rubbery with stage fright if he was assailed by it and did not handle it right.

Some of the best players, running onto the field at Croke Park and finding themselves at the bottom of a huge bowl of 60,000 or 70,000 faces, had attacks of nerves. Ned Wheeler of Wexford, who played before crowds of over 80,000 in the All-Irelands of '54 and '56, said, 'You could feel that they were all closing in on you, that the weight of the huge crowd was on your shoulders. If you didn't cope with it your game could suffer.'

Seasoned Galway

One team who could claim to know Croke Park on All-Ireland day was Galway. They knew what nerves could do to good players. In the final of '75 the game had gone away from them before some of their players recovered a sense of composure and began to play up to their capabilities. 1980 was Galway's second final in a row and they were bound to have learned how to cope better with all the pressures both before and during a game. Only Jimmy Cooney of Sarsfields, their left corner back, and the player in front of him in the half back line, Seamus Coen, had not played in an All-Ireland.

For John Connolly, Frank Burke, P.J. Molloy, Sean Silke and Niall McInerney, this was to be their third final. So Galway very definitely had the edge in final day experience. This, however, might not be enough to overcome what many saw as their unpredictability. Sometimes they seemed to play well, sometimes they played poorly. Sometimes they played both well and poorly in the same game.

The last time they had met Limerick had been in a National League game the previous November. Limerick had easily swept aside much the same team they now opposed in the All-Ireland. The score was 6-8 to a paltry 5 points. Ominously, Joe McKenna had by far the better of the duel with Conor Hayes and slammed in three goals while having a hand in all the others.

Winning Tradition

However this Galway side had begun to develop a winning tradition. Several of its players — Iggy Clarke, Frank Burke and P.J. Molloy — had been on the first Galway side ever to win an under-21 title in 1972. Conor Hayes, Steve Mahon, Seamus Coen and Bernie Forde had been on the under-21 side that had beaten Tipperary to win the title again in a replay in 1978. And players like McInerney, McDonagh and Silke had played on the successful teams that came out of UCG and Maynooth to break the traditional stranglehold on the universities championship held by UCC and UCD.

There were two heartening achievements early in 1980. Connacht, made up of all Galway players, beat Munster in the Railway Cup final to win the trophy for the first time since 1947. Then Castlegar became the first Galway side to win the All-Ireland club championship when they beat a hard-hitting Antrim side, Ballycastle.

Semi-Final Victory

Galway had shown real mettle and character in overcoming the tough challenge of Offaly in the semi-final. Only in retrospect did people realise just how fine a side this midland team was that day. They had beaten Kilkenny in the Leinster final — the first time they had ever beaten them in a championship game — and were on their way to contest every provincial final in the 1980s and to win two All-Irelands. Although Galway had outplayed them for much of the game, Offaly with the steady, never-say-die play that was to be so characteristic of them, kept in the game right up to the end. It took a good team to keep them at bay in the last five minutes of play as Galway did.

Clarke Injury

That semi-final triumph for Galway was won at some cost. The best left half back in the country, Iggy Clarke of Mullagh, had suffered a serious shoulder injury which effectively ended his role on the team for the final. It was a big loss. Clarke had an uncanny sense of position and anticipation. Any ball that came along the left wing seemed to be his. He had an effortless style, able to win the ball without much apparent bother, making breaks into midfield and the half forward area. It was his calm, imperturbable presence and unobtrusive power play that Galway needed most.

It has to be said, however, that his replacement in the semi-final, Seamus Coen, also from the Mullagh team, proved to be very competent. Behind him was the stocky Jimmy Cooney from the Sarsfields club. His job was going to be to mind the mercurial Ollie O'Connor. Some Galway followers expressed reservations about the left side of the defence because of the lack of All-Ireland experience. So the duels between Coen and Paudie Fitzmaurice and Cooney and O'Connor were seen in Galway as of crucial importance.

Goalkeeper

There was some criticism of the performance of Michael Conneely in the semi-final. The Sarsfields player, 6 ft 3 ins and 14 stone, had had some unsure and uneasy moments between the posts. Two goals had gone past him that some felt he should have stopped. But Cyril Farrell, Inky Flaherty and Bernie O'Connor, the triumvirate in charge of the team, put their judgment and their trust in the big man from Bullaun.

Daunting Tasks

When the Galway team was announced, with Niall McInerney at full back and Conor Hayes in the right corner, there was much comment about the capability of both to mind their respective opponents, McKenna and Cregan. There was real pressure on the tall, rangy full back from Clare, who played for the city team, Liam Mellowes. Anybody who had seen both teams playing over the previous two years knew that McKenna could devastate Galway with two or three crucial goals. Hayes, at 22, would be marking a man thirteen years older than himself, a crafty, nippy veteran who could draw on years of experience. As well as that the corner back had been out of the team with injury and had not built up his speed. But the Kiltormer player had a certain good humoured self-confidence, a coolness in his play that allayed some of the fears.

Half Backs

How Sean Silke would handle the bustling Flanagan was another point of comment. Silke was among the very best centre half backs, a great reader of the ball, strong, a swift striker. The Meelick-Eyrecourt player, so easy for spectators to identify by his bushy moustache, was very consistent. He had been an All-Star in 1975 and had vast experience.

On his right was a stocky, ginger-headed player, who was coming to epitomise the new confident, aggressive Galway approach to the game — Sylvie Linnane from Gort. His thick wrists enabled him to control the hurley well. He had perfected the art of the sideline cut, sending balls in a long trajectory forty or fifty yards up the field. He had a tigerish competitive approach, did not pull back from a challenge and often cleared the ball up field to a great cheer from the crowd, who saw him as a skilled, combative bantam with a bristling, ginger moustache.

Centrefield

Holding the fort at centrefield were Michael Connolly and Steve Mahon. Connolly had captained the Castlegar side in its club championship campaign. He was a forceful player who often went into the attack. Like his opposite number, Jimmy Carroll, he was speedy and had good ball control. On the other side was Steve Mahon from Kilbeacanty. A big strong man, he was adept at first time striking, sending the ball into the opposition half. Forwards loved to play with him because he let the ball fly before backs had time to settle and the ball came in low over the grass. In almost every match he played in, he found one or two occasions to send over long-range points

Forwards

Left half forward on the Galway side was the Athenry player, P.J. Molloy. Small and fast, he was one of the leading scorers on the Galway side for several years and had been selected on the All-Star side in '78. He held the hurley in the right-hand-under grip and took a wide swing on the ball but it did not stop him sending the ball over the bar or goalwards. In the centre of the attack was the captain, Joe Connolly. He himself would not claim to have the same level of skill as his brother John. But he was an inspirational player, full of force and bravery, and he drove his men onwards by example. The captaincy he found not a burden but a further incentive for leadership.

On the right was one of the big hefty men of the side whom Sean Foley would have the task of marking — Frank Burke. The Turloughmore man was popular with all the club players everywhere because they recognised in him an honest player who had to work to bring his hurling skills to their peak. He was a powerful runner with the ball once he got away and, near goal, the ball went off his stick like a rocket.

In front of him was a slight, red-headed player who was one of the least known in the wider hurling world — Bernie Forde of Ardrahan. He was a speedy forward and had raced away to make some spectacular scores when he played on the victorious under-21 team in '78.

John Connolly

At full forward was the most famous Galway hurler of the era, the tall, exceptionally skilful John Connolly. Aged 32, he was the veteran of the side. For fourteen years he had soldiered, mostly at midfield, often single-handedly keeping Galway in the game by his forceful play. He was almost automatically selected at centrefield for the first All-Stars team of 1971, the only Galway player on the side. Because of his great experience and personality he was looked up to as a father figure by the others, a steadying influence.

In the other corner was a tall, lithe player from Ballinderreen, Noel Lane. Like the other players he had shared in the team's triumphs and disappointments over the previous few years. He had great ball control, rose it neatly into the hand and could send over points from narrow angles.

'A team is only as good as the whole panel', said Cyril Farrell in one of the many interviews he gave. 'We have a very good bunch of fellows who make a big contribution to the team as a whole.'

In the Galway panel were the Ryan twins, John and Paschal, from Killimordaly, Joe McDonagh of Ballinderreen who had been captain in '79 but whose hurling career had been hampered by a serious illness, Padraig Connolly whose presence in the squad along with his three brothers constituted a kind of record. Gerry Glynn, another Castlegar player, was on the panel as were Michael King of Padraig Pearse's, Finbar Gantley of Beagh, Jackie Dervan of Kiltormer, Jack Lucas of Meelick-Eyrecourt, Michael Mulkerrins of the Sarsfields club and Gerry Curtin of Kinvara.

Limerick were to play in the first half with the advantage of a good breeze blowing from the Canal end. The teams spread out, markers shook hands tensely and at 3.15 the referee, Noel O'Donoghue, from Dalkey in Co. Dublin, threw in the ball.

First Save by Conneely

There was some indecisive pulling on the part of the Galway backs and a roar of delight from the Limerick supporters when their Munster final hero, Ollie O'Connor, raced out to the right wing, gained possession and sent a dangerous lob into the Galway goalmouth, just the kind that big Joe McKenna revelled in. But Michael Conneely pulled the ball down with a great flourish of confidence and sent it away down the field with a long stroke. It was the kind of positive start that he needed and it gave him a great boost at the start of the game.

Galway Goal

The Galway team and supporters got a tremendous uplift a minute later. Joe Connolly pulled on a ball and sent it high through to his brother in the

The teams as they lined out were:

GALWAY

Michael Conneely
(Sarsfields)

Conor Hayes	Niall McInerney	Jimmy Cooney
(Kiltormer)	(Liam Mellowes)	(Sarsfields)

Sylvie Linnane	Sean Silke	Seamus Coen
(Gort)	(Meelick-Eyrecourt)	(Mullagh)

Michael Connolly   Steve Mahon
(Castlegar)   (Kilbeacanty)

Frank Burke	Joe Connolly, capt	P.J. Molloy
(Turloughmore)	(Castlegar)	(Athenry)

Bernie Forde	John Connolly	Noel Lane
(Ardrahan)	(Castlegar)	(Ballinderreen)

Substitutes: Finbar Gantley (Beagh); John Ryan (Killimordaly); Joe McDonagh (Ballinderreen); Gerry Glynn (Castlegar); Padraig Connolly (Castlegar); Michael Mulkerrins (Sarsfields); Jackie Dervan (Kiltormer); Jack Lucas (Meelick-Eyrecourt); Gerry Curtin (Kinvara); Paschal Ryan (Killimordaly); Michael King (Padraig Pearse's); Iggy Clarke (Loughrea). *Manager/coach*: Cyril Farrell. *Selectors/mentors*: M.J. Flaherty (Liam Mellowes); Bernie O'Connor (Oranmore-Maree); Tom Callanan (Kilconieron); Frank Corcoran (Sarsfields). *Team doctor*: Dr Mary McInerney. *Masseur*: Willie Bennett.

LIMERICK

Tommy Quaid
(Feohanagh)

Donal Murray	Leonard Enright	Dom Punch
(Croom)	(Patrickswell)	(Patrickswell)

Liam O'Donoghue	Mossie Carroll	Sean Foley, capt
(Mungret)	(Garryspillane)	(Patrickswell)

David Punch   Jimmy Carroll
(Patrickswell)   (Na Fianna)

Paudie Fitzmaurice	John Flanagan	Willie Fitzmaurice
(Killeedy)	(Feohanagh)	(Killeedy)

Ollie O'Connor	Joe McKenna	Eamonn Cregan
(Ballybrown)	(South Liberties)	(Claughaun)

Substitutes: Brian Carroll (Garryspillane); Pat Herbert (Ahane); Eamonn Grimes (South Liberties); Seamus O'Sullivan (Tournafulla); Ger Mulcahy (Dromin-Athlacca); Paddy Kelly (Kilmallock); Pa Foley (Patrickswell); Con O'Keeffe (Ballingarry); Mike Grimes (South Liberties). *Coach*: Noel Drumgoole. *Trainer*: Tim Crowe (Sixmilebridge). *Selectors/mentors*: Kevin Lynch (Patrickswell); J.P. Ryan (Garryspillane); Timmy Horgan (Tournafulla); Vincent Byrnes (South Liberties). *Team doctor*: Dr Richard O'Flaherty (Na Piarsaigh). *Masseur*: Vincent O'Connor.

The referee was Noel O'Donoghue from Cuala, Dalkey, Co. Dublin.

full forward position. There was the first of many aerial battles between Connolly and his tenacious marker, Leonard Enright, as the ball came in. Connolly won this one and tried for a point. Enright bravely blocked his shot. Then, after a bout of pulling and scrambling, during which Mossie Carroll broke his hurley, the ball ended up at the feet of Forde out on the right. Gathering speed, he slipped like a wisp past Sean Foley and Dom Punch, heading goalwards with the ball on his hurley. Punch whipped round and raced after him, waiting for a chance to hook. Nearing the square Forde, under pressure, took a quick decision. He kicked the ball. It sped across the goal, brushed off Tommy Quaid's chest went in under his arm and ended up in the net.

This was the settling goal that Galway needed and the worst kind of start for the Limerick side, especially for those with no experience of the tensions of an All-Ireland.

Galway in Control

Galway had come out in full flight, running hard, and though Limerick tried to keep them at bay, the Westerners were in control in many areas of the field. After Forde's stunning goal the Galway midfielders tried to get the ball in low to him whenever they got the chance. When it came into his corner two minutes later he got possession but Dom Punch baulked him and the Ardrahan man had to hit the ball on his weak right-hand side. He did not connect properly but just the same the ball headed goalwards. Tommy Quaid, trying to recover from the shock of the goal, blocked it nervously and it went out for a 65.

Sean Silke, who even at this stage was stamping his authority in his area of the field, came up to take the puck. He had to hit it hard into the good breeze but it veered off wide. It was clear that the wind was a factor and clear that Limerick had better make use of it while the going was good.

Yet it was Galway who were making all the running. And running was the reality. Joe Connolly kept moving all the time, racing and backpedalling, bringing Mossie Carroll with him. Carroll made one or two very telling clearances during that first half but a great deal of his energy went to chasing after his man to make sure he did not get a clear path to goal.

Connolly did manage to make some progress but was fouled 25 metres out. He took the free himself. It was the first free to Galway and it gave Connolly and the team a good boost that he sent it unerringly over the bar.

Midfield Battle

Both Jimmy Carroll and Michael Connolly showed touches of skill and dash at centrefield. The honours between them were about even. Carroll covered a great deal of ground and his stylish play should have helped to settle the side down. But some of the younger players were playing well below their Munster final form.

Another Galway Goal

After nine minutes Michael Connolly gathered a ball from a free taken by Silke. He feigned a shot from 50 metres out but then sidestepped his opponent and raced into the heart of the Limerick defence. He was on the right hand side when he sent a strong shot across the field. It seemed headed for the sideline but P.J. Molloy tore after it and rose it into his hand. He deftly dodged two opponents to make enough space for himself and thundered into the square. There he was upended by a hefty shoulder and ended up on his back. There was some doubt about whether he had been fouled but as some of the Limerick backs stood awaiting the whistle Molloy hopped to his feet and smashed a powerful shot into the net.

This second goal set off a reverberating roar. The Galway supporters were in ecstasies of delight. The Limerick backs looked at one another in dismay. It was a question of playing to the referee's whistle rather than anticipating what the official in black might do.

'This could be a runaway win', said a flushed Galway follower, hardly daring to believe not just that the team was roaring along at such a pace but that this was reflected on the scoreboard as well. The score now stood at 2–1 to no score.

Limerick Reply

But any western euphoria was dampened down somewhat in the eleventh minute. Jimmy Carroll controlled a moving ball beautifully, raced over along the right wing of the Limerick attack and then sent a fast ball just over head high into the Galway square.

Eamonn Cregan came running in, closely policed by Conor Hayes. He might have whipped on the ball but he made a quick decision to meet it not with his hurley but with his palm. He leapt in the air between Hayes and McInerney and sent it to the left of Michael Conneely. There was a huge cheer of relief from the massed Limerick supporters and shouts of 'Good man, Blondie' at the fair haired Cregan. This was the wily old fox in action, showing how dangerous he could be with a half chance. He had palmed to Conneely's left because the Galway goalkeeper, with his unorthodox grip, had the hurley at his right shoulder as the ball had come in.

Limerick badly needed that score badly because the game was not going well for them. John Flanagan, whose success in breaking the ball out to his fellow forwards in the Munster final had ended Cork's dominance at the back, found himself in difficulties against the resourceful Silke. He was switched with Willie Fitzmaurice in an attempt to break the centre back's control of the territory.

When Limerick were awarded a free 55 metres out Cregan came trotting out to take it. There was something reassuring about the careful but confident way he spread his legs over the ball, totally concentrated but seemingly unhurried. He struck the ball with great precision and it floated between the posts.

It was clear that Cregan was the greatest threat in the full forward line. Up to this Niall McInerney had stuck like a leech to Joe McKenna, reading the play without error, anticipating how the ball was going to run and keeping it away from the big Shinrone man. In the other corner Jimmy Cooney was proving to be as fast as Ollie O'Connor and was giving him little scope. But it was taking Hayes all his tactical sense to handle Cregan. He dare not let him go past on a run, for the Claughaun man was lethal in front of goal.

When Mossie Carroll made a great clearance the ball came out to the left wing of the Limerick attack and Cregan ran on to it, with Hayes at his shoulder. Cregan pretended to hit it from one side then suddenly twisted and turned and from 50 metres out sent over one of the best scores of the match.

Limerick were beginning to come into the game a little more. Willie Fitzmaurice broke through the middle after the ball dropped favourably to him. Despite being buffeted about, he pulled hard on the ball and sent it flying towards the goal. Conneely, with superb reflexes, made a marvellous save — the first of many he was to make that day. He was to vindicate his selection and lead many to wonder why he hadn't been in goal the previous year.

Foley and Burke

Galway kept hurling with great fire and control. On the right wing Frank Burke and Sean Foley fought out a battle of wits and weight. The scales tipped this way and that but not by much. Burke, always unselfish, tried to clip the ball across the field since his own way was invariably blocked by the Limerick captain. All this meant that Foley, with his hands full trying to stop the big Turloughmore man going on a run, could not be the attacking half back that he normally was.

Carroll v. Connolly

There were great Limerick cheers when Mossie Carroll made two great raking clearances, typical of this player at his best. It was a hopeful sign that he was beginning to come into his own. However, Joe Connolly kept running and gathering and sending the ball out to the corners and Carroll was given few other opportunities to get in a long puck.

When the ball came up Galway's right wing of attack from centrefield Frank Burke jumped for it with his hurley held over his right catching hand. He got it and hit a hard shot into the wind. It went in fast to the right corner. The ball seemed on its way over the end line when Noel Lane caught up with it, trapped it and lifted it in one graceful movement, cut back to give himself a chance. It was still a narrow angle but he sent it over with great precision. The score now stood at 2–2 to 1–2.

John Connolly Point

Almost from the puck out Michael Connolly raced across the midfield, angled the boss of his hurley to clip the ball off the grass and send it goalwards. His brother John and Leonard Enright came racing out to it together. The Limerick full back was the speediest of all the backs but on this occasion the Castlegar veteran got to the ball before him, tapped it into his hand, whirled round and struck it with the dead centre of the boss and sent it over from 35 metres.

The two small men, Molloy and O'Donoghue, were fighting a battle royal, blocking one another's shots, scrambling and tussling for every ball. In the Galway half back line Sylvie Linnane was playing well on the bustling Flanagan. On one occasion he raced forward to clear the ball and sent a long accurate shot right across the field to the left corner. Lane's long legs and his speed were causing problems for Donal Murray and this time the Ballinderreen player ran onto the cross almost on the sideline. He rose to make a fine catch and sent over another narrow-angle point.

More Limerick Changes

Limerick continued to alter their attacking forces, with Flanagan moving to full forward and Joe McKenna coming out to the centre forward position in an attempt to break the dominance of McInerney and Silke down the middle. At this stage Galway conceded another free and Cregan put it over from 60 metres with another carefully struck ball. A minute later Joe Connolly replied with a free from 35 metres from directly in front of the posts.

Connolly, roving and urging his men on, fired in a speculative shot goalwards. Tommy Quaid, recovered from his nightmare start, handled with great authority. When he came racing out he was charged by both Lane and Forde and went down injured. This was one of the few moments of rancour in this game. Referee O'Donoghue put Forde's name in his book.

The game flowed back and forward but Galway continued to play with the greater composure. Cooney and Coen hurled solidly and their opposite numbers, Fitzmaurice and O'Connor, had a hard time trying to make any space for scoring chances.

With a few minutes to go to half time John Connolly came flying out to the right to meet an incoming ball. His marker, Enright, was right behind him. Connolly, 50 metres out on the sideline pretended to hit from his right then suddenly changed stance and sent a marvellous point over the bar from his left hand side. It was one of the best points that this immensely skilful player had scored in his long career.

John Flanagan, who just could not get into his stride, was replaced by Brian Carroll, brother of Mossie. As he walked to the Limerick dugout the Feohanagh farmer got a consoling clap from the Limerick people who were aware that their side would not be in Croke Park at all but for his display in the Munster final.

'Bomber' Carroll

The newcomer's first touch was an inspirational one. He cut infield, gathered the ball, raced across the field with it and sent over a good point. 'Bomber', as he was known, was a tough, aggressive player and was to help Limerick back into the game in the second half.

However, the game almost went beyond redemption when the ball sped into the Limerick goal area. John Connolly whipped in a cracking ground shot. For a fraction of a second it seemed a certain goal. Instead it ricocheted off the underside of the crossbar and flew away to the safety of the right wing. A goal at this juncture would have made a very steep hill for Limerick to climb in the second half.

From the clearance a free was awarded to Limerick. Cregan, whose scores were keeping his side in the game, put it over the bar once again. The puck out sent the ball up Galway's left wing of attack. Lane came running out to it and from the sideline sent over another beautifully angled point to end the scoring for the half.

The score stood 2–7 to 1–5 in Galway's favour as the teams trooped off the field.

Half Time Thoughts

'There was no doubt about it but some of our younger players were unnerved by the occasion in the first half. Our aim was to try to get the nerves out of the system and come back into the game in the second half', recalled Eamonn Cregan. 'In every game there is always a time when one team or the other gets in control for a period and we wanted to have this kind of a spell in the second half.'

Some of the attendance, sensing this also, wondered how much energy the westerners had burned up in that lung-searing first half. They wondered if Galway could keep it up. Among the western supporters and others who wished them well there was this deep hidden fear that they were capable of throwing their advantage away. But it was reassuring that the full back line was coping so effectively with Limerick's lethal full forwards.

When Limerick came back out on the field Cregan was at full forward. The Limerick followers, waving their green and white flags, urged the team to get going the way they had done in the Munster final.

Another Galway Point

But first blood of the second half went to Galway. Michael Connolly, gathered a ball at midfield, spotted his brother Joe free and sent him an accurate pass. The captain belted it over the bar from 50 metres.

Limerick were now playing against the wind but Tommy Quaid was still managing to send the puck outs well beyond midfield as was Conneely in the other goal. As a result a lot of the play by-passed midfield. Steve Mahon and David Punch did not see much of the ball.

Three minutes into the second half a free was awarded to Limerick. Mossie Carroll took it and sent it into the Galway half. His brother Brian pulled it down and hit it. Though he mishit, the ball went into the square travelling high. Cregan pulled overhead and connected crisply with it. It might easily have shot into the net but went just over the crossbar.

Mossie Carroll, who had tired following Joe Connolly all over the place, swapped positions with Sean Foley. But it did not seem to make a great deal of difference and Galway were still in control. Shortly afterwards Pat Herbert came on to replace the leg-weary Carroll.

Forde Scores

Noel Lane raced out for the ball on the left wing of the Galway attack. Donal Murray was on his heels so he had no option but to send the ball across the field. There the red-haired Forde grabbed it 40 yards out and struck another great point off his left.

A very strong Limerick attack was broken up by McInerney who came out with the ball, weaving and side-stepping past three opponents with great confidence and sent a long clearance down field to an exultant roar from the Galway followers. Forde, roaming at will, chased it over to the left side and struck a really telling point for Galway. The manner of the build-up and the score itself showed Galway to be still the superior side.

McKenna Dangerous

Now, however, there were signs that Limerick were at last, after great effort, pulling themselves back into the game. McKenna, for the first time in the match, won clean possession ahead of his tenacious marker. He set off with the ball on a long-legged diagonal run towards the left post and let fly a rasper. To the relief of the Galway backs and supporters Conneely blocked the screamer in great style. But it showed how dangerous the big Shinrone man could be.

Conneely again came to Galway's rescue a minute later when a free was awarded 21 metres out. It was expected that Cregan would take his point. He stood back deceptively, suddenly ran forward, lifted the ball on the run and shot for the net. Only Conneely's marvellous anticipation saved a certain goal.

A Limerick Goal

A few seconds later Conneely had no chance when McKenna took the ball out of the air from a long lob by Brian Carroll and, despite being fouled by McInerney, turned to shoot low into the right corner of the goal. A huge cheer of delight went up from the Limerick followers. For the first time in a long while the green and white flags waved with some vigour.

At right half back Liam O'Donoghue was clearing anything that came his way, off his left and off his right. There was a perceptible rising of Limerick performance elsewhere about the field. And they set off on another attack. It ended with a free being awarded to them from 35 metres out. Once again the ever-reliable Cregan in his dark helmet came out to take it and put it over the bar.

This now left only three points between the sides, 2–10 to 2–7, just as the game entered the last quarter. The excitement among the 65,000 attendance rose palpably. Limerick, so long outplayed, were back in the hunt. Galway, despite their superiority, had not been able to kill them off.

It was at this juncture that Bernie Forde showed his mettle. He pressurised Dom Punch into losing possession on the right, snatched the ball and ran fleet-footed in a display of exceptional speed. Though he had two colleagues free inside him he shortened his grip on the hurley to avoid being hooked and, swinging close to his side, sent a relieving point over for the westerners.

Linnane, Silke and Coen continued to play with great anticipation and grit but more and more ball was going over their heads into the full forward line.

Limerick struck again almost immediately. O'Donoghue burst forward shaking off all challengers and hit a long ball which went high into the Galway goal area. This was a McKenna ball. He reached up for it and, taking it out of the sky, turned and struck over a point from 25 metres.

Forde Restores Lead

Once again however it was Forde who restored a four-point lead when he nipped in to collect a ball which had gone over the upstretched hurleys of the backs. Forde, to a great cheer, hit the ball over from 21 metres out.

The Galway selectors, aware that Jimmy Carroll and David Punch were beginning to come into their own at midfield, moved John Connolly there. He could slow the pace down there and keep team morale up by his experienced presence out the field. His brother Michael went in to full forward in his place.

Jimmy Cooney, now totally in command of the left corner, made several forays out the field, to the great joy of the followers as they watched the burly, curley-headed man come charging along the sideline. From one of these clearances the ball went near Steve Mahon. He struck it quickly and accurately off the ground, sending it straight to Forde. Dom Punch threw himself bravely into the swing and blocked the shot for goal. But the ball ricocheted into the Ardrahan man's hand and he struck it over to leave five points between the sides: 2–13 to 2–8

Grimes Comes On

With ten minutes to go Limerick brought on Eamonn Grimes, the veteran South Liberties player who had been leader in the county's year of glory, 1973. He replaced Willie Fitzmaurice who had run himself into the ground with little to show for it. All the Shannonsiders' substitutes were now used up.

Limerick now threw everything they had into the game. Many of the younger players who had been hampered by nerves in the first half were getting more and more into their stride as the game went on.

In a midfield battle Jimmy Carroll doubled skilfully on a ball and sent it flying into the Galway square. There the redoubtable Cregan, ever full of fire and determination, fought for possession and gained it. He was immediately bottled up by the Galway backs. The referee blew for a penalty.

Cregan Penalty

There was a great buzz of excitement all round the ground. In the stands people rose an inch or two off their seats, leaning forward expectantly.

Cregan placed the ball carefully. He backed away a few paces. Then he trotted forward, jab-lifted the ball, threw it forward and from 18 yards hit it waist high with all his power. It billowed the net, the green flag went up and 10,000 green and white flags waved zestfully all over Croke Park. Suddenly Limerick were only two points behind and Galway seemed to be running out of steam.

Game in Balance

The players of both sides now flung themselves into the fray with renewed vigour, aware that the game was in the balance. Limerick were at last playing like they had played in the Munster final. Liam O'Donoghue raised great cheers from the supporters whenever he tackled tigerishly, invariably got possession and cleared the ball well upfield. Foley, the captain, had given a display of steady performance under great pressure all through the game and he began to get stronger as the game went on.

Galway Stay Cool

However there was no question of a Galway collapse under pressure or of signs of panic. They were less energetic but the experience of previous All-Irelands was now standing them in good stead. John Connolly's presence in the centre of the field, using all his skill and sense of positional play, helped to stabilise the team. His brother Michael who, like many players, had taken severe blows across the shins, began to slow down and was replaced by the farmer from Beagh, Finbar Gantley.

On the left wing of the Galway attack, Frank Burke foraged endlessly. He was one of the unselfish workhorses of the side who let the backs come charging into him and then got the pass out to the unmarked man at the last second. Now, with about eight minutes to go, he brushed aside opponents and went on a run of his own. From 30 metres he swung hard on the ball. It sped goalwards but Tommy Quaid raised a great cheer when he saved very confidently and got the ball away.

Captain Scores

Galway attacked again. P.J. Molloy grabbed the ball near the Nally stand side of the field and raced goalwards. Tommy Quaid had no option but the

The Cork team of 1976 that defeated Wexford in the All-Ireland final. Front row (*left to right*): Charlie McCarthy, Brendan Cummins, Gerald McCarthy, Ray Cummins, Martin Coleman, Pat McDonnell, Sean O'Leary. Back row (*left to right*): Jimmy Barry Murphy, Mick Malone, Johnny Crowley, Pat Barry, Martin O'Doherty, Pat Moylan, Denis Coughlan, Bertie Troy, trainer.

All-Ireland final 1976: The captains, Tony Doran of Wexford and Ray Cummins of Cork, flank the referee.

Galway, All-Ireland winners of 1980, the first Galway team to win the title in 57 years. Front row (*left to right*): Niall McInerney, Seamus Coen, Jimmy Cooney, Joe Connolly, Sylvie Linnane, P.J. Molloy, Bernie Forde. Back row (*left to right*): Conor Hayes, Steve Mahon, John Connolly, Michael Connolly, Michael Conneely, Frank Burke, Noel Lane, Sean Silke.

All-Ireland final 1980: Niall McInerney of Galway and Eamonn Cregan of Limerick challenge for the ball.

The Limerick team that lost to Galway in the All-Ireland final of 1980, surely one of the finest teams never to win the title. Front row (*left to right*): David Punch, Ollie O'Connor, Donal Murray, Jimmy Carroll, Sean Foley, Tommy Quaid, John Flanagan, Liam O'Donoghue. Back row (*left to right*): Joe McKenna, Mossie Carroll, Eamonn Cregan, Willie Fitzmaurice, Dominic Punch, Leonard Enright, Paudie Fitzmaurice.

The Offaly team that won the All-Ireland final for the first time ever when they beat Galway in 1981. Front row (*left to right*): Tom Donoghue, Johnny Flaherty, Damien Martin, Padraig Horan, Ger Coughlan, Pat Carroll, Mark Corrigan, Brendan Birmingham. Back row (*left to right*): Paddy Kirwan, Pat Fleury, Joachim Kelly, Liam Currams, Pat Delaney, Eugene Coughlan, Aidan Fogarty.

The ball drops into the Galway goalmouth in the All-Ireland final of 1981.

All-Ireland final 1981: Eugene Coughlan of Offaly challenges Bernie Forde for the ball. John Connolly is in the background.

Noel O'Dwyer of Tipperary in the thick of the action in the Munster hurling final of 1984, in which Cork were the victors.

Munster final 1984: Michael Doyle of Tipperary under pressure.

The Offaly team of 1985 that won the Leinster semi-final replay against Kilkenny after the epic drawn game. Offaly then went on to win the county's second All-Ireland. Front row (*left to right*): Danny Owens, Pat Cleary, Pat Carroll, Ger Coughlan, Jim Troy, Mark Corrigan. Back row (*left to right*): Pat Fleury, Joachim Kelly, Eugene Coughlan, Tom Conneely, Pat Delany, Joe Dooley, Padraig Horan, Aidan Fogarty.

Munster final 1984: Hurling as ballet!

Tom Conneely of Offaly takes the full pressure of a Kilkenny caman in the Leinster semi-final of 1985.

Christy Heffernan of Kilkenny and Eugene Coughlan of Offaly contest the ball.

The Tipperary team that won the replayed Munster final of 1987 to take the Munster hurling title back to the premier county for the first time since 1971. Front row (*left to right*): Nicholas English, Gerry Williams, Aidan Ryan, Richard Stakelum, Pat Fitzelle, Seamus Gibson, Pat Fox, Paul Delany. Back row (*left to right*): John Kennedy, John Heffernan, Conor O'Donovan, Ken Hogan, Colm Bonnar, Donie O'Connell, Bobby Ryan.

Munster final of 1987: Nicholas English and Jim Cashman in the thick of the action.

race out and stop him. A 26-metre free was given against the goalkeeper. Every score was now crucial. All eyes were on Joe Connolly, whose hair at the back of his head was matted with blood and who also had a mouth injury. He bent, lifted the ball well and struck it carefully over the bar. He raised his hurley in a gesture of resolution to his men. His total commitment and the way he carried the mantle of captaincy reflected well on the judgment of those who decided he should lead the team.

'Bomber' Carroll, always chasing and challenging for every ball that came anywhere near him, set up a Limerick attack. The ball came back to him and he pulled hard on it. It rocketed in at crossbar height. But the hero of the game, Michael Conneely, took it out of the air and cleared it away. As he was doing so he was charged by Joe McKenna, whose name was taken by the referee.

The play was going from end to end. These two sides were now locked in an even combat. The difference was that Galway's dominance in the earlier part of the game had given them great confidence and, most importantly, had them three points to the good with five minutes to go.

This was the worst time for their followers. Time and time again they had seen their side almost have victory in its grasp and yet let it drop, out of foolishness or panic. In the minds of many there was a dread inevitability that once again their side would be labelled 'gallant Galway' while the other team were victorious.

Yet Galway came within a few inches of tying up the game there and then. Noel Lane again got possession but again Donal Murray kept after him so that the Ballinderreen man had to strike across the goal. Forde, off balance, just got to it before it went wide, whipped quickly on it and saw it hit the side netting.

Almost a Crucial Score

Then, with only two minutes to go, came the most crucial piece of play in the whole game. Limerick went on a fast running attack, all the forwards racing into positions to strike, spurred on by a great surge of roaring support from the massed crowd. People stood up from their seats when the wily Cregan got the ball thirty yards out, spun like a top and raced goalwards. To the agony of the Galway supporters, the unmistakable gangling figure of the lethal McKenna appeared behind all the defenders. He waited to accept the pass that would have given him an open run. Not even the heroic Conneely would have stopped a certain goal. Cregan handpassed the ball in a high lob towards his colleague — but Conor Hayes raised up his hurley and pulled the ball out of the air in mid-flight. A great sigh of relief went up from the western followers.

Almost from the puck out Limerick came charging in again. And again McKenna was the danger man. He clipped in a smart shot but Conneely, saving and clearing with utter composure, took good care of it.

A minute later came a clinching score. A tiring P.J. Molloy had been replaced by John Ryan to try to counter the inspirational play of O'Donoghue. In an all-out Galway assault Finbar Gantley sent the ball to Ryan, who was fifty yards out, not far from the sideline. It was Ryan's first and only touch of the ball but he scored a splendid point that put his side four points ahead and almost out of reach of their opponents.

Last Limerick Attack

In the very last minute Limerick threw everything they had into a final attack. Their faithful followers rose to them and the green flags waved with great pride. They had got off to a bad start but here they were battling it out to the very end, never beaten.

David Punch, who had kept hurling away despite a difficult game, had begun to play very well in the last fifteen minutes. He came racing into this last attack, whipped the ball into 'Bomber' Carroll who sent it in to Eamonn Grimes. The fair-haired South Liberties man was pulled down. A penalty was awarded.

Cregan had to go for a goal in the hope that if he scored it there still might be a few seconds left for an equalising point. But even as he stood back from the ball the western followers had set up a howling gale of whistles and Noel O'Donoghue keep glancing at his watch.

The veteran Cregan, who had taken thousands of 20-metre frees, ran into the ball, scooped it up and swung hard on the ball. It sped in at head height, no more than a blurred white streak to most spectators. The hurleys in the goalmouth converged on its flight and it was deflected over the bar.

That was it. When Conneely took the puck out it was the last stroke of a tremendous game.

Western Celebrations

Next afternoon, after the lunch for the teams at the Burlington hotel in Dublin, the Galway team boarded a bus at 2 pm to take them to a county ablaze with bonfires, awash with emotion, gratitude and joy and a tinge of sadness for all the unrewarded warriors of the past. It was a full twelve hours later before the team were able to leave the bus in Eyre Square and stand before a crowd of tens of thousands who had been assembled there before the fall of night.

All the way to the West the bus had had to crawl past roadsides bedecked with flags and full of cheering people. It seemed that people from every county and from all walks of life wanted to celebrate the long-awaited triumph of the perennial losers. A huge crowd had gathered at the bridge over the river Shannon at Athlone, the boundary to the west and to Galway. The McCarthy Cup was hoisted into the air for all to see again and again by Joe Connolly.

Frank Burke, one of the droll wits of the side was heard to say, 'If we had known it was going to be like this we would have won years ago.'

Limerick Still Proud

The Limerick team got a warm welcome when they returned home. They had given hurling a great boost of excitement that year and they had played themselves back into the game when all seemed lost. Their grit and character in adversity gave a great sense of pride to their disappointed followers.

'Don't worry — we'll be back', said Eamonn Cregan into the microphone at one of the gatherings. Sure enough the team won the Munster crown the following year as well and this time met Galway in the semi-final. Before a huge crowd, eager to see these sides in another trial of strength, they battled to a draw on a hot day in August. Limerick were badly handicapped in the replay, with five key players on the wounded list; even then, they succumbed only after another titanic struggle.

Sadly, those two epic games, full of excitement and incident, were the last hurrah of one of the great sides of hurling which never won an All-Ireland. Limerick had given hours of enjoyment and delight to hurling followers everywhere and when that team broke up and its great players retired from the game there was a void that was not easily filled.

For Galway, winning the All-Ireland of 1980 was a great release from the years of being haunted by the spectre of inevitable defeat. That victory released a great surge of energy in the county, no long stifled by fear of failure. They were to win more All-Irelands in the 1980s. They were to lose All-Irelands as well but they were now counted among the giants of the game. They could never again be patronisingly dismissed as hopeful challengers and gallant losers.

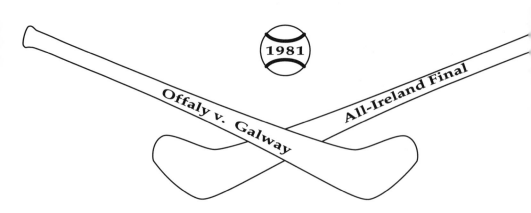

CLASH OF AMBITIOUS NEIGHBOURS

A s darkness fell over the Shannon and the flat lands on either side, it was possible to pick out the pinpoints of flickering red light here and there on the Connacht side. These celebratory bonfires, lit for several evenings in September 1980 were for the Galway heroes who had at last brought the senior trophy to the county after fifty-seven long years.

The bonfires could be seen from across the broad black river in Co. Offaly. The hurling lovers in that county did not begrudge their neighbours' joy. Indeed many crossed the river to join in the celebrations in places like Meelick, Eyrecourt and Portumna. The local pubs of many of the Galway celebrants were on the Leinster side, in Banagher, and they came across the bridge to share their triumph.

The Offaly followers were happy for Galway and for the boost it would give to hurling in all those areas where the game was played without having achieved national honours. If Galway could beat the odds, beat the weight of tradition, so also could counties who had never won an All-Ireland or not won one for years and years — counties like Clare, Antrim, Dublin and Offaly itself.

New Leinster Champions

If Galway were the main celebrants in 1980 their neighbours across the Shannon also had something to celebrate. They had won their first ever Leinster senior title, having beaten the powerful reigning All-Ireland champions Kilkenny in a cliff-hanger of a game. They had contested their very first All-Ireland semi-final against their friends and rivals, Galway.

1980 Semi-Final

Against all expectations it turned out to be a close run thing. The westerners, who had contested the All-Irelands of 1975 and '79 were on their way to their triumphant final. Offaly had not the same experience of the big scene. In addition they were not fully attuned to such an occasion. The effort to win their first Leinster title and the endless gatherings in town and village to share the triumph with the faithful populace, had taken their toll.

Just the same, when all seemed lost to the greater experience and skill of Galway, the midlanders had kept battling away and edged their way back into the game. At the end they were going full out and had hauled back their rivals to a mere two points as the final whistle went.

That refreshing game, between two of the outsiders of hurling who had not met before in the championship, seemed to signal that two new forces had arrived on the tradition-bound scene. But both of these counties would not be fully accepted by many until they had stamped a more distinct seal on the scroll of honour.

Offaly Begin Preparations

That momentous semi-final was hardly over when Offaly set about continuing the task of growing in skill and experience. They wanted to learn from their Leinster win and semi-final defeat. They had now set their sights on an All-Ireland, impudent as this may have seemed to the many doubters of their ability.

The team made a great effort in the National League of 1980–81. They won match after match, honing their abilities, adjusting and adapting. Under Diarmuid Healy and Andy Gallagher they were becoming more astute with each game.

First League Final

That spring the county team reached its first league final ever.

They faced Cork, one of the long-established teams, on a day at the beginning of May. It was a Sunday of gale-force wind and torrential showers in Thurles. With the wind behind them Cork got off to what was almost a freak start — they scored 2 goals and 3 points within a few minutes.

The crowd, huddled for shelter under the cover of the stands, expected the midlanders to succumb easily after such a disastrous beginning. This was when Offaly showed their grim, never-say-die attitude. Although outplayed in many positions, they never gave up. Cork were far ahead but the Offalymen kept going, giving it all they had. They earned a lot of respect that day for their doggedness and their persistence. They were going full steam at the end, matching Cork score for score, but they were unable to overcome the bad start. Cork were victors by 3–11 to 2–8.

Galway, still relishing their All-Ireland championship status, did not take the league very seriously and had to make a great effort to avoid the humiliation of relegation.

Forecasts

When the 1981 championship began the usual favourites were posted. Cork and Kilkenny came first because both counties had great reservoirs of talent; then the reigning champions Galway, then the team they had conquered in the 1980 final, Limerick. In Leinster the pundits were hedging their bets by saying that Kilkenny would be seriously challenged by the county which was always a tough challenger, Wexford. Offaly, although reigning provincial champions were seen as 'in there with a chance' and no more.

This almost proved to be true in the semi-final against Laois. With four minutes to go a Laois side led with great heart by P.J. and Martin Cuddy, Christy Jones and Billy Bohane were two points ahead in a thrilling match. Then, in a dramatic finish Offaly scored two points to draw level.

Almost on the call of time Offaly were awarded a free well inside their own half. One of the longest strikers of the ball in modern times, Paddy Kirwan of Ballyskenach, went across to take the free. The previous year against Laois he had scored the winning point from a free over 90 metres out. He repeated the feat this time as well to win the game.

Kirwan was using one of the light Neary hurleys that Diarmuid Healy had introduced. His feat proved the point that hitting the ball right is what matters, not the weight of the hurley.

Against Wexford

After the semi-final, when Wexford beat Kilkenny on a scoreline of 4–12 to 1–8, the Slaneysiders were installed as firm favourites for the Leinster final against Offaly. They were seen as a stronger, more determined team, hungry for the success that had eluded many very good Wexford sides in recent times.

No other team had given such a succession of strong challenges to the great Kilkenny side of the late '60s and early '70s. With tremendous spirit and grit, Wexford had beaten Kilkenny in 1970, 1976 and '77. They had gone on to contest, unsuccessfully, the All-Irelands of those years, against Cork on each occasion. Because of their great band of sporting followers and the way their predecessors had changed the static hurling scene 30 years before, there was a great residue of goodwill towards them.

Offaly had virtually the same side that had won the provincial title the previous year. But they were not quite the same. They had developed cohesive teamwork. They had worked hard on their skills. They had developed character.

Exciting Game

They were now being taken seriously by hurling followers. The previous year only 9,600 had turned up for the final against Kilkenny. This year the number had swelled to 29,000. A great section of these were, of course, the loyal followers from the south-east, fully expecting their side to win and go straight into another All-Ireland.

This was a wholehearted and exciting game. Every ball was fiercely contested. The pace was frenetic. Against expectations Offaly were the power side and went into a six point lead. A big blow to Wexford was the sight of Tony Doran being carried off after a fearsome bout of tackling and pulling in the square. Despite that, Wexford hauled themselves back into the game in the second half. George O'Connor gave a great display of high hand-catching and great delivery of the ball that went within an ace of taking the title for the Slaneysiders. With two minutes to go, Wexford were only one point behind after a 70 taken by Colm Doran had gone all the way into the net.

Offaly refused to panic. Damien Martin pucked out the ball to centre-field where the captain, Padraig Horan collected it and sent a fast ball goalwards straight into the hand of the elusive Johnny Flaherty. The 35-year-old corner forward put it over the bar. In a last desperate Wexford attack a ball from one of the most skilful ball-jugglers of the side, Johnny Murphy, almost reached the in-rushing George O'Connor. But Offaly's centre back, the redoubtable Pat Delaney, intercepted the pass and ensured a place for the midlanders in their first All-Ireland.

Semi-Final Saga

Galway were scheduled to take on the Munster champions in the semi-final. Once again Limerick emerged from the southern province. Then began one of the most enthralling semi-final sagas. The two sides which had battled so entertainingly in the previous year's All-Ireland now ran out on to the field for a re-match.

A huge crowd of over 40,000 came to Croke Park for what many decided was the virtual All-Ireland final. The tension was palpable. When the national anthem finished the rising roar was like a great release of pent-up competitive emotion. When the game was started by referee Noel O'Donoghue from the Cuala club in Dalkey, every ball was competed for with such intensity that the yelling of spectators was continuous.

Unfortunate Incident

It seemed inevitable that a distressful incident should occur. P.J. Molloy, the Galway half forward, snapped up a ball, put it on his hurley and flew towards the Limerick goal. Sean Foley, the Shannonsiders stalwart half back, went in hard on him. In trying to sweep the ball off Molloy's hurley he instead connected with Molloy's face. The Galwayman collapsed on the ground, blood pouring from above and below his right eye. The referee judged that this was dangerous play on the part of Foley and sent him to the line.

Only eight minutes had gone and now Limerick were down to fourteen men. Yet they battled away with fierce intensity, showing immense courage in the face of adversity. Galway, who seemed to have the advantage, could not put their opponents away and were lucky enough to draw the match.

Great Replay

The replay, on 16 August, was an even more enthralling contest. Played on a blazing hot day before 42,000 spectators it was an occasion when the raw courage of the Shannonsiders won them a place in the annals of the game. They were short several key players, including the suspended Sean Foley and the injured half backs Dom Punch and Pat Herbert. Five minutes before the interval of a bone crunching, lung-searing encounter, Mike Grimes went off injured.

For the replay the Galway players and mentors had prevailed upon the veteran John Connolly to come out of retirement. It was felt that his authority, his great game-experience and his deft touches would make a significant difference to the performance of the team. So it proved in the replay. Even though he was not fully match-fit for a contest of this exacting kind, his presence on the field gave a great boost to the westerners. He got telling scores at key moments.

Despite their diminished strength Limerick gave everything they had in this game and stayed in it until almost the final whistle. The biggest blow they had to endure was when their great full back, Leonard Enright, could carry on no longer with an injury and had to leave the field.

End of the Line

There was sadness among the Limerick team and supporters after this tumultuous match. They sensed that it was the unrewarded end of the line for this great team of supreme entertainers and hurlers. 'We simply ran out of men', said one of the Limerick mentors, sorrowfully.

Galway Favourites

Galway had drawn and won in two of the most stirring contests seen in Croke Park for a long time. They were immediately installed as favourites to beat Offaly. They had shown all their skill and resolve in beating this fine Limerick side. But some of their own supporters were uneasy that the forward line did not really get going until the last quarter of the replay, when four of the first-choice Limerick backs were no longer playing.

They went into training in Athenry a few days later under the tutelage of Cyril Farrell, Bernie O'Connor and M.J. 'Inky' Flaherty. The feeling all over Galway and indeed among hurling followers elsewhere was that they had their second All-Ireland in a row for the taking.

Doubts About Consistency

Yet even in Galway there was unease about their likely performance on the first Sunday in September. This may have been a residue of the many times in the recent past that the side, with everything going for them, could do everything but win. Even the great win of the previous year could not erase the legend of the team's inconsistency.

In previous years they were exhilaratingly effective in one game and could not get going at all in the next. Now it was somewhat different: they could be going all out and then be frustratingly ineffective in the same game. This happened in both games against Limerick. The heat and the exertion during the replay had seen some of the veterans of the side, who had backboned the team since 1975, slowing a little in the last hectic quarter.

Non-stop effort was a quality that Offaly had in abundance. It would need concentration, consistency during the entire game to overcome the champions in the All-Ireland. Not alone that but it would require that vital instinct — the capacity to deliver telling blows to the opposition when in a position of advantage.

Offaly In Training

No one who visited the Offaly team training in Tullamore had any doubts about the commitment of the side. All their players were honing the skills that had brought them two Leinster titles and a place in their first league final earlier in the year.

'We concentrated 75 per cent of our effort on skills training — standing in lines of four or five, pulling on the ball, meeting it, controlling it', said Diarmuid Healy.

They were all immensely fit. Many were big, strong players. They now had more talent in terms of skill and astuteness than ever before. Players like Martin in goal, Delaney at centre back, Kelly at midfield and Carroll, Flaherty and Mark Corrigan in the forwards had to be rated among the very top practitioners in their positions on the field.

When the names and the positions of the players became known the followers tried to assess the relative merits of the teams, to figure out how they might measure up to one another.

In the semi-final encounter the previous year Michael Conneely had been most unsure of himself and was blamed for two goals that let Offaly back into the game. However, the Sarsfield's man had answered his critics in the All-Ireland. He was the hero of the game, giving one of the great goalkeeping displays on All-Ireland day. Since then he was full of confidence and the team had full confidence in him.

Conneely would need to be at his best. Among the Offaly forwards were fast runners like Paddy Kirwan, Mark Corrigan and Pat Carroll who could strike on the run from far out and send in dangerous dipping balls that would trouble any keeper.

Flaherty Danger

In the semi-final of the previous year the Galway full-back line had been very much in command for most of the game. Seamus Coen had proved himself a very good replacement for the injury-plagued Conor Hayes. He had vigilantly marked Johnny Flaherty. However the problem would

The teams as they lined out were:

GALWAY

Michael Conneely
(Sarsfields)

Seamus Coen	Niall McInerney	Jimmy Cooney
(Mullagh)	(Liam Mellowes)	(Sarsfields)

Sylvie Linnane	Sean Silke, capt	Iggy Clarke
(Gort)	(Meelick-Eyrecourt)	(Loughrea)

Michael Connolly	Steve Mahon
(Castlegar)	(Kilbeacanty)

Finbar Gantley	Joe Connolly	P.J. Molloy
(Beagh)	(Castlegar)	(Athenry)

Bernie Forde	John Connolly	Noel Lane
(Ardrahan)	(Castlegar)	(Ballinderreen)

Substitutes/panel: Frank Burke (Turloughmore); Paschal Ryan (Killimordaly); Michael King (Padraig Pearse's); Brendan Lynskey (Meelick-Eyrecourt); John Ryan (Killimordaly); Pearse Piggott (Gort); Conor Hayes (Kiltormer); Joe McDonagh (Ballinderreen); Padraig Connolly (Castlegar); Michael Mulkerrins (Sarsfields); Michael Earls (Killimordaly); Syl Dolan (Ardrahan); Andy Fenton (Kiltormer); Frank Canning (Tommy Larkins); Tommy Grogan (Castlegar). *Manager/coach*: Cyril Farrell (Tommy Larkins). *Selectors/mentors*: M.J. 'Inky' Flaherty (Liam Mellowes); Bernie O'Connor (Oranmore-Maree); Tom Callanan (Kilconieron); Frank Corcoran (Sarsfields). *Team doctor*: Dr Mary McInerney. *Masseur*: Willie Bennett.

OFFALY

Damien Martin
(St Rynagh's)

Tom Donoghue	Eugene Coughlan	Pat Fleury
(Ballinamere)	(Sier Kieran's)	(Drumcullen)

Aidan Fogarty	Pat Delaney	Ger Coughlan
(St Rynagh's)	(Kinnity)	(Kinnity)

Joachim Kelly	Liam Currams
(Lusmagh)	(Kilcormac Killoughey)

Paddy Kirwan	Brendan Birmingham	Mark Corrigan
(Ballyskenach)	(Lusmagh)	(Kinnity)

Pat Carroll	Padraig Horan, capt	Johnny Flaherty
(Coolderry)	(St Rynagh's)	(Kinnity)

Substitutes: Brendan Keeshan (Shinrone); Danny Owens (Kilcormac Killoughey); Jim Troy (Lusmagh); Christy King (Killavilla); Sean O'Meara (Shinrone); Mick Kennedy (Birr); Martin Cashin (Birr); Liam Hogan (Coolderry); Sean Whyte (St Rynagh's). *Coach*: Diarmuid Healy. *Trainer*: Andy Gallagher. *Mentors/selectors*: Tom Errity (Coolderry); Charlie Daly (Na Piarsaigh); Padge Mulhaire (St Rynagh's); Mick Spain (Drumcullen); Fr Sean Heaney; Tony Murphy. *Team physician*: Dr Brendan White. *Masseur*: Ossie Bennett.

The referee was Frank Murphy of Cork.

be to mark the wily Kinnity player for all of the game. He had a will-o'-the-wisp style, almost unseen until he snatched a ball from under a back's nose and slammed or hand passed it to the net. And Coen would have to be fast on the turn because the amazing Flaherty had retained his speed on short bursts.

In that game Niall McInerney had got the better of things with Padraig Horan. There was no question that the St Rynagh's man would win any easy balls on the ground or in the air or, if he did, find room to hit them. But he had an indomitable will to win and he had a great capacity to block and hook and harrass and harry. Backs did not find it easy to make long clearances when he was around.

Pat Carroll in the right corner was a forceful hurler. This red-haired player challenged fiercely for any ball that came his way, often won it and could hit the ball deftly left or right. Jimmy Cooney, one of the stars of the previous year's All-Ireland, was due another storming game. He was very like Carroll in his appearance and vigorous play.

Galway Half Line

For many Galway followers the Galway half-back line, once the sheet anchor of the side, was a cause for some concern. Sean Silke, one of the great centre backs, was at the veteran stage. The anticipation and positional play for which he was famous had not been evident in the games against Limerick. He was now up against a bustling centre forward in Brendan Birmingham, who himself had had some difficulty striking form but who, on his day, broke up the play very well so that Mark Corrigan and Paddy Kirwan were able to pick up good balls.

Iggy Clarke, who had suffered a serious shoulder injury in the semi-final of 1980 against Offaly, was now plagued with a delicate hamstring. He had been an outstanding wing back and all hurling followers were hoping he would regain his form, for he had a delightful style about his play, could race into the attack, send long balls into the opponents' square. He would be marking Paddy Kirwan, a very skilful striker who, once he got the smallest space, was able to send high soaring balls over the bar.

Sylvie Linnane had the task of marking Corrigan. A fiery battler, his power play had an inspirational effect on the players and indeed on the spectators. He had great skill, could clip the ball off the ground and send it away down the field. But Corrigan had proved himself one of the most opportunitstic half forwards in the game. He had a quiet, unobtrusive style of play but he scored many points in match after match. Once he got the ball within forty yards of goal it was almost certain he would put it over.

Midfield Battle

Offaly were considered to have greatly strengthened their midfield by the arrival of the stylish Currams to partner the endlessly foraging Joachim

Kelly. Kelly's courage and stamina were by now part of the folklore of Offaly hurling. This left-hander ran vigorously about the field, finding the pace and the energy to join in the attack or to get back in defence.

The bearded Currams, who was equally talented as a footballer and was a member of the senior side, was a natural athlete. He had a beautiful stroke on the ball and he had scored some great long-range points since he came on the team. He ranged freely about the field of play and was difficult to mark. Offaly had also reached the football All-Ireland that year and Currams would create something of a record by playing in both.

Their opponents were Steve Mahon and Michael Connolly. Mahon was one of the best midfielders of that era. He was strong. He was full of running. He could race into the attack. From midfield he invariably sent in low fast balls to the forwards. And he waited his opportunity and then struck some great points from long range. His partner was Michael Connolly, a stylish player who was capable of playing in many positions. In the replayed semi-final against Limerick he had gone centre back after the departure of Sean Silke, who had been slowed by injury. Connolly had played a great game, reading the play well, striking the ball quickly and forcefully.

Offaly Defence

The Offaly defence was seen as a phalanx of solid, reliable players. They placed great emphasis on team work, on supporting one another in difficulties. They had developed a sound way of playing, of giving little away, of trying to avoid unnecessary frees under pressure.

Undoubtedly the most visible of the six was the tall, sinewy centre back, Pat Delaney of Kinnity. A hardy outdoorsman, his curly blond head was here and there about the half back line, clearing the ball with great determination. He had developed into one of the most reliable centre backs in the game. One of his greatest assets was his ability to send over long-range frees. When under pressure with the ball he was strong enough to shoulder his way out of danger. But he had also developed the quick flick out to Fogarty at one side and his Kinnity team mate, Coughlan on the other.

Joe Connolly, very determined, a great battler for the ball, a powerhouse centre forward was going to be fully tested in his duel with the Kinnity man. Connolly had had some really great moments in both the draw and replay with Limerick, winning difficult balls as well as snapping up loose balls, sending the side into attack. He had leadership qualities, yelling encouragement to the players about him.

On one side of him would be Finbar Gantley, a stocky farmer who had worked for several years in London and played a lot of his hurling there. He had been on the team in the All-Ireland of '79 but was among the subs the following year. He had regained his place because he was a solid, steady player who was not easily shouldered off the ball in tussles along the sideline.

His marker, Ger Coughlan, would be giving him a two and a half stone advantage in weight, but not in speed or skill. One of the smallest and lightest players to play senior hurling, Coughlan's performance in every game was full of courage and nimbleness.

He tipped the ball away from opponents, pulled with unusual confidence on fast incoming balls, was a tenacious tackler who was so slight that he could never be knocked over and, when he got possession, slipped under the elbows of opponents to clear the ball away.

On the other side the duel would be between Aidan Fogarty and P.J. Molloy. Despite his bad facial injury in the first game against Limerick, the broad-shouldered Athenry player had hit a great spell in the replay. He held the hurley in the right-hand-under grip and had a similar opportunistic style as Mark Corrigan. He could expect little change from Fogarty, who had emerged as a solidly reliable half back who was rarely beaten in the air and had an astute sense of positioning.

Strong Galway Line

It was thought that Galway's full forward line would be the one from which Offaly had most to fear. At full forward was one of the great Galway hurlers, John Connolly. He was skilful, and had a great first touch of the ball. He was tall and determined. More than that, he could draw on the experience of hundreds of games. He was being marked by a man who was also tall and strong, Eugene Coughlan. The Clareen man had played his way onto the team by a series of sound, cool performances and had now made the full back berth his own. The big test for him was supposed to be the Leinster final when he had to put the shackles on the most feared full forward in the game, Tony Doran from the Buffer's Alley club in Wexford. However, Doran had gone off injured early in the game and there was a feeling that this relative newcomer had yet to be really tested.

Corner Duels

In the corners Galway had two players who had created lots of difficulties for defences. Bernie Forde and Noel Lane had played a big role in the defeat of Limerick in the 1980 All-Ireland and they had played well subsequently. Forde's greatest asset was to whip round in possession and run like a hare for the goal. Pat Fleury, the strong sinewy Drumcullen player, would have to stop him getting possession without giving away the kind of frees that Joe Connolly would be only too happy to put over the bar. Fleury and Forde had played on one another before and had come out evens. Fluery knew that Forde was a player who invariably hit the ball off his left-hand side and was certain to keep that side of him.

In the other corner was the rangy Noel Lane, a great player for getting and keeping possession by weaving and turning. He could do so because he had first-rate ball control. He was fast and had good direction with a first-time pull. His marker was going to be a former colleague, Tom

Donoghue. He had been on the first Galway team to break the losing tradition — the under-21 side that won out in 1972. He was a member of the senior panel from 1976 to '78 and gained great experience as Galway grew in strength and resolve. When he had taken up an appointment in Offaly as a PT instructor he had thrown in his lot with the county. He was fast and alert but he would need to concentrate for the full seventy minutes if he was to stop Lane doing real damage.

Damien Martin

Offaly's last line of defence was Damien Martin. The veteran goalkeeper had emerged as one of the finest in the game. It was not just that he had great anticipation and lightning reflexes. He was a player who radiated determination to his colleagues and who showed it the way he faced up to the ball. He was one of the influential members of the side. He had been on the point of retiring before he achieved what often seemed like an impossible dream — winning a Leinster championship. Now, when most of his contemporaries, with the exception of Flaherty, had long hung up their boots, here he was in his first All-Ireland final.

Westerners Given Vote of Confidence

When the media commentators, and indeed the hurling followers, looked over the teams most unhesitatingly made Galway firm favourites. They were seen as, man for man, having the edge in hurling skills. Their All-Ireland experience would stand to them. They had been through it all, knew something about handling the nerves that assailed so many players on the big day. They had star players like John Connolly, Sean Silke and Iggy Clarke who would be playing in their fourth All-Ireland.

'If they are in the right mood on the day they'll do it. If they are in the peak of mental and physical condition there will be no beating them — their defence is the best in the country and the forwards will get the scores. After all it's Offaly's first All-Ireland. No team wins out the first time. But Galway better have the right mental approach.' This was a reported comment of a western follower.

Offaly Conviction

Offaly were given full credit for their teamwork and fighting spirit. They were a unified side and had displayed great resolve over the past two years. They were growing with each game, their cohesion getting better, their stickwork improving from week to week under the tutelage of Diarmuid Healy and their own unremitting efforts.

Diarmuid Healy did all he could to convince them that they could beat the champions. 'I told them that if they were within six points of Galway with ten minutes to go then they could win because Galway would weaken.'

Pre-match Celebrations

Most of the huge crowd of Galway supporters streaming into the city from Thursday onwards were in a celebratory mood. This was the first time ever that they could come to a final where their team had been installed as firm favourites. It was the first time ever that they were contesting an All-Ireland as well-deserved champions. They might have been less assured if their opponents had been Cork, Tipperary or Kilkenny. The western supporters felt that their side would be well able to handle the newcomers on the championship scene.

The Aisling hotel, across from Heuston railway station, near the road to the west, was where the Galway team stayed. On Saturday night it was jam-packed with supporters, laughing and joyful, sometimes surrounding those players who emerged into the foyer. The players went to their rooms early but the sound of revelry echoed in the corridors and streets outside into the early morning.

Offaly Pre-conditioning

How does a manager ensure that his team is as settled as it possibly can be in the 24 hours before they run in to the gale of sound that surrounds the pitch at Croke Park on All-Ireland day? What if it is the team's first All-Ireland? Shortly before the final Diarmuid Healy sought some advice from Noel Skehan, the veteran Kilkenny goalkeeper, whom he met by chance outside Nowlan Park.

As a result of their conversation Healy made a number of decisions. The team would stay in Power's Hotel, where they normally stayed and with which they were comfortably familiar. When they set out for Croke Park on Sunday the players were in one coach and the wives and girl-friends were in another. The players had enough inner tensions to handle without worrying about their loved ones gaining admittance through the huge moving streams of people heaving outside Croke Park; that was being looked after by someone else and they had not to think about it.

Healy had also tackled head-on the often-avoided subject of how intimi-dating, if not fear-inducing, the emergence on the field can be for players. He told the players that a massive wall of sound would surround them as they ran out from the tunnel, that the level of noise from the voices of 70,000 people would be throbbing throughout the game. They were to expect it and not to take any notice of it but to concentrate on the puck about, to look only at the ball and their fellow-players, to talk reassuringly among themselves. As far as possible they were to shut out all the sur-rounds and to focus on the ball, on the game and on their opponents.

The Galway players had been through all this before, some of them several times, and they took the field and pucked about with a certain panache.

The Game Begins

After all the unavoidable but, to players, tiresome ceremonials had been got out of the way the referee, Frank Murphy of Cork, called the two captain together. Silke and Horan knew one another well. They lived within sight of one another, separated only by the Shannon. The McCarthy cup would eventually come home to the same area, no matter which side won it.

Galway would be playing into the Canal goal in the first half and had some advantage from a crossfield breeze. The grass was dry and the day perfect for a game of hurling.

When the ball was thrown in there was some scurrying about in the first anxious seconds. Sean Silke and Brendan Birmingham had their first tussle for the upper hand. The referee judged that the Galway captain had pushed his opponent and a free was awarded. It was 70 metres from the Galway goal. Pat Delaney, who was assigned the long-distance frees, cantered up to take it. This was a significant moment for Offaly. It would be great for morale if they could score off such frees. The tall, sinewy Delaney, rose the ball carefully and swung accurately on it. The ball soared away and went over high between the posts. It was first blood to the midlanders and a spur to the whole team.

Then Galway, to a roar from their supporters, went into the attack. From the puck out Joe Connolly got hold of the ball and sent it flying low through legs and hurleys towards the Offaly goal-line. But he topped his shot and Martin, concentrating intently, saw it coming in time. In his characteristic style, the Banagher man got down to it, putting hurley and body in front of the ball. He caught it. Backs and forwards were glued to one another and Martin decided to make a run out the field in a defiant gesture. He got to 35 metres but there was a lot of jostling and a free was given against his team.

First Galway Score

Joe Connolly, captain of the previous year and taker of close-in frees stood over the ball 40 metres out. Like Delaney a minute before, it was important not to miss such frees, especially at an early stage in the game. But Connolly was consistent and he slotted it over the bar with aplomb.

From the puck out the Galway half back line sent the ball back into the Offaly half and in towards the left corner. The long-legged Lane won the race against Tom Donoghue for the ball. Donoghue stayed goalside of him, hustling him out to the corner but Lane passed the ball back to the midfielder Steve Mahon, who had raced forward along the left hand side. From about 37 metres out the strong man from Kilbeacanty hit an angled shot smartly over the bar. Galway were in the lead.

Both teams were playing cautiously. Offaly were tentative in their approach. Galway seemed to be playing well within themselves. The excitement level for spectators was moderate.

In an Offaly attack the ball went over the sideline off a Galway hurley on the left. Johnny Flaherty, who held the hurley in the right-hand-under grip, cut the ball and flighted it into the square. The ever-running Joachim Kelly pulled on it. Niall McInerney took the force of this ball on his legs and deflected it out over the end line for a 65 metre free. Another test for Delaney. Another point for Offaly.

Danger For Galway

There was a moment of danger for Galway some time later. When the ball came goalwards McInerney and Iggy Clarke went for it together, fluffed it between them and allowed the alert Pat Carroll to snap it up. He struck it hard. This was the first real test for Michael Conneely and he handled the difficult ball well. But he could only bat it away and Flaherty was lurking outside, waiting for such a chance. He was hard pressed by Seamus Coen and sent it wide.

Galway went into another attack and were awarded a free 40 metres out. Joe Connolly, being well contained by Pat Delaney in play, came over, lifted the ball well and struck it accurately over the bar.

Galway were getting in control, hurling better than their opponents. Even at this stage it was clear that they had a clear upper hand at midfield where Mahon was playing powerfully and Michael Connolly showed many stylish touches.

A Heartening Offaly Goal

Not much good ball was getting in to the Offaly forwards but in the 12th minute a quickly struck ball from the tenacious Ger Coughlan ended up on the left hand side of the attack. Mark Corrigan, well marked though he was by Sylvie Linnane, sent it further in. Flaherty, very fast in short bursts despite his years, was first to reach it, controlled it deftly and made an elusive run goalwards. At the last second he passed it across the square to Pat Carroll who pulled hard and accurately on it. It flew in low, ricocheted off the inside of the near post and went into the goal behind Conneely, who had little chance with this kind of shot.

This goal, by the gingery-haired farmer from Coolderry, raised a huge cheer from Offaly supporters and gave a great impetus to the team, who were feeling the burden of being in a first All-Ireland. It was an additional boost that it had been scored by the fervent Carroll, a man totally dedicated to hurling, to the team, to fitness, to honing his own skills.

Galway move Up a Gear

Galway responded by moving up a gear and putting more pressure on the Offaly defence. In an attack, Bernie Forde went up for a clean catch but caught Pat Fleury's hurley on the face. He had to leave the field for medical attention and returned looking somewhat battered with a bandaged head and nose. Meanwhile, Joe Connolly had scored a point from a free awarded for the incident.

Shortly afterwards the Galway centre forward, who was having a gruelling time with Delaney, fought for possession and though under great pressure sent over a fine point from 55 yards out. Aidan Fogarty was playing soundly on Molloy but the Athenry man got away from him two minutes later and sent over a well-struck point from near the sideline, fifty yards out.

The game was strangely subdued at this stage, though it was enjoyable enough for the spectators. There was a feeling that it might be won rather easily by Galway. However, the vaunted half back line was not getting the attack under way as it had done in previous games. Brendan Birmingham kept whipping the ball away from Silke and the Galway captain was making few of his long raking clearances. On his left, Iggy Clarke found his hands full with Paddy Kirwan. He played soundly but there was no question of his assuming his familiar role of attacking half back. John Connolly was being very closely policed by Eugene Coughlan and he got few opportunities to make use of his great skills and experience. Coughlan played a calm game, displaying an unexpected amount of skilful touches in flicking the ball out of danger, batting it away from Connolly.

However, at midfield, Mahon was playing one of his best games in the maroon jersey, challenging for and winning a lot of balls and sending them fast and low into the path of the running forwards. Twenty minutes into the game he scored a point himself, clouting a ball from midfield that soared away from his stick and passed high between the uprights.

When the ball came in to John Connolly, he got hold of it with only inches to spare in front of Eugene Coughlan. The Offaly full back was to give a display of hooking and blocking that placed him among the great full backs of the era. This time he partially blocked down his opponent's shot but it rebounded out to Joe Connolly who scored another fine point.

Offaly Now Being Outhurled

Offaly were being outhurled in many parts of the field and the full forward line were getting a meagre supply of ball at this stage. With the kind of gritty determination that was to characterise the team in the years ahead, they were hanging on grimly.

Pivotal Incident

Twenty-five minutes into the game came one of those pivotal incidents on which games swing. P.J. Molloy got the ball on the wing but Fogarty was goalside of him. However, the Athenry man managed to lob the ball goal-wards. John Connolly fielded it superbly, broke to the left and raced for goal, with Eugene Coughlan in hot pursuit. Offaly supporters held their breath. Damien Martin faced the incoming full forward. Connolly, fearing his hurley would be hooked by Coughlan behind him, handpassed the ball towards the goal. Martin managed to partially smother it. Connolly, unable to stop his momentum, crashed into him. The loose ball trickled over the line.

Frank Murphy judged that the goalkeeper had been fouled. To the dismay of the prematurely jubilant Galway followers he gave a free out.

This incident was the subject of a good deal of after-match discussion. Damien Martin said that if Connolly had hit the ball a yard before he did or had handpassed it a yard after he did, then the full forward would have scored a certain goal. Joe McDonagh maintains that Connolly had been hampered by injury in his efforts to get back to sharp match fitness after almost a year in retirement before the replay with Limerick.

'All the skill and experience of this great player could not overcome this handicap in an All-Ireland. I believe that if it had been a month later, as Connolly proved by his performances with Castlegar, he would have scored that goal', he said.

A goal at that juncture might have effectively sunk Offaly, despite their never-say-die grit. Coming from Connolly, it would have been a great boost to the western side and gone some way to deflating the opposition. The fact that the goal was missed, that Martin made a courageous save and that a free out was given raised a great cheer from the hard-pressed Offaly followers.

And a minute later the midlanders were awarded a free 75 metres from the Galway goal. Pat Delaney, who was having a toe-to-toe battle with Joe Connolly, stood over the ball, lifted it, took account of the crossfield breeze and struck it hard. It rose and rose and then began to curve and fall but went between the uprights for a heartening point. Despite Offaly being outclassed for so much of the time, they were only two points behind: 1–3 to 8 points.

Two Long Range Points

Two of the best scores of the game came next. When the ball came into the Offaly goalmouth John Connolly got the ball but had it flicked from his hurley by the vigilant Coughlan, who then cleared it upfield. Connolly's brother Michael ran onto the clearance, swung around to elude his marker and hitting the ball on the turn, put over a great point from 50 metres out.

Shortly afterwards the ball came between Finbar Gantly and Ger Coughlan. Coughlan, light and lithe, got the better of the brief tussle and sent the ball into the midfield area. There Liam Currams, who was finding it hard to come into the game, lifted and struck in one movement. To a great cheer of delight from the hurling-lovers in the crowd the ball shot straight as a die over the bar.

Galway Switches

At that stage the Galway mentors decided to switch Lane and Gantly. The Ballinderreen man had hardly come onto the right wing when he pulled on a ball that hopped almost on the sideline under the Hogan stand. It went over the bar for a fine point and a great cheer from the Galway supporters. It seemed to indicate that Galway only needed to go up a gear to take full control of this somewhat subdued game.

At that time Joe and John Connolly switched positions. On the Offaly side Mark Corrigan went to the ailing midfield while Joachim Kelly went to left half forward.

Eugene Coughlan got possession of the next ball that came in between himself and Joe Connolly. He came racing out but with Galway forwards in pursuit the referee reckoned he had held on to the ball too long. Joe Connolly put the free over the bar.

Galway were on top and moving into attack regularly. In one of these inrushes Gantly got possession and sent the ball to John Connolly. He fell but managed to tip the ball into the path of Lane who scored another good point.

Bernie Forde was having a hard time making progress against Fleury who kept glued to the Ardrahan man's left — his striking side. But just on the half-time the bandaged forward snapped up a ball and was heading goalwards when he was fouled by his marker.

Joe Connolly took the free to leave the score Galway 13 points to Offaly's 1–4 at half-time.

Half-time

As the teams trooped off the field thoughtfully there was an air of expectant satisfaction among the Galway followers if not the members of the team itself. They had played reasonably well, were very much on top and were six points up. There was no reason to believe that the pattern of play in the second half would be any different.

Many of the Offaly supporters were satisfied enough. Their team had certainly not fallen asunder under the tensions of a first All-Ireland and the experience and skills of the champions. They were still there and even if they did not win at least this dogged side would not disgrace the county.

It was hard to imagine the Galway side escaping the weakening drug of complacency. They were red-hot favourites going into the game and had well justified that rating. They were now even hotter favourites at half time.

When the teams ran back out on to the spacious sward the cheers from the crowd was lacking the decibels of tension and aggressiveness that marked the more closely fought All-Irelands.

Game Resumes

The second half resumed with all the players in their original positions, with the exception of Lane and Gantly who stayed as they were.

There were some wides by both sides before Mahon, still playing powerfully at midfield, went running down the middle with the ball on his stick. He created an opening for Joe Connolly who slapped it over the bar to put Galway seven points ahead. People in the crowd were wondering if this was to be the start of a steady scoring process by Galway which would effectively end the game as a real contest.

However Offaly showed no sign of despondency. They kept hurling away steadily. It also began to be noticed at this stage that they had no intention of giving away frees in their own half, gifts for the marksmanship of Joe Connolly.

Instead, it was Offaly who were awarded a close-in free. The dangerous Flaherty got the ball and was fouled in possession. Horan had the unhurried, calm temperament to take the close in frees under pressure. The St Rynagh's man took this one from 21 yards and sent it over the bar.

Tom Donoghue who had been playing well in the right corner had taken a knock over the eye at the start of the half. The blood began to run into his eye, hampering his vision. He was replaced by the stocky, hard-striking Brendan Keeshan who took over at left half back while Ger Coughlan moved from there back into the left corner.

In the same position for Galway, Jimmy Cooney was proving to be a tenacious marker for Pat Carroll for much of the time but now the Coolderry man came bursting out for an incoming ball, grabbed it and hit it as he was turning, 25 yards from goal. Another point for the midlanders.

Galway Missing Scores

At that time the Offaly backs kept harrassing the Galway forwards, marking them tightly, frustrating them. The western players, who were able to score regularly in the first half, were already beginning to find it increasingly difficult to get any kind of clean possession. When they did they were so closely pursued that they had to hit hurriedly. They began to send balls wide.

One player who managed to get possession was Lane. He ran fast with ball on hurley and scored one of the best points of the game from 40 yards out.

Just over a minute later, Currams, who never stopped running and foraging despite his difficulties at midfield, gathered and ran and shot over an excellent point. This score raised Offaly hearts.

'Oh — they're not dead yet', said a man from Birr hopefully, in his flat midlands accent.

With Birmingham often pulling and connecting just before Silke, more low balls began to go in to Flaherty, Horan and Carroll. Sometimes he flicked the ball out to Kirwan or Corrigan. The tall Ballyskenach man was proving well able for Iggy Clarke but Sylvie Linnane was having a good game on one of the most prolific of the Offaly forwards, Mark Corrigan.

Offaly pressure resulted in a 70-metre free against Linnane. Delaney had the slight benefit of the crossfield breeze when he cantered up and straddled the ball. This was an important effort because Galway were beginning to get into a missing cycle and it would be great for the midlanders morale if the Kinnity man put it over. He did just that. There were now only four points between the sides, fifteen minutes into the second half.

Eight Scoreless Minutes

For the next eight minutes play swung from end to end of the field without a score. Offaly were fighting with remarkable grit but their efforts were not being rewarded by scores. To try to improve matters, the mentors switched Flaherty and Horan. The tempo of the game increased. Spectators sensed that while Offaly were far from finished a goal or a series of points at this stage would put the game out of their reach. The Offaly supporters set up a resonant chant — Offaly, Offaly, Offaly — to spur their stalwarts to greater effort.

Paddy Kirwan, who had taken a series of knocks, had no option but to go to the sideline. He was replaced by a tall, fair-haired player, Danny Owens, a strong, fast-running ball-carrier.

Significant Switch

The most significant change of the entire game was now made by the Offaly mentors. Both Aidan Fogarty and Pat Delaney had been finding it difficult to get going. Delaney had to cope with two great players, Joe and John Connolly, and it was taking him all his time to limit the kind of damage of which they were both capable. Fogarty had countered the clever darting and feinting of P.J. Molloy for much of the time but, like Delaney, his role had been that of damage limitation. The mentors decided to switch them.

Why do players sometimes come into their own when they switch positions? Some see it as a new phase, a clean page which engenders an enthuasism to do better this time. Some are goaded by the thought that they have been switched because they were not doing well in their original positions. And, occasionally, a player finds that he can do much better against his new marker.

This certainly happened for both players but particularly for Pat Delaney. He was taller than P.J. Molloy. He was good under the high ball, had an excellent catch. And a lot of the ball from the Galway puck outs were falling on that side of the pitch.

The Galway mentors, aware of how shackled their forwards now were and concerned about the number of wides being struck, switched Forde and Gantly in the corners. But their dogged markers changed places with them. Then the mentors replaced Gantly with the strong, thrusting Turloughmore player, Frank Burke. And John and Joe Connolly were signalled to swap positions again.

It was Offaly who now seemed to have got the measure of their opponents and the play was now beginning to be divided equally between the two sides. Michael Conneely, who had had little to do up to now was forced to show his quality on two occasions. A 95-metre free by Pat Delaney kept soaring and soaring after it left his stick and then dipped hazardously just below the crossbar. The Sarsfield's man handled it confidently. Not long afterwards Brendan Birmingham, now causing problems for Silke, came bursting through and hit the ball hard on the run. The tall goalkeeper got to it and held it with great assurance.

Crucial Offaly Score

The first of Offaly's crucial scores came in the 26th minute. The fighting spirit of Kelly and Currams at last began to bear dividends. Outclassed for most of the match by Michael Connolly and by Mahon, they now began to win more ball to send their side attacking.

After one such attack a clearance by Jimmy Cooney came towards Delaney and Molloy. The rangy Kinnity man reached high over his opponent's head to grab the ball and then shouldered his way forward to go on a solo run and send over a heartening point from 45 metres. He was beginning to revel in the freedom of movement afforded him on the wing. Fogarty was now beginning to command the centre.

Galway had seemed slightly complacent in their game up to this. Now their opponents were only three points behind. For the first time it looked as if the midlanders were there with an equal chance. At this juncture the champions went into a dangerous attack. Frank Burke jumped high to make a great catch on the wing and cut inside in a strong, hard-running stride. He fell after a tackle but, on his knees, scooped the ball precisely to Molloy who kept going down the middle. The backs had to challenge him and at the last second he flicked the ball across to the unmarked Lane on his right.

The Ballinderreen man now sent in a shot that was a goalkeeper's nightmare — rising and moving fast across the length of the goal. Galway supporters were ready to give a great cheer at what would have been a game-clinching goal. But the redoubtable Martin leapt agilely, turning his body in midair to parry the hard shot and to deflect it just wide.

This was one of the great All-Ireland saves, one that in retrospect made the difference between defeat and victory. It had been made by a veteran goalkeeper who had won no major honours until the previous year. The reshowing of this pivotal incident on TV showed that the rising bullet from Lane may have just gone over the bar if it had not been saved. But at the time it raised the spirits of all the Offaly players and evoked a massive roar of admiration from friend and foe alike

A Critical Miss

Now came another key moment. Iggy Clarke, very good on the long ball, got ready to take the 65. The Galway forwards, now fully alive to the unthinkable prospect of losing, positioned themselves intently near the goal. The expectation was that Clarke would put it over and give them a four point lead. Instead the half back's effort tailed away near the end of its flight and was waved wide by the white-coated umpire. The Offaly side were spurred on by this miss.

The play surged from end to end but then in an Offaly attack Pat Carroll controlled the ball and sent it goalwards. Johnny Flaherty got possession but with the vigilant Niall McInerney at his heels showed his ball-juggling skills to keep possession on the run, weaving and side-stepping away from goal until, 30 yards out he turned to strike a splendid point. With only five minutes remaining Galway's comfortable lead had been cut to two points.

Match-Winning Score

Ninety seconds later came the remarkable score that electrified the attendance and, more than that, won the All-Ireland for the midlanders at their first attempt.

Danny Owens got the ball and raced goalwards. Only the expert hooking of Iggy Clarke prevented a score. The ball was got away in a high clearance. It came down between Delaney and Molloy. The Athenry man, back-pedalling quickly, still could not overcome the advantage of height and reach held by the fair-haired Kinnity player. Once again Delaney took the ball safely in his hand and began to move forward in a long, loping stride, while the Offaly supporters yelled encouragement. He kept going and drew the defence until the last split second when he parted with the ball to Brendan Birmingham, running parallel to him. Niall McInerney, fierce in his determination, had no option but to race out to challenge him. Meanwhile the quick-thinking Flaherty was clear before goal.

Just before the full back collided with him, Birmingham handpassed the ball over his head to Flaherty. The veteran caught it in his right hand with his back to the goal. Next thing Conneely, knowing he had no choice, leapt off his line and flung his arms about the full forward. But Flaherty managed to extricate his right arm, threw the ball up just above his left shoulder and then hit it hard with the palm of his hand. It flew back behind him into the empty net.

'Let me go for fuck's sake — the ball's in the net', he said in his high-pitched voice to the distraught Conneely. A huge exultant roar rocked Croke Park. This was an astonishing turn of events. All over the terraces and stands the Offaly supporters roared and danced with delight.

In the Hogan stand an elderly man, who had kept his heavy coat on all the time, while he sat there silently for most of the game, now struggled to his feet and shouted again and again, 'Good man, Flattery, good man Flattery' until someone told him to sit down and let other people see the game.

There were some who marvelled at the alacrity and skill of the low-sized 35-year-old in scoring this match-winning goal. Some felt there was something lucky about it. The reality was that the Offaly side, under Healy's direction, had endlessly practised handpassing the ball to one another with the man at the end, on the full forward line, striking it into the net with his palm. This was far from being the first time Johnny Flaherty, with his back to the goal, sent the ball into the net off the rim of his left shoulder.

Offaly Now Moving

Offaly now had the momentum. Up to this they did not seem to be able to win at their first attempt. They had been unable to take advantage of Galway's prodigal waste of scoring chances, of the fact that Lane's score in the 12th minute of the second half was the westerner's last. Now they came out with all guns blazing.

From the puck out the ball came back from the half back line, and in tremendous tussling was struck towards the sideline near midfield. Currams had the speed and reserves of energy to chase it and whip on it just as it was about to go over the white line. It went up to Danny Owens. Jimmy Cooney hesitated, appealing for a line ball, but the referee waved play on and now Owens raced forward. Once again Flaherty was like a cougar waiting to pounce at the edge of the square, but from well out the field Owens struck a fine point to put Offaly two points ahead with only a few minutes remaining.

In the final minute Offaly were again on the attack, all the tension of their play suddenly released by the winning goal. The Galway defence conceded a free. Padraig Horan, the tough-minded captain, came up, settled his feet carefully and hoisted it over the bar from 35 yards out.

Galway, the champions, were stunned by the unexpected reversal of play. Their opponents had taken the lead and left them little or no time to compose themselves and strike back. They made two frantic attempts to retrieve the situation. Micheal Connolly got hold of the ball from a puck out and went soloing towards the Offaly goal. He drew the backs and sent it in but the Coughlan and Fleury were fast and effective and they combined to get it out again.

Diarmuid Healy had run along the sideline and around the back of the goals to lend moral support and shouted advice to his hard-pressed charges.

Brave Block by Kelly

With the Offaly supporters whistling for full time Galway made one final desperate assault. Mahon now came charging up along the right. From 20 yards out he swung hard on the ball. However, Joachim Kelly, who had played second fiddle at midfield for much of the game, now came to his side's rescue. With great bravery he jumped into the flight of the ball. This bullet-like shot, which might have gone into the net, ricocheted off Kelly's hand, flew high in the air and went over the end line.

It should have been a 65 but Galway's luck had run out. The umpire erroneously signalled a wide. Mahon was still protesing vigorously when the puck out was taken and the referee blew the last long whistle.

In a matter of seconds, half the playing area of Croke Park was full of jubilant supporters of the underdogs. The players were surrounded in the tumult, slapped on the back, raised rapturously on the beefy shoulders of heavy men. The players radiated delight all the more extreme in that it seemed unexpected. Padraig Horan led the team up the steps to receive the McCarthy cup but it was fully ten minutes before the great waves of noise and celebration died down. This was one of the great moments in the history of hurling, when a team from a relatively small area of countryside put a team on the championship field and, against the odds and general expectations, won out.

The intensity of joy and emotion could only be compared to the previous year, when today's vanquished were being feted as the new champions. Yet it was somehow different. Galway had always been seen as good hurlers who could not get it right on the day and had endured years and years of disappointment. For Offaly it was a case of a territory on the edge of the hurling area from which good hurlers and winning teams were not expected to emerge.

Now here they were on their very first try, only the second time as provincial champions, with Pat Delaney singing a name-place song called 'The Offaly Rover' at the microphone on the presentation stand at Croke Park.

Offaly's victory was one for the disadvantaged, for the good hurlers who had never played in an All-Ireland, let alone won one, for teams from counties that were always championship cannon-fodder — Clare, Westmeath, Roscommon, Antrim, Down, Dublin, Kildare, Kerry, Waterford, Carlow.

Messages

Offaly's win had a message. If you tried hard enough, improved your skills and your game by effort, believed in yourself then there was every chance of winning.

There was another message. Counties had gone outside their own boundaries before to find a knowledgeable manager but Diarmuid Healy's involvement with the Offaly side opened official minds a little wider on this subject.

It was to give an impetus for people to seek out the best trainers and managers irrespective of where they came from. It was a blow against county chauvinism.

Men in crumpled suits and women in crushed dresses, children barely aware of the import of the occasion, milled about the field at Croke Park long after the speeches were over and the television cameras were being hauled away and the seagulls began to scour the littered steps of the terraces.

Bitter Disappointment

The Galway supporters were bitterly disappointed. They were dismayed by the way their side had let the game slip from their grasp when they seemed to have it there for the taking. But they did not begrudge the victory to their neighbours. They had a west of Ireland generosity of spirit about them.

While the Offaly dressing-room reverberated with yells and laughter and shouts of joy the scene in the Galway quarters was one of stunned dismay. The players sat there quietly, inconsolable, trying to work out what had gone wrong. Being red-hot favourites for the first time ever in an All-Ireland had not been good for them. It was hard to escape the conclusion that, despite the team's best effots, a certain cloying complacency had affected them.

'That may be so — but we must give full credit to a great Offaly team', says Joe McDonagh, who was a sub on the Galway team that day. 'They proved just how good they were in the next nine years, contesting every Leinster final, winning some, being barely beaten in others. And they had this indomitable will to win, to keep going no matter how bad the game might be going. And they had real stars as well.'

In the anguished post-mortems of a baffled and incredulous county there was great dismay that the win of the previous year had not dispelled the Galway penchant for losing games they should have won. There was criticism of the older players like John Connolly and Sean Silke whom some felt had gone on too long.

This was unfair to these players and unfair too to the great players with whom they had to grapple — Eugene Coughlan and Brendan Birmingham. These latter emerged as the most powerful players in their positions for the next five years. Coughlan was recognised as a full back on a level with any of the best of the past twenty-five years.

When the Offaly team came back home on the Monday night there were scenes of joy-filled celebration in Tullamore and Birr which had never been seen before. Thousands of delighted well-wishers from those towns and the surrounding countryside crushed into the streets as the team arrived with the cup.

Bonfires

Near the top of the slopes of the Slieve Bloom, on Knocknaman and Knockbarron, two great bonfires twinkled redly in the dark of the night. These and other bonfires were visible across the Shannon in Meelick and further back into Galway.

When the cup, after many wanderings about the pubs, hotels and dancehalls of the county, eventually came home to rest in the home of Padraig Horan it was almost within shouting distance of the home of the Galway captain, Sean Silke. Indeed many Galway followers crossed the bridge and joined in the celebrations of a famous victory, even if their side had been the losers on this occasion.

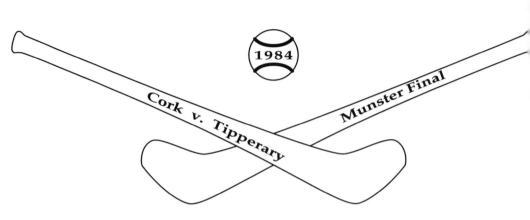

FROM IMMINENT DEFEAT TO INCREDIBLE VICTORY

Six minutes from full time a thunderous roar went up from the Tipperary supporters in the huge crowd of over 50,000 frantic followers. Inside Semple Stadium this detonation of massed sound was almost alarming, ear-stunning. A mile away the great surge of sound disturbed a flock of crows in the dark green woods of Brittas; they rose into the mild air and wheeled about cautiously.

What set off that explosion was the marvellous inspirational point, struck with wholehearted fire, by the big red-haired man from Borrisoleigh, Noel O'Dwyer. His shot, from out on the right wing, had soared between the high white wooden uprights at the Killinan end of the ground. It put Tipperary four points ahead. This lead was a true reflection of the power of a resolute side which, after a titanic battle, now seemed about to wrest the Munster title from the red-hot favourites.

That great boom was the last of a succession of huge, exultant roars as Tipperary had taken control and gone on the attack, again and again, sending one, two, three and then four points over in succession during a nine-minute period of inspired hurling.

On the stands and terraces the Tipperary followers, aching beyond description for a win after years of failure and disappointment, shouted and yelled their lungs out. Some, unable to contain their excitement, stood up, completely heedless of the curses of those behind whose view of the match they were blocking.

This was no ordinary crowd of hurling followers atremble at the prospect of a win. These were the proud ones, who loved hurling, who loved Tipperary to always be in the front rank, but who had had to swallow the bitter dregs of defeat year in year out since 1971.

The Cork followers were yelling too as the game entered its last five minutes. Many were concentrated in the place they had made their own over the past twenty years of Munster final participation in Thurles — at the town end, under the scoreboard. There they were, a huge slope of red and white flags, waving under the gale of passion and exhilaration. They urged their side not to go down without a last-gasp effort.

At the start of this game these supporters were full of jollity and humour, looking forward to a very likely win against a county that had failed, often dismally, to make any kind of showing in the championship over the previous ten years. Now they tried to outshout the endless fusillades of the Tipperary followers, who outnumbered them by at least three to one.

All that week-end the hurling lovers had been converging on Thurles for the Munster final. The Cork followers were full of confidence as they marched about the streets of the town, singing and swapping shouted witticisms.

There was however a serious competitive side to the Cork ebullience. This was their third final in a row in Thurles. The previous two years they had completely overwhelmed Waterford in games that diminished the stature of the Munster final by their one-sidedness. Cork's power-packed performance in both those provincial finals made them favourites to win the All-Ireland.

All-Ireland Favourites

In both finals they came up against what many considered to be moderate Kilkenny sides — and were beaten by the Noresiders on both occasions. These were humiliating defeats. Star Cork hurlers like Jimmy Barry Murphy and Tony O'Sullivan were played out of the game by the forceful tactics of their rivals. The Leesiders seemed unable to match Kilkenny for astute play, clever hurling and, some said cuttingly, for the grit and spirit that it takes to win All-Irelands.

The Cork players were hurt and stung by these allegations. They were hurt too by the less than compassionate welcome they received when they came home to Glanmire railway station empty-handed after promising so much.

Now they were coming to Thurles determined to win decisively and then move on to make amends by taking the All-Ireland trophy in the centenary year of the GAA.

Good Munster Record

Despite their All-Ireland defeats of '82 and '83 the Cork followers swarming in from the roadways and the railway station had much to be proud of. Since Tipperary's last Munster title in 1971 their Leeside rivals had won no less than eight. They had won five-in-a-row between 1975 and '79, going on to win three All-Irelands in '76, '77 and '78.

Many of their side were players of national renown, men who had won every honour in the game. It was little wonder that just about everyone in the hurling world installed them as most likely winners of the 1984 Munster final.

There was another reason that many felt this was going to be an easy victory for Cork — the poor record of once-proud Tipperary over the last eleven years. Here was a county that had fallen on hard times.

Tipperary had been a dominant force in hurling since the start of the senior hurling championship in 1887. A side from Thurles had brought the first of many All-Irelands to the county that year. Tipperary followers were so used to their side winning that the seven year gap between the victorious All-Irelands of 1937 and '45 was regarded as a bleak and barren period.

Fall From The Top

Then two great sides came successively on the scene. In 1949 an exciting team led by Pat Stakelum won the first of three All-Irelands. It was followed by another victory in 1958. In the 1960s a power-packed juggernaut of a team contested one All-Ireland after another, winning in '61, '62, '64 and '65. It was said of that side that they simply got weary of winning.

It was a regular, familiar ritual for the winning team to come back to Thurles from Croke Park on a special train which drew into the station on the Monday night to rousing welcomes, bands playing, triumphal processions, speeches of praise and the assurance that Tipperary would always be at the very top of the hurling ladder.

Then, after the thrilling Munster final of 1973 in which they lost by a last-minute point to Limerick, something went amiss in Tipperary hurling. For nine years in a row they did not win a single first round match. There were near misses, some agonisingly close matches. But in many cases the side played poorly, left its dejected supporters dwindling in numbers as the years went by.

All sorts of theories were put forward. They just did not have the quality players or the necessary leadership among the mentors. The new rules, introduced at the start of the '70s, which protected the goalkeeper and did away with the big stopper full backs, opened up the play in the goal area and put the big Tipperary players at a disadvantage.

Some old hurling sages in the Thurles area pointed to the fact that this stronghold was no longer producing the kind of hurlers who once backboned the county team.

Those were exciting years for hurling — outside of Tipperary. Limerick had splendid sides in the '70s and at the start of the '80s. When Galway at last took the Liam McCarthy trophy back across the Shannon huge crowds of supporters followed their every game. Then Offaly, once Tipperary's lowly neighbour to the north, won an All-Ireland. In those years two marvellous sides from Cork and Kilkenny played thrilling hurling, providing great delight and joy to hurling lovers everywhere.

Tipperary was left out of this feast. The pride in the team declined. For some players it was no longer an ambition to wear the county colours. After some defeats there was pressure to remove players who had not done well. There was scathing criticism of the selectors and those in charge of the team. One day in 1981 a man was arrested in Thurles for blocking the footpath against passers-by 'shouting and roaring about the state of Tipperary hurling' as the Garda reported in the subsequent court case. This unfortunate received fourteen days in prison for his concern about the state of the game in his native county.

However, the Tipperary under-age sides kept hope alive. The minors won the All-Ireland of 1976 for the first time in eighteen years. They won again in 1980 and 1982. And the under-21 sides were very successful, contesting final after final and winning three in a row from '79 to '81.

There was rejoicing in the county when, in 1983, the Tipperary seniors at long last won a first round match. They beat Clare. There was a resurgence of team support and a big crowd assembled to see the side play Waterford in the Munster semi-final. It ended in yet another galling defeat. The Tipperary followers dispersed from that game despondent. What made it even worse was the way their conquerers that day were subsequently annihilated by Cork.

By 1984 Tipperary were now among the outsiders of the hurling world. Yet Tipperary pride, wounded though it might be, was still there and in the centenary year they were determined to make a huge effort to regain their place at the top.

The GAA had decided to honour the birthplace of the Association by staging the final in the fine setting of a transformed Semple Stadium, now capable of housing 60,000 people in comfort. A great daydream began to take hold in the county — that the men in blue and gold might be on that renowned sod on the first Sunday in September and that they might actually win!

Euphoria

A euphoria took hold in the county. Five good men were appointed to select a side: Pat Stakelum, Fr Ray Reidy, Len Gaynor, Liam Hennessy and John Kelly. Donie Nealon was brought in as coach-trainer. There was a feeling that Tipp were going to make a bold bid this year, to honour all their past heroes who had done so much to make hurling part of the weft and weave of the national sense of being.

Team motivation was important. Tipperary were down in division two of the National League that year. Excessive fantasising about their prospects was curbed when, in the special centenary competition, they went out to Laois in the quarter-final. It was a ragged game that did not promise much for the Tipp side.

In the Munster championship they were drawn against Clare. They won but not very convincingly. Even the most hopeful of their own supporters said they were lucky to win. Cork, on the other hand, had gone to Limerick and beaten the Shannonsiders very soundly, displaying much of the talent and ability which had kept them at the top for so long.

The Square in Thurles

By noon the wide long Square in Thurles was crowded on that mild, overcast Sunday in July. The air crackled with the static of expectancy. Old adversaries from both counties greeted one another warmly, once-fierce rivals now bonded by the camaraderie of the game. There were more All-Ireland medal winners per square metre there than anywhere else in the country on any other occasion. There were hoary old veterans, some hobbling from old leg wounds, gnarled, knuckle-scarred hands that could no longer comfortably hold a hurley. Many of the fine Cork side of the mid-'70s were there. Their memories of winning at Thurles were recent.

There were young Tipperary followers there who had never seen the county side play in a Munster final, let alone win one. There were former players now moving into middle age who were so full of longing for Tipperary to win that the pain and disappointment of losing year after year made them cautious.

One of the great hero-figures of Tipperary and Thurles, Tommy Doyle, made his way through the shuffling, moving throng in the Square.

'Well Tommy, what do you think?' many people asked of him. He shook his head a little doubtfully and said in his familiar nasal drawl, 'Oh I don't know about this team. But I hope they do it.'

English and Dwyer

The Tipperary side were not well known even within the county. The outstanding figure was a lightning-fast, lithe figure who could side-step neatly and whose skills were a delight to watch — Nicholas English. The previous year he was the sole Tipperary representative on the Bank of Ireland All-Star selection. He had a magic first touch on the ball, could take the high ball out of the air, running at full speed, cushion it on the upraised hurley, take it down into his hand and strike it over the bar. English had a great instinct for seeing the gap even before it opened up. Then he was through at full stretch, leaving defences stranded.

The other hurler of national renown was Noel O'Dwyer. He was one of the last links with Tipperary's last All-Ireland win in 1971. Strong and determined as a player, he had given his all in the thirteen years since then, knowing little but defeat. This was going to be his last chance to win another Munster medal or indeed an All-Ireland medal.

Goalkeeper and Backs

Tipperary's goalkeeper was an alert, acrobatic player, John Sheedy from Portroe in the north of the county. They had three sound full backs in

Jack Bergin, the tall fair-haired stalwart of the Moycarkey team, Jim Keogh who had helped put Silvermines to the forefront of Tipperary hurling and Dinny Cahill from Kilruane. Keogh and Cahill were two of the experienced, long servers on the Tipp side who had been called back into service for this supreme centenary year effort. There was a question mark over Cahill. He had been labouring with a leg ailment. It would certainly be put to the test in the scorching hot pace of a Munster final.

A lot of Tipperary hopes rested on their half back line of Pat Fitzelle on the right, John McIntyre in the centre and Bobby Ryan on the left. Fitzelle, tall and vigorous, had been one of the mainstays of the side over the previous years, with his powerful hurling. Now however, on the big day that he had looked forward to so much, he was doubtful because of an ankle injury. The Tipp supporters were hoping it would hold out. In the centre was John McIntyre, a sturdy player, and neat striker. Some people in the county said he was inconsistent, but the same could be said for many of the players. The match would tell. On his left Bobby Ryan, a clubmate of Noel O'Dwyer, had always given his best even in the worst days of defeat. He was brave, sporting and skilled. When he came bursting out with the ball and cleared it off down the field it inspired his colleagues and raised a cheer from spectators. He was a worthy captain of the side.

Ralph Callaghan and Philip Kennedy manned the midfield berth. They were both good players but many of the media commentators could not see them getting the better of the immensely skilled John Fenton and his Midleton clubmate, Pat Hartnett, a hard tackling player who revelled in the rough and tumble at midfield.

The star player, English, was on the right wing of the attack. In the centre was a tough, hard-running ball carrier, Donie O'Connell. He grabbd the ball when he could, drawing backs as he thundered forward, then sending the ball out to English or the man now on the other wing, Liam Maher of Boherlahan. Maher had been playing well since the start of the year.

Tipperary had a strong full forward line. Here were three muscular players who were expected to challenge vigorously for every ball — Michael Doyle, Seamus Power and Noel O'Dwyer. Power was one of the best Tipperary players of those years. This dark-haired, stocky player was a fine striker of the ball, especially off the ground. The selectors hoped he might upset the experienced Cork full back line.

O'Dwyer manned the left corner while in the right was Michael Doyle, a vigorous bustling player who had first come to prominence as one of the stars of the All-Ireland-winning minor side that had started the under-age resurgence of Tipperary hurling in 1976. He had come on as a sub in the match against Clare and had played well enough to keep his place.

Cork Better Known

The Cork side was much better known to the hurling public. Ger Cunningham was one of the best goalkeepers ever to man the gap for the Leesiders.

'He had great footwork. He was nimble and fast. He had a great eye for the ball. Above all he worked day and night on his game', says Gerald McCarthy, who was a spectator at the match. 'He never stopped practising.'

Of the Cork full back line Denis Mulcahy was the most prominent. He was an alert player, fast off the mark. He was tall and used his weight to knock opponents off the ball. The full back, Donal O'Grady, had played very well in the All-Ireland of the previous year, curbing the dangerous Christy Heffernan of Kilkenny effectively and it was hoped he would do the same with Power. John Hodgins in the other corner was one of the leading players with the St Finbarr's club, but he had not a great deal of experience at this level.

The Cork half back line had three of the best hurlers in the country in it. At right half was Tom Cashman, who had an astonishing instinct for where the ball was going to land or break. He had fast, supple wrists and clipped the ball, left or right, so close to his body that he was difficult to baulk. 'Even in the tightest situation you would rarely see him being blocked or hooked', says Jimmy Barry Murphy, who himself was still starring among the forwards.

In the centre was one of the most deceptive and under-rated players on the field. Johnny Crowley was a big strong player who sometimes gave the impression of lumbering about ineffectively. Yet he cleared the ball again and again, sometimes almost unseen.

Gerald McCarthy says of Crowley: 'There were times, near the end of games, that he looked as if he was out on his feet. Yet the ball just seemed to keep coming to where he was standing and he belted it away. All this hid the fact that he was an astute reader of the game, knew where to position himself.'

On the wing was a stocky, fast player, Dermot McCurtain. He raced to the ball and set attacks going by his careful deliveries. 'McCurtain was a very clever player, very adroit', says Nicky English, who was being mark-ed by him that day.

Good Midfielders

The Cork midfielders seemed likely to dominate the scene. In John Fenton they had one of the great stick artists of the modern game and beside him was a hard-running, aggressive player, Pat Hartnett, who revelled in the tough going. In those years nobody could hit a 20 metre free as hard or as accurately as Fenton. He was totally reliable with the dead ball. He had the most astonishing facility to cut sideline balls from centrefield that took off and landed in the opposing goalmouth or even went over the bar. It was fitting that he should be captain.

In the centre of the half forward line was the swashbuckling Tim Crowley, the workhorse of the side, who did a lot of the heavy work from which the other forwards could feed. On either side of him he had vigorous forwards in Kevin Hennessy and Pat Horgan. Hennessy, tall and strong, was very hard to stop when he came running in with the ball. He had scored some memorable goals in the previous three years. Pat Horgan was one of the long-range point scorers on the side. He was good on the ground ball, pulling on it accurately to send it low and fast into the full line.

Cork had a full forward line of proven quality. The tall Tomas Mulcahy was an endless forager for the ball. He could carry the ball goalwards at full speed, dodging and riding tackles, and send in shots that went across the face of the goal and, often, into the net. At full forward was one of the most skilful opportunists ever to play for Cork, Jimmy Barry Murphy. He had an uncanny ability to know where and how the ball was going to break near goal and struck like lightning, left or right, off the ground or from the hand.

In the other corner was Sean O'Leary, one of the best corner forwards of the era. Over the years he had got goals for Cork at vital stages. He never strayed far from goal. He was a supreme opportunist, with the experience to know what to do and where to be for the incoming ball.

Incredible Scene

'Cork were seen as the likely winners that day', reflects Nicky English. 'So we did not really feel under that much pressure — even though we knew eveyone in Tipperary was willing us to win.' When the Cork team ran out on the field that afternoon it seemed to them that their own support was submerged, like scattered red poppies in a field of blue and gold flowers. Even the concentrated Cork followers under the scoreboard seemed hemmed in by a semi-circle of Tipperary flags and banners.

'It was an incredible scene. Tipp had a huge following. They came from everywhere. They were shouting and waving flags even before the game began', recalls Jimmy Barry Murphy. 'It was no wonder the Tipp lads were lifted up to play the kind of game that they did.'

There was a slight breeze blowing from the Killinan end of the ground and Cork were to play into it. The air trembled with excitement as the players took their places and shook hands with their markers. Then came the national anthem. As the last notes were being sounded a huge tidal wave of sound began to break around the stadium. In it was tribalism, deep longings, aggressiveness, pride and hope. Very few Munster finals had heard such a unique sound made with such intensity.

Explosive Start

The referee took a brief look about the field and nodded to his linesmen and threw the ball in to begin the game. From the very start both teams played hurling with abandon. There was little time for a sizing-up period. Tipperary tore into the game as few had seen them play for years and years. There were neck and neck races for every ball as players sought to get a good first touch, to get off to a good start, to establish some kind of dominance over their markers.

The teams as they lined out were:

CORK

Ger Cunningham
(St Finbarr's)

Denis Mulcahy	Donal O'Grady	John Hodgins
(Midleton)	(St Finbarr's)	(St Finbarr's)

Tom Cashman	Johnny Crowley	Dermot McCurtain
(Blackrock)	(Bishopstown)	(St Finbarrs)

John Fenton, capt   Pat Hartnett
(Midleton)   (Midleton)

Pat Horgan	Tim Crowley	Kevin Hennessy
(Glen Rovers)	(Newcestown)	(Midleton)

Tomas Mulcahy	Jimmy Barry Murphy	Sean O'Leary
(Glen Rovers)	(St Finbarr's)	(Youghal)

Substitutes: Tony O'Sullivan (Na Piarsaigh); John Blake (St Finbarr's); Denis Walsh (St Catherine's); Bertie Og Murphy (Sarsfields); Ger Power (Midleton); John Buckley (Newtownshandrum); John Hartnett (Midleton). *Coaches*: Justin McCarthy; Fr Bertie Troy. *Trainer*: Noel Collins (Newcestown and Cork RTC). *Selectors*: Joe Desmond (Midleton); Denis Hurley (Sarsfields); Fr Michael O'Brien (Carrigaline); Justin McCarthy (Passage); Tom Monaghan (Kildorrery). *Team doctor*: Dr Con Murphy (UCC). *Masseur*: John 'Kid' Cronin (Glen Rovers).

TIPPERARY

John Sheedy
(Portroe)

Jack Bergin	Jim Keogh	Denis Cahill
(Moycarkey)	(Silvermines)	(Kilruane)

Pat Fitzelle	Jim McIntyre	Bobby Ryan, capt
(Cashel)	(Lorrha)	(Borrisoleigh)

Ralph Callaghan   Philip Kennedy
(Carrick Davins)   (Nenagh)

Nicky English	Donie O'Connell	Liam Maher
(Lattin)	(Killenaule)	(Boherlahan)

Michael Doyle	Seamus Power	Noel O'Dwyer
(Holycross)	(Boherlahan)	(Borrisoleigh)

Substitutes: John Doyle (Holycross); Brian Heffernan (Nenagh); Paul Dooley (Borrisokane); Tom Waters (Carrick Swans); Austin Buckley (Cappawhite); Gerry Stapleton (Borrisoleigh); Pat McGrath (Loughmore); John Grace (Silvermines); Mick Ryan (Borrisoleigh). *Mentors*: Pat Stakelum; Len Gaynor; Ray Reidy; Liam Hennessy; John Kelly. *Coach*: Donie Nealon. *Masseur*: Ossie Bennett.

The referee was John Moore of Waterford.

There were tremendous aerial clashes between O'Connell and Crowley and between McIntyre and Tim Crowley, with hurleys smacking sharply against one another while other players shouldered one another, waiting for the break of the ball.

Each clash, each shoulder-charge, each race for possession was willed on by the frantic roars of the spectators so that the whole stadium, players and spectators, were bound together in a whirling maelstrom of excitement. It was for this reason that many players and spectators were afterwards incoherent about the ebb and flow of the game, could hardly remember much in sequence. Only the very calmest personalities were later able to discuss the details of this game with any kind of authority.

Cork Composure

Tipperary were playing with tremendous spirit in those first few minutes but Cork seemed the most effective. The men in red were less frantic than their opponents, used their superior experience to conserve their energy. And they got the first score from the big red-haired player from Midleton, Hennessy. It was an ominous sign for Tipperary when he rounded Pat Fitzelle with a stylish side-step and cracked a fine point over the bar.

'He wouldn't do that if Fitzelle was in the full of his health, I can tell you', said a Tipperary supporter in the open stand, face contorted with anger and anxiety. Even in the pre-match puck around the Tipperary stalwart seemed uneasily tentative as he ran about. His ankle had been in plaster for much of the previous week.

The two vigorous midfield men, Callaghan and Hartnett, began their duel. They raced about the area, sometimes shoulder to shoulder, other times charging into the broken play to try to get the ball and send their side on the attack. There was a succession of exultant roars from the blue and gold supporters when it began to emerge that their man was getting the better of things.

Callaghan's dominance was needed because Fenton was extremely effective from sideline balls and any frees although in the man-to-man duels Philip Kennedy was holding his own against Fenton's fast and accurate pulling on the ground.

Tipp Goal

Kennedy epitomised the raw courage of the players on both sides in this game. On one occasion he jumped in front of one of Fenton's powerful ground strokes and took the force of the swing on his lower legs. That was the kind of game it was. Players forgot about personal safety, forgot about weals and wounds. The adrenalin was flowing so fast some did not know they had been hurt until the match was well over.

Cork seemed more composed and competent. Yet it was Tipperary who scored the first goal. With a rousing shoulder charge Callaghan knocked a Cork player off the ball, got hold of it and centred it to the square. The lightning-fast striker, Power, whipped it straight into the net from in front of goal.

This was the kind of start that the underdogs needed. The whole team was fired by this score. It did a lot for the confidence of Power who even at that stage looked dangerous in his tussles with Donal O'Grady.

And Tipperary were heartened by the fact that McIntyre began to get in control in the centre back position. He was well able for the power and drive of Tim Crowley and moreover displayed great skill in the air and on the ground. It was a performance reminiscent of one of the most stylish centre backs of the recent past, Mick Roche.

McIntyre's opposite number, Johnny Crowley, had caught a tartar in the form of the moustachioed Donie O'Connell. The Killenaule man crouched low for the ball and, with his muscular thighs, was very hard to shift. And he began to carry the ball forward ever so often to great cheers from the Tipp supporters, who loved his tearaway style.

For all that, Cork still looked overall the more convincing side. When a sideline cut was awarded 65 metres out the backs and forwards became glued to one another as the man in the white helmet stood back from the ball. Here was a side-line artist who had taken tens of thousands of practice cuts over a ten year period. 'Fenton was so good at it that it was the same as if Cork had been awarded a free every time he came over to take one', said Michael Keating, who was later to play a key role in the resurgence of Tipperary hurling.

Fenton brought his hurley down on the ball, clipping it sharply so that it rose up fast over the up-stretched hurley of the Tipperary player standing ten metres away. To a gasp of admiration the white ball travelled straight as a die. Only at the end of its long flight did the breeze begin to bring it down on the swinging hurleys waiting below for it. On this occasion Jack Bergin, whose crinkly fair hair made him easy to identify, grabbed the ball and swung hard on it to send it away down the field. It was one of many sound clearances the Moycarkey man was to make that day.

The Tipperary followers were becoming alarmed when twice in succession Hennessy left Fitzelle behind and, further in, Tomas Mulcahy beat Dinny Cahill for speed. And Pat Horgan was playing well on the other wing, positioning himself for long range points.

Barry Murphy Goals

In the eleventh minute the supreme opportunist, Jimmy Barry Murphy, got a half chance when Tomas Mulcahy passed a high ball over the full back's head. 'I raced on to it and got in a good strong left-handed shot', he recalls. John Sheedy twisted his body to try to stop it but it was going too fast from that range. The Cork supporters responded with a great cheer. It was reassuring to see one of their great stars performing this way.

Tipperary followers were anything but reassured when they saw the mentors calling off a limping Dinny Cahill. There was some shaking of heads when the captain of the side, Bobby Ryan, was sent back into the corner. He had begun to play with conviction and he had twice sent the attack rolling with well-struck balls. His place in the half back line was taken by John Doyle of Holycross, who was to have a splendid match in the position. Just the same it seemed to many that an inspirational player like Ryan should be kept well out the field.

And Cork were beginning to pick off points at this stage. They went two points ahead. Any frees within 65 metres were invariably sent over the bar by Fenton.

Then Barry Murphy struck again in the 16th minute. In broken play near the goal Pat Horgan put him in possession and he struck the ball off his right, and it flew into the net.

'He was able to disappear from his marker. Then suddenly there was a gap and there he was, as fast on the draw as the most legendary pistolero of the American West', said a contemporary account of this player.

Barry Murphy's score put Cork five points ahead on a scoreline of 2–4 to 1–2. The game seemed to be going away from Tipperary. Two of their class players were being well controlled. Nicky English was having a difficult time with the tenacious Dermot McCurtain who knew his opponent's style of play very well while Denis Mulcahy was effectively marking O'Dwyer in the corner.

Tipp Reply

'Come on Tipp — don't fade away whatever you do', shouted a man who feared that the fire might go out of the men in blue and gold as they began to fall behind.

Tipperary did not wilt. They gave it all they had. In the 23rd minute O'Dwyer got clear of Mulcahy. The big man sent in a cannonball of a shot. Only a player of Cunningham's agility would have been able to parry it. Parry it he did and saved a goal but the shot was so hard that he could not get it under control but flew away from goal. Rushing in to meet it was O'Connell and he lashed the ball back into the goalmouth and into the net.

That was the score that finally convinced many waverers that this was to be a battle right up to the last seconds of the game.

There was going to be no runaway victory for Cork as had happened the previous two years when Waterford faded out after an initial effort.

One of the features of the half was the way the experienced Cork players were able to pick off points against the breeze, some from far out. O'Leary, Horgan, Fenton and Hennessy were on the mark during the half.

With six minutes to go the Tipperary selectors decided to take off Pat Fitzelle. Slowed by his injury, he was unable to contain Kevin Hennessy. It was a pity for Tipperary followers to see one of the intrepid warriors of the side having to go off. But whether he should have been on in the first place was one of the talking points in heated post mortems. The conventional wisdom said 'Unless you are in the full of your health, in body, mind and spirit you are likely to be caught out in the Munster final.' He was replaced by Brian Heffernan.

The Cork selectors tried to curb the effectiveness of McIntyre in the centre by switching Pat Horgan on him but the Lorrha player was almost unbeatable under the high ball and was indomitable that day. Just the same Horgan came with a few inches of scoring a goal nearing half time. His shot whizzed across the goal and went just wide.

Stylish Goal

Cork had gone into a five point lead playing against the breeze. There were only a few minutes to go to half time when Tipperary went on another attack. Michael Doyle got the ball. The backs converged on him and as they did, Nicky English, who had gone into the corner, ran free in front of the goal. Doyle sent the ball to him. A player of his calibre was not going to miss such and opportunity and he lifted and struck the ball in one stylish movement to give Cunningham no chance.

A great roar reverberated about the stadium. The underdogs, many of them unknown figures in the hurling world, were taking the game to the provincial champions. Cork were now only two points ahead, 2–10 to 3–5 as the half-time whistle went.

As the players left the field they got one of the loudest and most prolonged rounds of applause ever heard in this famous stadium. All the hurling lovers — from the contesting counties and all the other counties — realised they were seeing a stirring battle that was restoring the fading reputation of the Munster final as one of the great events of the sporting calendar.

The terraces and stands were abuzz with excited conversation, gesticulation and prediction. 'If Tipp can keep up the effort — you never know what they might do', said a man in the stand. He hoped against hope that what they might do was win their first provincial title in thirteen years. But he was afraid to mention the word 'win' in case by doing so his expectations would be raised too high.

Thunderous Restart

From the throw-in Tipperary again thundered into the game. It was where they had left off but there was an even greater urgency about their play. Cork responded and the tempo and heat of the game went up several notches. With only half a minute gone the ball came flying into the Cork goalmouth. As backs and forwards back-pedalled, Cunningham raced off his line and caught the ball. There was a collective intake of breath when Seamus Power reached forward and tipped the ball away from the goalkeeper just as he was about to send a clearance down the field. The ball ran loose, Power pulled on it. It could easily have been a goal but instead it whammed into the side netting. Power was proving to be the most forceful of the forwards.

With Callaghan now rampant and Philip Kennedy gradually outplaying Fenton, the ball kept coming into the Cork goal area. Tipp had three wides in the first few minutes. Cork were using all their game-wisdom and the astuteness that only comes from experience to try to keep the roaring challengers at bay.

Power pointed a free for Tipperary four minutes into the half. Cork's response was a point by Kevin Hennessy, who was set up by a pin-point pass from Barry Murphy.

Critical Move

Ten minutes into the second half came an incident that had an important bearing on the game. The lion-hearted Bobby Ryan, blocking and clearing with great verve, ran into a tackle and ended up with such a bad injury that he had no alternative but to go off.

There was consternation among the Tipp followers at the departure of the captain and team-rouser. Thousands of eyes were riveted on the bench where the five selectors and coach consulted urgently. People were surprised to see a messenger go racing down the sideline to tell Seamus Power to come back to replace Bobby Ryan.

'It looked an extraordinary move to us', recalls Jimmy Barry Murphy. 'We were relieved to see Power leaving the area where he had been causing a lot of trouble to our backs.'

Questions were to be asked about the wisdom of this move and whether there was not a good back player among the list of substitutes. Noel O'Dwyer went full forward while Paul Dooley was sent on as an attacker.

It was ironic that at this time the Cork selectors decided to replace Donal O'Grady, who had had a difficult time on Power. Denis Mulcahy moved to full back — again marking O'Dwyer — while John Blake went into the corner.

O'Sullivan Comes On

Only a minute later came a significant move by the Cork mentors. Tim Crowley, tiring after his wholehearted efforts, was replaced by the most promising stick-artist on the side, Tony O'Sullivan. He had been ill and had not been picked on the first fifteen but this nimble-footed, neat striking forward now took his place in the side. He was to play a vital role in the minutes ahead. Going into the third quarter it was clear that Tipperary were getting the upper hand, now playing with more confidence while the Cork effort was becoming more ragged. McIntyre was playing a storming game and there was little Horgan could do about it; it was a once-in-a-lifetime performance by the Lorrha man.

Doyle and Bergin were so effective that the loss of Bobby Ryan did not seem so bad. Yet the reality was that Tipperary had lost half of their selected backs and the others now had to play out of their skins every minute of the match to keep the impetus going.

That impetus was driven on by the swaying roar of the Tipperary supporters who sensed that this might be their great day, unbelieveable as it
had seemed that morning. Tipperary slowly hauled back the Cork lead,
point by point. English, restored to the wing, was now playing better
hurling.

Tipp Draw Level and Lead

In the thirteenth minute of the half Paul Dooley, with his first puck of the
ball, sent a fine point over the bar to level the scores at 2–12 for Cork to 3–9
for Tipperary. The faces of the Tipp followers were taking on a victorious
flush as they yelled and clapped. Then Liam Maher put Tipperary into the
lead for the first time since the early minutes of the match with a fine point.
But Hartnett, battling on valiantly against Callaghan and the tide of play,
got a ball well out the field and sent it over to equalise.

This was the period when nearly everything was going Tipperary's way.
They went on the attack and were awarded a penalty. Seamus Power came
running up from the back to take it. He had a powerful shot and the backs
tensed — as did the spectators — as he lifted the ball and struck it hard. He
sent it over the bar. A point at this stage was more important than the risk of
a resoundingly saved penalty which might hand back the initiative to Cork.

Tipp Move Ahead

Yet Cork kept in the game. Tomas Mulcahy was sent out to the centre
forward position to try to keep McIntyre preoccupied and, to some
extent, succeeded. At that stage the limping Pat Horgan was replaced by
Denis Walsh. However, in the next Tipperary attack Denis Mulcahy
fouled O'Dwyer. The Borrisoleigh man took the free himself and sent it
over the bar to put Tipp two points up.

Another Tipperary assault. In a scramble on the end line the ball went
over off a Cork hurley. Philip Kennedy took the 65. The Tipp supporters
held their breath as he lifted it well, struck it well and sent it soaring away
towards the uprights. There was enough power in it to breast the breeze
and it crossed the bar, pushed along by the decibels of thunderous sound
from the Tipperary supporters.

One minute after that Noel O'Dwyer struck over a point from the
right wing that put Tipp four points up with six minutes to go and
which seemed to hoist the victory signal for the blue and gold.

The score at that point was 3–14 for Tipperary to 2–13 for Cork. The
Tipp scores had come via Power (1–6), O'Connell (1–2), English (1–0),
O'Dwyer and Kennedy (2 points each) and points from Maher and
Dooley. The Cork scorers were Barry Murphy (2–0) Fenton (0–5), Horgan
and Hennessy (0–3 each) and points from Hartnett and O'Leary.

Jubilation

At this stage Tipperary were playing so well that it did not seem possible
that they could be beaten. Thousands of jubilant supporters began to run

along behind the sidelines, ready to race on to the field to congratulate their heroes. They looked at their watches and willed away the remaining five minutes. Some were no longer watching the game with any concentration, such was their ecstasy. All they wanted to see was the referee put the whistle to his mouth to sound the end of the game.

Many of the Tipperary players seemed stunned by the prospect of actually winning, as if the unbelievable was about to happen. But there were others who had given so much of themselves that they were now utterly exhausted. The most significant area was at centrefield where Ralph Callaghan, so dominant for most of the game had now run out of steam. His opponent, Hartnett, now came into the game with a vengeance. His resurgence made the point that if a player of stamina and determination keeps hurling away doggedly, despite being outplayed for much of the game, his time may eventually come. Yet Hartnett's power play did not seem enough to turn the game Cork's way.

Cork were awarded a free near the centre of the field. The ever-reliable Fenton rose it and struck it with great assurance and authority and nobody was surprised to see it sailing over the bar. Cork were now a goal behind with some four minutes remaining.

Cork Goal

Then Hartnett came racing in towards the Tipperary goal. The tiring Tipp backs seemed slow to challenge him. He swung hard on the ball and sent in a pile-driver. Sheedy got his hurley to it but it was going so fast that it was difficult to cushion and control. Instead it flew back out into the path of O'Sullivan, who had slipped into open space. His lightning fast reflexes and wrist-work served him well. The ball billowed the back of the net and raised a great cheer from the outnumbered and outshouted legions of Cork supporters. 'Mark up, mark up for God's sake', shouted Tipp followers at their backs.

In an almost unbearable welter of excitement every ball, every challenge, every clash of bodies and hurleys was greeted with resounding roars. This was an epic battle such as had not been seen in a Munster final for many years. And the outcome of the game rested on every puck of the ball. Many supporters were now hoping that it would end in a draw. It would be agonising to lose such a game. Even the most ebullient Tipp supporter was now prepared to settle for a replay. Their side had no more substitutes to deploy, fresh players who could have replaced men who had given their all and were now leaden-legged.

Misdirected Handpass

Yet the men in blue and gold seemed about to sow the game up when Michael Doyle raced out to the left wing, collected a ball and turned for the goal.

Doyle kept running with ball on stick, roared on by the crowd. He now ran in to a cul-de-sac of surrounding Cork players. On his right English and O'Dwyer were running parallel to him with English calling for the ball. Doyle, now under great pressure, got a handpass across. It was, however, too far forward for English. Instead, the redoubtable Denis Mulcahy, reading the play so well, came racing out and intercepted it. He kept going for 20 metres and then unleashed a mighty puck which sailed well down the field. O'Sullivan of the balletic footwork, got it, sidestepped despairing Tipp markers and clipped a neat ball towards the Tipp goal.

The followers from both camps held their breaths. This could be the winning score for Cork. It was just about to drop over the crossbar when Sheedy jumped with upstretched hurley to stop it. He was unable to cushion and control it at full stretch. The ball hopped off his hurley and down to where the old fox O'Leary was lurking, unmarked, looking for his chance. The Youghal man had scored vital goals at vital times for Cork but none more important than the one he now struck with great force to the back of the net. Against all the odds Cork were a goal ahead. The Tipperary team and followers were stunned and speechless. When the ball was pucked out there was a tussle near the centre of the field and the referee awarded a free to the Leesiders.

Fenton, immaculate all day off the placed ball, sent it over the bar to put Cork four points up. The scoreline stood at 4–15 to 3–14 as the referee blew his whistle.

Great Come-back

This was one of the most memorable comebacks in the history of the game. Cork grit and spirit, allied to skill and game-experience had enabled them to snatch victory from defeat just as the second hand of the clock began its final round. It can rightly be described as a sensational victory. Their supporters, who had been resigned to defeat only five minutes before, were now racing onto the field to congratulate their warriors. This was a time of broad smiles, of the laughter of victory, of great pride and exhilaration.

The Tipperary team was utterly dazed. For some the disappointment would only sink in hours later. On the stands and terraces many of the supporters stood there speechless. Some, so utterly devasted by disappointment, shuffled away from Semple Stadium, straight to the railway station or to the car-parking areas. They did not feel like indulging in any after-match analysis in pubs and hostelries; all they wanted to do was to take a direct line home.

The frustration engendered by this traumatic match crystallised into criticism of the selectors in the post mortem period. Lots of critics were wise in hindsight. The move of their most effective forward, Power, to the backs was seen as a serious blunder especially as they had established back players like Gerry Stapleton on the bench. If Tipperary had won it might have been acclaimed as a good tactical move.

'Lack of big-time experience is as much a disadvantage for team managers and selectors as it is for players', says Jimmy Barry Murphy. 'In a close match there is a need for calm nerves and an icy detachment that only comes with lots of experience — the ability to sit tight and not panic.'

Cork went on to win the centenary final impressively, beating an Offaly side that did not do themselves justice. That win was a triumph for Fenton, a talented player who had known a lot of disappointment and disillusion in his playing career; an early nose injury had hampered his breathing and he became a perennial sub, sitting on the sideline or being substituted when things were not going well for Cork at midfield.

Positive Results

It took Tipperary a long time to get over losing this game. But it had positive results. The richness of the side's hurling that day and their assurance restored county pride in hurling and in the hurling team. It engendered a spirit of rejuvenation which eventually resulted in a completely new system and culture of team management. In time, a strong-willed trio would be entrusted with putting Tipperary back on top of the hurling world. They would be given unprecedented powers and backing from a united county and its GAA officials.

The Munster final of 1984, now accepted as one of the best of all time, restored the reputation of this great occasion. It also proved that the new Semple Stadium and its management could handle even the biggest event with style. Most important of all it began a renewed period of Cork-Tipp rivalry which was to result in some of the most thrilling games seen in the '80s and early '90s.

The legacy of that July day still lives on to the benefit of hurling lovers everywhere.

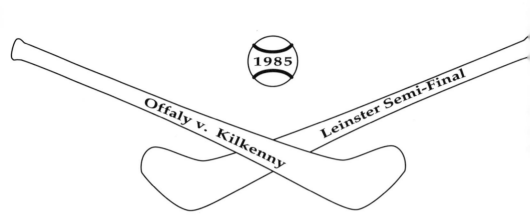

'LET'S MAKE OUR OWN TRADITION'

When the Kilkenny midfielder, Ray Heffernan, made a superb run from near midfield into the Offaly goal area and then fired over a fine point it looked like the end of the road for the midlanders. They were the reigning Leinster champions but they were now nine points behind to a good Kilkenny side at the start of the second half.

'Offaly are well gone out of it now', said several spectators, and few from Offaly would have disagreed with them. Up to this point the match had been tense, dulled by tight marking, as if both sides were afraid of making mistakes at the first hurdle in the championship race. Now it looked as if it were going to be a one-sided game as well, devoid of the kind of excitement that games between these sides had generated in the recent past.

The hurling world is both strengthened and shackled by tradition. The winning tradition of the dominant three counties Kilkenny, Cork and Tipperary seems to give sustenance to their sides. It is as if they can reach back into the past and draw upon a rich repository of experience to help them in the present. It lends them confidence. They are used to winning.

The winning tradition for few means a losing tradition for many. Up to 1980 Offaly was one of those counties which had never won a provincial championship in senior hurling, let alone an All-Ireland. Then in 1981 they had surprised the hurling world by overcoming the reigning champions Galway in the final. Yet even after that well-earned victory they were not fully accepted as equals in the narrow field of hurling endeavour.

Failure of '84

In 1984, with almost the same side as made the breakthrough, they were back in the All-Ireland again. This was an exceptional occasion. To mark the Centenary of the foundation of the GAA the final was held in Thurles, where the Association was founded in 1884.

Cork were their opponents. The Leesiders had been losers in the two previous All-Irelands and they had no intention of making it a three-in-a-row. They had learned a lot from their defeats. They had matured and were vastly experienced.

There were great expectations of a thrilling game to give a fitting climax to the Centenary celebrations. Semple Stadium had a brand new stand. The terraces had been expanded. That Sunday it looked in the peak of readiness for its first All-Ireland.

The town of Thurles was totally submerged by hurling followers. All morning a steady stream of motor cars converged on the town along every road from every direction. The heavy hum of diesel engines vibrated in the air near the railway station as many excursion trains drew into the station.

The hurling-lovers crowded the streets, laughing and greeting one another. There was a great air of expectancy about. Cork followers exuded their usual ebullience but they were anxious as well, remembering the two successive defeats of previous years.

The Offaly supporters were confident. They had a well knit side and, in the Leinster final, had overcome a very good and very determined Wexford team. They had beaten a strong Galway side in the semi-final.

Everything seemed set for an exciting and intriguing game. Unfortunately as the game got under way it was soon evident that Cork were by far the superior team. They were in control from beginning to end. Offaly were struggling from the start. They played well below their form. It was a disappointingly one-sided game.

Among the dyed-in-the-wood traditionalists there was some grumbling that the great occasion had been diminished by the presence of a team from one of the 'weaker counties'. Offaly had collapsed under the pressure of the big day.

Despite their emergence from Leinster three times in the 1980s they were not fully accorded top ranking by many in the hurling world. This All-Ireland defeat seemed to bear out this grudging view of the newcomers in green, white and orange.

Emotional Return

Yet that defeat was to evoke moving and emotional scenes in the towns of Tullamore and Birr. Huge crowds turned out to cheer their beaten heroes when they returned from Thurles. Many estimated that there were greater numbers thronging the streets and squares that night than when the side had returned with the Liam McCarthy cup in 1981.

'It was very touching to see all the faithful followers there, full of pride in the side', said Diarmuid Healy, who as coach had had a significant influence on the team since he began his association with the county in 1980.

'Here they all were, offering their consolation and encouragement when the team were feeling down, knowing they had played well below their capability. It brought tears to our eyes', he recalled.

There and then the downcast players were filled with a resolution to reward their loyal supporters. They would be back the following year. They would work might and main on their skills, on their team cohesion. They did so in the league campaign of that winter and spring. They reached the semi-final where they were beaten by two points by Limerick. Then they got ready for the championship and the first key game, against Kilkenny.

Double in '82 and '83

For Kilkenny 1984 was a dormant year. They had achieved a remarkable double in 1982 and 1983 — winning both the All-Ireland and the National League titles. They had taken a lot out of themselves in doing so and after their failure to retain the provincial championship in 1984 the team went through a period of rest and recuperation. They did not take the 1984–85 league very seriously. Their sights were set on coming back on the scene in the 1985 championship.

The team that took on Offaly in the first round was a very good one. Most of them were part of the combination which had so dominated the scene in '82 and '83. These were All-Ireland medal holders who had been through it all before.

There were some, like the Henderson brothers, Ger and John, Paddy Prendergast, Ger Fennelly and Joe Hennessy who had been on the side that had beaten Galway in the final of 1979. There was one player, now a sub, who had captained the winning side in 1975 — Billy Fitzpatrick of Johnstown Fenians.

Kilkenny Side

Many of the players had made their way to the team through the fine under-21 championship sides that had won in '74, '75 and '77. Some, like David Burke the goalkeeper and Ray Heffernan, had been part of the winning under-21 combination of the previous year.

Burke, nicknamed 'Stoney' had taken over the mantle of Noel Skehan. He had a goalkeeper's temperament — confident, outgoing, devil-may-care.

At right corner back was John Henderson. He was an unobtrusive player but anyone who ever played on him could tell how difficult it was to get scores off a player who was so fast on the ball, made few mistakes, was tough and agile.

The full back was Paudie Brennan of Conahy Shamrocks. He was sound, big and strong. He was very fit because he had to give much time and energy to managing a large farm. In the left corner was a right-hand-under player, John Marnell of the Dicksboro club in Kilkenny city who had won an under-21 medal ten years before.

The Kilkenny half back line was one of the strongest of that time. On the right was Joe Hennessy. From the mid-'70s he had been one of the mainstays of Kilkenny sides. He had developed into a great wing back — fast and sharp. He knew what to do and where to be, often putting himself into a position to take a pass from a colleague in trouble, particularly his centre back. He was an attacking half back, sometimes scoring dashing points at the end of solo runs.

At centre back was Ger Henderson, the steely-minded, fiercely competitive farmer from Johnstown. This left-handed player revelled in the tough going, could catch the ball among hard-pulling hurleys and come bursting out for a rousing clearance. On his left was another farmer, Paddy Prendergast from Clara. Like Henderson, he was physically strong. He could read the play up the field and know where the ball was likely to break. Prendergast weighed up each of his opponents and decided how best to curb them. He had frustrated many good forwards by decisive blocking and hooking and then taking possession to clear the ball away.

At centrefield Kilkenny had the quietest of the Fennelly brothers, Ger. They had brought the Ballyhale Shamrocks team to the fore in the county. The high balls seemed to drop straight into his hand, such was his anticipation. He was a tough player with fine sharp skills. His partner was Ray Heffernan, who was fast and skilful and a brother of the full forward Christy. He played great games for his south Kilkenny club, Glenmore, over a long club career.

Right half forward was a broadshouldered player from Windgap, Pat Walsh. He was forceful, long striding and could score from far out. In the centre was another forceful, hard running player, Richie Power. One of the most dedicated players on the team, his powerful displays against Offaly in 1982 and '83 had done a great deal to put paid to the midlanders' championship ambitions. On his left was Kieran Brennan, another of the stars of the '82–'83 side. He was fast and vigorous, good at taking passes and flying up the wing.

The full forward line had great power and penetration, unmatched by any other team. In the corner was a small, fast player, Harry Ryan. His lack of stature was compensated for by his courage and his skill. At full forward was the towering Christy Heffernan, by far the biggest player on the field. He was dangerous with the overhead pull in the square, where his weight enabled him to hold his position under the incoming high ball and his height gave him great advantage. He was a team player, sending out passes to his colleagues when he found himself bottled up.

In the other corner was a player who epitomised Kilkenny hurling, Liam Fennelly. He had first-rate ball skills, he had balletic footwork that enabled him to twist and turn and side-step when he got the ball. Fennelly had an inbuilt instinct for the breaking ball; in front of goal he could whip it off the ground right or left. Some said he was far more dangerous at full forward than in the corner but he roved at will wherever the ball might be.

Healy's Role

Nobody knew the abilities of the Kilkenny side better than Diarmuid Healy. He was part of Kilkenny hurling as a trainer of college and under-age sides. He had an astute eye, watched the members of the county team playing in the club championship Sunday after Sunday. He knew many of them personally. This insider's knowledge of the opposition was of special importance as the Offaly team went into training for this critical game.

After the county had made the historic breakthrough in winning the final of 1981 Healy had entertained thoughts of relinquishing his post of coach. It took a great deal of his time and energies, going up and down to Offaly from his home in Kilkenny.

It was the reluctance of the tradition-bound hurling world to give Offaly full credit for that win that spurred him to stay on until they won another. This reluctance sprang in part from a perception that they had caught an over-confident Galway unawares.

It was also said that in '82 and '83 when Kilkenny beat them in Leinster, the Noresiders had what it took to go on and win successive All-Irelands. When Offaly came back on the All-Ireland scene in 1984 they had failed.

'Beating Galway in an All-Ireland is one thing but look what happened to them when they met Cork', was said often enough.

Challenging Accepted Tradition

Since he had taken over the coaching of the team Healy had scoffed at any idea that Kilkenny or any other side had an in-built superiority.

'We made a joke about tradition. I told the players, "Look — the present teams from the main hurling counties didn't win twenty All-Irelands. If Offaly has not won twenty that certainly is not your fault. You won one against all predictions and you can win another." I said to them, "Let us make our own tradition. And part of that tradition is not being in awe of any other county and never, but never giving in, no matter how bad things may be going during a game" ', he recalled.

With Healy's urging the players had put paid to any idea that the Offaly side were not entitled to win an All-Ireland. This notion often assailed teams from outside the Big Three, especially coming into the final ten minutes of a game. They might be leading but something inside them said, 'What's this! We are not meant to win, not expected to win.' And such teams often faded out, to their own chagrin and that of their frustrated followers. Healy had exorcised that fatal trap from the team mentality.

They were now hardened with determination to make amends for the failure of 1984. But like all teams approaching the first outing they were uneasy about themselves and their doughty opponents.

Skills Training

The team was already fighting fit after the league campaign so 75 per cent of the time was given to skills training. Hitting the ball on the ground or in the air, rising it, catching it, hand passing, taking sideline cuts and frees. Pat Delaney practised the long range shots with the dead ball while his Kinnity team mate, Paddy Corrigan, took the medium range efforts and Padraig Horan the near-in frees. Many of the players were now using the light Kilkenny hurleys that Healy had introduced.

There was a strange advantage in the fact that the pool of players upon which the county team could draw was extremely limited.

'A lot of the time we only had 13 top-class players. The selectors and team management were always searching about to fill the other two places. This meant that if any of our thirteen played badly in a game he was not dropped as he might have been in Kilkenny or Cork or Tipperary. We took him aside and told him where he had fallen down and to go out and do better next time', recalls Healy.

'This helped immeasurably in building up a player's confidence — he knew he would not be penalised for making a mistake. It helped engender a player's determination to improve his game all the time. It also generated a great team loyalty among the players and towards myself and the team management', he says.

Eight of the side selected for the game had been part of the ground-breaking team of 1981 while several more were among the substitutes.

Offaly Team

In goal was a stocky, red-haired player from Lusmagh, Jim Troy. He had proved a worthy successor to Damien Martin who, after almost twenty years minding the net, was now the substitute goalkeeper. Troy typified the tough-minded Offaly approach. He had a weight problem which left him less than agile, but with great self-discipline he dieted until all excess weight had been shed.

In the right-hand corner of the defence was a player from the Kinnity club, Liam Carroll, who had come to attention because of good displays in the club championship. At full back was Eugene Coughlan, a man who had emerged as one of the best full backs of the era. He had a calm, resourceful way of playing. He had an astonishing capacity to reach forward and flick the ball away from a forward just as he was about to hit it. Despite being tall and strong he had a delicate touch, able to control the hard-hit incoming ball by a loose-gripped cushioning action with his hurley. His duel with Heffernan was looked forward to.

In the left corner was the captain of the side, Pat Fleury. By this time he had established himself as a strong, hard-tackling, very reliable corner back. He was a rock-solid inspirational figure on the team.

Offaly's half back line was of equal stature to their Kilkenny counterparts. The three had been together for five years, now had an instinctive knowledge of one another's play, worked as a unit, backing one another up. On the right was the tenacious Aidan Fogarty. He was rarely beaten for a ball especially the high balls. The St Rynagh's player was resilient, able to win back the ball that had escaped him.

In the centre was one of the linchpins of the side, Pat Delaney. He was tall and strong and skilful. Centre forwards did not find him easy to pass. Even when he was having a difficult game he could always come up to take a long-range free and put it over the bar. This well-practised facet had often kept his team in the hunt when they were being outplayed.

On the left was Delaney's Kinnity team-mate, the small, slightly built Ger Coughlan. All hurling followers loved to see the fearless way he went into the tackle on taller, heavier opponents; his featherweight nimbleness enabled him to grab the ball, ride the shoulder-charges and race off to clear it.

At centrefield were Danny Owens and Joachim Kelly. These were two hard working players, of the never-say-die mould that was becoming part of the Offaly tradition. Kelly was an inspirational player, winning balls in tough encounters around centrefield to the admiration of the crowd. He roamed purposefully about the field, helping the attacks and back in defence at critical times. Owens had a similar style. He liked to run with the ball, speeding along on a long-legged stride. His introduction in the closing stages of the All-Ireland of 1981 was one of the factors that helped tip the scales in his county's favour.

Paddy Corrigan, Mick Coughlan and Pat Carroll made up the half forward line. Coughlan's good performances at club level had brought him onto the panel. He was a tall, earnest player who could fit into a number of positions. Carroll was the ideal wing forward, a red-headed player who raced out to the sideline, battled for possession and fired over points, usually off his left. His wholeheartedness had an encouraging effect on the whole team. One of his attributes was that he could perform well at centre forward and midfield — and was often shifted about to shore up leaky positions.

On the right was Paddy Corrigan. He had come on as a sub in the All-Ireland of the previous year. He had the same small build and similar opportunistic style as his more experienced brother, Mark. He was fast and scored points in every game in which he played.

Mark Corrigan, in the right corner, had proved himself one of the most effective forwards of the '80s. He made scoring points seem simple, with his wide, measured swing. In the Leinster final of five years before it was his scoring feats that had helped sink Kilkenny, then the reigning champions.

The teams as they lined out were:

OFFALY

Jim Troy
(Lusmagh)

Liam Carroll   Eugene Coughlan   Pat Fleury, capt
(Kinnity)   (Clareen)   (Drumcullen)

Aidan Fogarty   Pat Delaney   Ger Coughlan
(St Rynagh's)   (Kinnity)   (Kinnity)

Danny Owens   Joachim Kelly
(Killoughey   (Lusmagh)

Paddy Corrigan   Mick Coughlan   Pat Carroll
(Kinnity)   (Clareen)   (Coolderry)

Mark Corrigan   Padraig Horan   Joe Dooley
(Kinnity)   (St Rynagh's)   (Clareen)

Substitutes: Tom Conneely (St Rynagh's); Declan Fogarty (St Rynagh's); Brendan Birmingham (Lusmagh); Damien Martin (St Rynagh's); Brendan Keeshan (Shinrone); Mick Clear (Kinnity); Joe Mooney (Seir Kieran); Pat Cleary (Kilmacud Crokes, Dublin); Martin Cashin (Portlaoise). *Coach*: Diarmuid Healy. *Trainer*: Andy Gallagher. *Selectors/ mentors*: Tom Errity (Coolderry); Charlie Daly (Na Piarsaigh); Padge Mulhaire (St Rynagh's); Mick Spain (Drumcullen). *Team physician*: Dr Brendan White. *Masseur*: Ossie Bennett.

KILKENNY

David Burke
(Emeralds)

John Henderson   Paudie Brennan   John Marnell
(Johnstown Fenians) (Conahy)   (Dicksboro)

Joe Hennessy   Ger Henderson   Paddy Prendergast
(James Stephens) (Johnstown)   (Clara)

Ger Fennelly   Ray Heffernan
(Ballyhale)   (Glenmore)

Pat Walsh   Richie Power   Kieran Brennan, capt
(Windgap)   (Carrickshock)   (Conahy)

Harry Ryan   Christy Heffernan Liam Fennelly
(Clara)   (Glenmore)   (Ballyhale)

Substitutes: Johnny Murphy (Glenmore); Billy Fitzpatrick (Fenians). *Trainer/coach*: Pat Henderson. *Mentor*: Mick O'Neill (Kilmacow), chairman of county board. *Team doctors*: Dr Kieran Cuddihy; Dr John Cuddihy.

The referee was Noel O'Donoghue of Cuala, Dalkey, Co. Dublin.

The Corrigan brothers had developed a finely-tuned understanding of each other's play and were a dangerous duo for any defence to face.

At full forward was one of the tough men of the team, Padraig Horan. He had been an exemplary captain of the All-Ireland winning side, battling relentlessly for every ball. He went into every tackle with great vigour, pulling hard on the ball, often disconcerting backs and goalkeeper by his glowering presence.

In the other corner was a tall, strongly-built player, Joe Dooley. He had a long-legged loping stride, running into position for the breaking ball, often going far out to take possession and swing over points with his right-hand-under grip.

Kilkenny Odds-on

On the morning of this Leinster semi-final, most of the media forecasters went for Kilkenny. It was understandable that they should do so, considering the quality of the players. The Noresiders had far greater achievements under their belts than their opponents. And they could be expected to have all the Kilkenny hurling attributes — great skill with the ball, clever team play, a great sense of the ebb and flow of a game, knowing when to make a headlong charge, when to consolidate a lead, when to take scores that raised their own spirits and demoralised the opposition.

This was a two game programme, with Wexford and Laois contesting the first match. It was a stirring encounter with Laois winning by two points to reach their first Leinster final since 1951.

Then the crowd of 29,586 turned to their programmes to survey the two sides about to do battle, on this warm, dry day with only a light breeze.

In fact, when the teams took their places it was seen that Offaly had had second thoughts about the forward line-up. Pat Carroll was playing at centre forward with Mark Corrigan on his left while Mick Coughlan was at full forward and Padraig Horan on the right of the line.

Rivalry of '80s

Even before the ball was thrown in there was an air of tension among the crowd. This was to be a clash between two sides which had developed a hard rivalry over the previous five years. Offaly, the newcomers on the high plateau of hurling, had against all predictions dethroned Kilkenny in 1980. In 1982, when Offaly were then going for three-in-a-row Leinster titles they were beaten in controversial circumstances by Kilkenny; at a crucial time in the second half a ball seemed over the end line, shepherded by Damien Martin, when Liam Fennelly raced in and flicked it back into play; Matt Ruth, left alone by a backline expecting a puck out, swept it to the net for a hotly disputed goal.

That was the hardest game Kilkenny had to play that year on the road to another All-Ireland championship. As a result, the following year a crowd of 37,707 turned up to see them meet again in another final. This was another thundering game, though the Noresiders pulled away near the end.

There was a feeling that another defeat by Kilkenny might put Offaly into the hurling backwater from which they had so defiantly emerged. Both sides knew that this would be one of the closest games they were likely to have during the championship. It all added up to a sense of strain that was evident as soon as play got under way.

Wary Start

Kilkenny, playing into the Canal end, forced a 65 in the first minute but the shot was sent wide. The sides were exceptionally wary of one another. The marking was so close that there was no room for style or imaginative hurling.

The first score came from Offaly when Horan, burly and bustling, cut in from the right and sent a point over the bar. Three minutes later Kilkenny responded. The fast running Brennan, racing along the wing, sent over a point.

Then came some moments of anxiety for Offaly. Richie Power, who was at the start of a battle of wits and muscle with Pat Delaney, sent in a low shot. This was the first real test for Jim Troy in the Offaly goal. He stopped it but the ball ran out, straight into the path of the giant figure of Christy Heffernan. With impulsive bravery Troy dashed out and threw himself in front of the powerful swing of the Glenmore man. The ball was smothered.

There was a sigh of relief from the Offaly supporters as the ball was pucked out. It could have been far worse. Yet Kilkenny were looking the more accomplished side and their thrusting captain, Brennan, sent a fine ball between the uprights from 50 metres out.

Fennelly Goal

It was in the sixth minute that the lightning skills and opportunism of Liam Fennelly were seen at their most lethal. Kilkenny were awarded a free in their own half. Ger Henderson, familiar brown helmet low over his forehead, came up to take it. This left handed player struck the ball well and it soared away, and came in over the upstretched hurleys of backs and forwards. Eugene Coughlan, unruffled but anxious to keep the ball out of the big hand of Heffernan, tipped the ball away. However, it ran across the front of the goal. It hit a Kilkenny forward and spun away. Fennelly, prancing for the break, pounced on the loose ball and whipped it decisively into the net.

That was typical Fennelly fare — nimble and hawklike, the fastest stroke off the ground, left or right.

A dismayed Offaly supporter in the stand roared out, 'Mark that shagging man, will you, for God's sake.'

This delightful piece of opportunism was a jolt for Offaly. But they fought back. Even at that stage the sound playing of Kelly and Owens was giving the midlanders the advantage at centrefield. They went on the attack and were awarded a free. Paddy Corrigan came up to it. He had taken hundreds of frees from all angles in the weeks of preparation and now he sent this one over with ease. Then he got one of the best scores of the day when he eluded his marker and, from 65 metres out, flighted over a long point.

Duels

The big crowd were being highly entertained by the tussles between Delaney and Power, two tall men of similar stature. The fair-haired Kinnity player stuck close to his man, trying to baulk him from starting on one of his dangerous runs.

The other great struggle was between Heffernan and Coughlan in front of the Offaly goals. From the start the big full forward came pounding well out from his position to battle for the high dropping balls, with his tall marker forced to chase after him, leaving lots of space in front of goal for Fennelly and Harry Ryan to exploit.

On one of his outfield forays Heffernan got the ball. With Coughlan on his back he passed the ball deftly to the in-running Power who clipped it over the bar before Delaney could block him down. It kept Kilkenny three points ahead.

In the left corner of the Offaly defence the captain, Fleury, kept goalside of the sharp, speedy Ryan. The small Clara player started to race well out to collect passes and from one of these he sent a neat point over the bar from 35 metres.

Joe Dooley, whose running style was cramped in the corner with the resolute Henderson at his elbow, also roamed out. In one of these long-legged sallies he dispossessed Ger Henderson and passed to Mark Corrigan, who sent it over the bar.

These same two Offaly players gave great heart to their side shortly afterwards. Dooley got the ball and played it on to Mick Coughlan, who in turn flicked a defence-splitting pass straight as a die into the path of the in-running Mark Corrigan. He made ground before whipping it low into the net. Offaly, after such a shaky start, were level.

Offaly Go Ahead

Then Offaly went ahead when Dooley and Joachim Kelly combined to set up Danny Owens for a good point. The Kilkenny midfielder, Ger Fennelly, hurling hard to try to keep his side in the race in the centre, got hold of a ball and sent over a fine, long-range point which levelled the scores.

Offaly's lead was restored with one of the best points of the game. Fleury and Ger Coughlan broke up a Kilkenny attack. The small Kinnity player passed the ball across to his team-mate Delaney. The Kilkenny goals were over 80 metres away but the sinewy centre back took a stylish stroke on the ball and it shot up and away and, watched by the fascinated crowd, kept going until it went between the uprights. This score drew a huge round of applause from the hurling lovers, those from Kilkenny included.

Any Offaly euphoria was swept away by a another near-goal by Liam Fennelly. Troy had to throw himself in front of the Shamrocks man and scramble the ball away to safety. Then, in the 23rd minute, the mercurial Ryan raced determinedly for a ball and sent it over the bar to level the scores at 1–6 each.

Another Fennelly Goal

Ten minutes from half time Kilkenny struck again for an important score. Ger Fennelly broke up an Offaly attack, and sent a great ball across the field into the left corner of the attack. Heffernan and Coughlan bumped and tussled together. When they fell in a tangled heap the ball ran loose. The predatory Liam Fennelly picked it up quickly, rounded Liam Carroll, and clipped the ball into the top corner of the net.

The Kilkenny supporters all round the ground gave a great burst of applause to this consummate opportunist. He almost got another immediately afterwards. He broke through with the ball but the grim-faced Pat Fleury blocked his shot. The ball ricocheted off his stick to Heffernan, who pulled quickly under pressure from Coughlan. The ball thumped off one of the uprights and flew away from goal.

A goal at this stage might have made it very difficult for Offaly to climb back. It would have given Kilkenny enough of a lead that they could play more relaxed, effective hurling. As it was, the reliable Delaney kept his side in the picture. He pointed a free from 65 metres out. A minute later he sent over a huge soaring effort from well inside his own half. Offaly were only a point behind.

Then came a very good Kilkenny spell. While Pat Carroll and Ger Henderson cancelled one another out in tough, hard-pulling tussles, Joe Hennessy and Paddy Prendergast came more into the picture. A better type of ball, fast and low began to go into the Kilkenny forward line, where Pat Walsh, vigorous and fast-running, was playing well. Ger Fennelly from midfield sent over a good point. It was followed by another quicksilver effort by Ryan.

In an attempt to get the better of the Kelly-Owens midfield combination the Kilkenny mentors sent Walsh there in a switch with Ray Heffernan. He reduced the Offaly dominance and, in addition, sent over a good point.

Offaly had also decided on a switch. To curb Liam Fennelly before he could do further damage, Aidan Fogarty moved back into the corner just before the half time whistle. When it sounded Kilkenny were ahead by 2–9 to 1–8 at the end of a taut and edgy first half.

Assailed by Strain

'No team can benefit from being uptight, afraid to make mistakes. It is no harm at all to be nervous but the fear of losing can be disastrous', says Diarmuid Healy, recalling the half-time scene in the Offaly dressing-room. 'In hurling you have to take risks and chances and you can't do that if you are paralysed by the spectre of failure.'

Kilkenny had certainly justified their rating as favourites and in the last five minutes had begun to play their own clever, adroit hurling. The two Fennelly goals had settled them down by then and some of the stiffness went out of their game. Offaly, on the other hand, seemed assailed by the strain of the occasion and looked anything but reigning champions.

Electric Restart

The game looked over as a contest within three minutes of the restart. Only 25 seconds after the throw-in a high dropping ball came into the Offaly goalmouth. Liam Fennelly reached up for it but the hard-tackling Fogarty was at his side and the corner forward dropped it. It fell right into Christy Heffernan's hand. Despite Eugene Coughlan baulking him the big Glenmore man twisted about and hand-passed the ball to the net.

To an increasing volume of cheering from the black and amber supporters Kilkenny piled on the pressure. Harry Ryan scored another point, followed by Ray Heffernan, after his run from midfield. Kilkenny were nine points ahead and opening out in their play.

The Offaly mentors replaced the luckless Liam Carroll at right half back with Tom Conneely and brought in Declan Fogarty for the limping Mick Coughlan; but changes at this stage did not seem to matter. Paddy Corrigan pointed a free and his brother fired over another to cut the lead to seven points; but Kilkenny, now playing confidently, struck back. Harry Ryan, darting and weaving, grabbed another ball and raced away to take another point. Two minutes later, Brennan, the Kilkenny captain, playing very forcefully, sent over another point to restore the nine point lead.

The dauntless Kelly, always at his best when Offaly were in a tight corner, got clear in the fifth minute and from 45 metres out sent a long ball over the bar at the Canal end. Eight points, however, seemed a formidable lead.

Fortunate Goal

It was at this juncture that Offaly got what could only be described as a lucky break. They were awarded a free about 45 metres out from the Cusack stand side of the field. Paddy Corrigan stood over the ball, rose it and belted it hard goalwards. It was intended to be a point but he misdirected the shot. The ball flew low over the heads of backs and forwards and before anyone had time to react, including the goalkeeper, 'Stoney' Burke, it ended up in the back of the net.

This fortuitous score, apart from reducing the Kilkenny lead to five points, was a lively stimulant to the Offaly side. There and then they threw off all their caution, opened their shoulders and began to hurl. Making the very best of their lucky break they stormed into the game to the great delight of their supporters.

Pat Carroll challenged for the ball at midfield, captured it under pressure, ran clear and off his left sent a long ball that went all the way between the uprights. Offaly were only four points behind.

Kilkenny now raised their game in response and the two sides began to play some of the best hurling ever seen between these rivals. A furious battle for supremacy began and did not end until the final whistle. Every player risked injury in the fierce melees that ensued. Yet not a single foul blow was struck in the white heat of battle. At this time Ray Heffernan was replaced by Johnny Murphy.

Pat Delaney stood over another ball to take a free awarded well into the Offaly half of the field. The backs and forwards raised their heads and jostled for position as as the ball rose and sailed goalwards. As it dipped down players got ready to pull hard. There came a jangling smack of ash on ash and the ball bounced clear. Joe Dooley pulled first time on it and it flew just over the bar. There was now only a goal between the sides.

Then the indomitable Delaney jogged over to take another free from well inside his own half, over 85 metres from the Kilkenny goal. Going about the country in his work for the Department of Agriculture he carried a hurley in his car. In spare moments, in lonesome places, in fields populated only by a few cattle, on the treeless heaths of the Slieve Blooms he practised striking the ball long and accurately. On this day of reckoning for Offaly his diligence stood him and the team well. The point he scored brought the difference between the sides to a mere two points.

At this time Joe Hennessy was relieving the pressure on the Kilkenny back line and as the game went on Paddy Prendergast became more forceful against a number of opponents. Pat Walsh, one of the least known of the Kilkenny players, having a great game, struck a point over the bar from 65 metres out to halt the relentless thrust by the midlanders.

Tactical Move

What was giving Offaly a clear advantage emanated from a very astute move by the mentors. They took Carroll out to midfield and Kelly went in centre forward. Both of these players could rise to the occasion and came into their own when the going got tough. Kelly had to battle all he knew just to keep the ball out of the magnet-like right hand of Ger Henderson but he effectively negatived the great match-winning potential of the Johnstown man.

Carroll, muscular and farm-hardy, hurled with great verve and vigour and controlled much of the play at midfield. He sent in ball after ball to the forwards and was at the heart of the astonishing recovery by his side.

By this time Eugene Coughlan was getting the better of his trying duel with Heffernan while Aidan Fogarty's tight and guileful marking had effectively diminished the danger of Liam Fennelly.

With fourteen minutes to go Kilkenny were still three points ahead in the relentless struggle which evoked a continuous barrage of cheering and roaring all round the stadium. Then Offaly were awarded a free well into their own half. Delaney took it and the ball flew up and away and only dipped down onto the waiting hurleys ten yards from the Kilkenny goal. There to meet it was the home-made stick of the square-jawed Kelly. His overhead pull sent the ball rocketing into the net for a spectacular goal to bring the sides level. The score was now 3–14 apiece.

Grabbing the initiative, the midlanders attacked again. Padraig Horan, now a full forward, snapped up a ball in front of goal. Paudie Brennan and John Marnell raced over and blocked his way to goal. The veteran Horan, with hurley holding off his opponents, kicked the ball over the bar.

Paddy Prendergast sent some fine balls to the forwards, low and hard and set up two attacks. Richie Power and Pat Walsh snapped up a ball but, under severe buffeting and baulking, could only shoot wide. Things looked bad for Kilkenny when Paddy Corrigan got the ball near the side-line and floated a fine point over the bar to put his side two points ahead.

It was at this juncture that the great Kilkenny fighting spirit in tight situations came to the fore. They were never afraid of being behind coming up to the final bell. Being in difficulty seemed always to bring the best out of the black and amber-clad sides. It made them dig deep into their repertoire of wristy skills, of clever play, of ploys to fox opponents.

Captain to Midfield

Mick O'Neill and the mentors made a key move in shifting out Kieran Brennan to midfield to stop the dominance of Carroll and Owens. He succeeded in doing so and hit some great balls in the final minutes of this game. Ger Henderson, never as redoubtable as when the team had its back to the wall, came into the game with strength and rugged will-power, blocking and clearing balls down the centre. Whenever he was trapped he found Hennessy racing out to his free side for a relieving pass.

Kilkenny's courageous comeback, after they had lost the momentum, was rewarded when Ger Fennelly sent an elegant point over from 50 metres. It was followed by another by the endlessly running Richie Power. The sides were now level and there was a sense that Kilkenny were now going to take this game. Their mentors took off the substitute Johnny Murphy and sent in the veteran Billy Fitzpatrick, who had scored many fine points for Kilkenny, many from the most acute angles in his long playing career.

Yet it was Offaly, now going at full steam, who regained the lead. Six minutes from the end Padraig Horan won possession in a bruising challenge; amid swinging hurleys he got a pass out to the in-running Paddy Corrigan who slapped it over the bar.

Then from a puck out the hand of Ger Henderson caught the ball amid elbows and hurleys, grunts and swear-words. He shouldered his way out of the affray and went on a loping run which ended when he sent a morale-boosting point over the bar. However, he had been fouled on his way forward and the referee did not allow the advantage. From the resulting free Kieran Brennan put the ball over the bar to bring the sides level again.

There was a tremendous scramble when Jim Troy's puck out landed past midfield. Joe Hennessy whipped the ball back into the Offaly half and his side went on the attack. The Offaly supporters cringed when the towering figure of Christy Heffernan closed on the ball and took possession of it. Eugene Coughlan, who had policed him well without resort to fouling, was right behind him. The big Glenmore man saw Pat Walsh running in and sent a neat and accurate pass to him. Walsh swept it over the bar to give Kilkenny the lead with little over a minute remaining. It was the Noresiders first time in front for fifteen minutes. A great roar of encouragement and admiration went up from the black-and-amber flag-wavers.

Saving Point

With less than a minute remaining Offaly went into a desperate last raid towards the Canal end. Joachim Kelly got the ball near the Cusask stand side, held on to it under pressure and was fouled. It was about 45 metres out, not at a very easy angle. Paddy Corrigan came over to take it. He had played well during the game and had put other frees over. The crowd saw the referee looking at his watch as the Kinnity player stood over the ball. He rose it well, struck it well and it went fast towards the centre of the uprights to a great sigh of relief from the Offaly followers. The sides were level for the eighth and last time in the game. Almost on the puck out, Noel O'Donoghue, who had had a good game, blew the whistle.

As the sweat-soaked players stood there, chests heaving with exertion, gasping for air, shaking hands with one another, there was a feeling of relief on both sides. They were still in contention after as hard a battle as they were likely to have for the rest of the year.

Offaly Go Forward

Some of the commentators said that Offaly had lost their chance. It was the opposite. When the sides met for the replay three weeks later, before a crowd of 22,171, it was Offaly who were victorious at the end of another great game of hurling. This time their back line had tightened up considerably and the Kilkenny forwards were held in check for most of the game. The midlanders won by six points to stamp their dominance on the Leinster scene once more.

These two games were by far the best of the championship season. From there Offaly went on to play and beat Laois in the provincial final. It was the first time since 1948 that neither Kilkenny nor Wexford were in contention.

From there Offaly went on to beat Antrim in the semi-final in Armagh and once again met Galway in the final. Galway were favourites, having ousted the All-Ireland champions Cork with a display of powerful hurling on a day of torrential rain in Croke Park. Once again Offaly emerged victorious to win their second All-Ireland.

When they lined out for that final there were two significant changes on the side — Brendan Birmingham of Lusmagh was at centre-forward and Pat Carroll was not even on the panel.

Birmingham and Carroll

Birmingham's story is one about hanging on and then leaping to grasp with eager hands a golden opportunity. He had played a key role in the 1981 All-Ireland win but at the start of the 1985 season had been thinking of retiring from the game. Healy persuaded him to stay on. He had done so but remained on the substitutes bench for game after game, to his own disenchantment.

The team for the final of 1985 had already been picked and Birmingham was not on it. Then, only a week before the big day, he took part in a training game between the first fifteen and a makeshift collection of subs and Kilkenny players. The Lusmagh man played with such flair and style that the mentors had no hesitation about putting him at centre forward. In that position he played a fine game against Galway and was instrumental in taking the Liam McCarthy cup to the Faithful County for the second time. His career thus ended on a high note and he was a local hero in his parish on the eastern bank of the Shannon.

Pat Carroll's story is one of a vigorous young life tragically ended by a fatal illness. He had played a fine game in the replay, scoring three good points and starred again in the Leinster final.

When they went to Armagh to meet Antrim in the semi-final he took part in a puck around in the grounds of a college. Diarmuid Healy noticed the red-haired farmer less vigorous than usual.

'He was the type of fellow who would never complain. But he told me that he had taken about 14 Anadin since morning to try to relieve a severe headache and that he could hardly see the ball. Brave man that he was he lined out for the semi-final but we took him off during the game.'

Carroll went to a specialist when the team got back to Dublin. He was found to have a tumour of the brain. There was nothing could be done for him and to the great sorrow of his family and his comrades on the team, he died six months later.

The stories of his dedication to the game and to the team, the sacrifices he made to keep himself fit, the amount of effort he put in to hone his skills were already part of hurling lore round Coolderry and Offaly when he died. He and the other players had helped to create the Offaly tradition of never being over-awed by honours-laden opposition, of never giving in, of persistent, resolute play from start to finish.

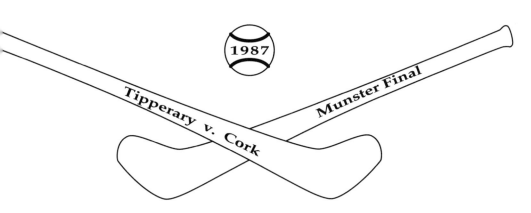

EERIE SILENCE BEFORE EXPLOSIONS OF ECSTASY

A strange silence, disturbed only by subdued murmurings, settled over the field of play and the great crowd assembled in Fitzgerald Stadium in Killarney. From the top tiers of the high embankment spectators could look across at the mountains, glowering dimly all of this afternoon of thrills and excitement but now suffused with strong evening sunlight as the game was about to go into the second period of extra time.

Down below some players lay on the grass while team masseurs and mentors desperately rubbed their cramped legs. Others stood there motionlessly, not talking, as if trying to conserve any last dregs of energy for the final minutes. The injured players sat quietly along the sideline, now waiting as weary, wealed spectators.

The silence of those few minutes, noted by many onlookers and commentators, was because the spectators were limp from excitement, from yelling and shouting. Almost as much as the teams in this titanic contest, which had begun one week before and had now passed the 155-minute mark, most of the onlookers were exhausted by the emotion of it all, drained of energy. They, like the players, were about to summon up their last reserves of spirit in order to cheer their heroes on.

When the referee, Terence Murray of Patrickswell in Co. Limerick, signalled the battered combatants to take their places to renew the contest, the players from Tipperary and Cork walked or limped into their positions. Then they flexed their muscles, breathed deeply, tried to get the adrenalin flowing again for the crucial last fifteen minutes.

Along with the unusual silence was another phenomenon. The day had been overcast and humid. Now, with the emergent evening sun shining down into the tightly-packed bowl of the stadium, the temperature went up noticeably. This unexpected heat was a further strain on lungs and limbs.

Then, as the referee, with ball in hand, looked at his watch and nodded to his linesmen, a cascade of hoarse, croaking shouts began to flow down from the stand and terraces. It grew stronger and louder as the four mid-fielders began to shoulder for position. All the players seemed to be re-energised by this great tide of tired emotion on the part of the Cork and Tipperary followers in the crowd of 45,000 jammed cheek-by-jowl into the stadium. They pulled themselves together for the last act of a great hurling drama that already had been so full of thrills and incidents, of unexpected twists of plot, of such heroic endeavour that it was to be regarded as one of the most memorable occasions in the history of hurling.

The score at that stage stood at 1–21 for Cork, now going for their sixth provincial title in a row, to 1–20 for Tipperary, who had not won a Munster championship for sixteen years. It seemed at that moment that the vastly experienced Cork side, the reigning All Ireland champions would retain their title, despite the most heroic efforts of the young Tipperary challengers.

Tipperary were lucky to be still in contention at the end of the seventy minutes. They had only levelled the match by a point on the call of normal time through a great effort by one of their star performers, Nicholas English. But they were still in there, having hung on desperately, and now they were but one point behind. Their supporters, who had been following their side in one of the longest championship campaigns in modern times, simply ached for them to win. The pent-up frustration and anguish was on every face. Many found it hard to enjoy the skills, the duels, the rampaging attacks and the great back play from both sides. They so much yearned to win that they would only be able to enjoy this game in retrospect if they actually won.

Predictions

At the start of the year, when people looked ahead to the championship, most predictions were that it would be between the two current power-houses of the game, Cork and Galway. The westerners had emerged as the most consistently strong side of the mid-'80s They seemed unbeatable in semi-finals but faltered under the burden of favourites when contesting finals. In 1986 they were odds-on to beat Cork in the final. Yet the Cork side, always dangerous as underdogs, outplayed and outmanoeuvred the Tribesmen. Hurling skill and artistry, allied to traditional grit and astute moves from the sideline, won the game for Cork.

Those who doubted the Leesiders' ability to capture yet another All-Ireland pointed to a number of key facts. Some of their most experienced, battle-hardened players were now in the veteran stage; tough cham-pionship games could cruelly expose players carrying the weight of old wounds and of years. Then, one of the most outstanding opportunists ever to play for Cork, Jimmy Barry Murphy, had retired after the 1986 All-Ireland win. His skill and his score-getting ability would be sorely missed.

There was yet another factor that made Cork supporters uneasy — they had become exceptionally dependent for scores from the hurley of their Midleton midfielder, John Fenton. His accuracy off the placed ball, frees and 65s, was unparalled by any other player of the '80s. His sideline cuts were as good as frees; they went over the bar regularly if they did not drop into the goalmouth. To be relying so much on Fenton was seen as a source of weakness in the side now bereft of Barry Murhpy.

Yet these were mere doubts about a team that bristled with All-Ireland medals and experience and had proved itself in 1984 as well as 1986. They had the will and the determination to go for a record six Munster titles and many could not see them being seriously challenged by Tipperary, the county that had once upon a time been their main rivals in Munster.

Spirit of Resolve

At the beginning of 1987 Tipperary were in the second division of the National League. But a great spirit of resolve had by now enveloped the county. The iron-hard will to get back to the top of the hurling scene had been engendered by their great performance against Cork in the 1984 Munster final, when only the inexperience of the team was their downfall in the final traumatic six minutes. The following year they again contested the provincial final against Cork in Pairc Ui Caoimh. Tipperary were not equal to the occasion, losing by six points. In 1986 Tipperary hopes were dashed at Ennis, when they lost to a very fine Clare side, which itself was unlucky to lose the provincial final to Cork.

These defeats only served to goad the Tipperary hurling powers to take drastic action. They appointed a resolute triumvirate who were given full power to do everything they could to restore the county's hurling fortunes. To the coach of 1984, Donie Nealon, was added the strong managerial personality of Michael Keating together with one of the most astute judges of players, Theo English.

These three men went to work with a will. They were old hurling friends. They had played together in the great years of Tipperary hurling, and knew what it took on the part of players and mentors to win major games.

They set about reviewing the ability of every player on the Tipp panel. They began to scour the county, looking for players of potential. They were often among a handful of spectators looking at some junior game played on a Saturday in a venue unknown to most. They looked especially at players who had been on the fine under-21 sides that had contested many finals between 1978 and 1985, bringing the title home on four occasions.

Once a good player was identified, his abilities, strengths and weaknesses assessed, he was brought into the panel. There was going to be a tough regime of training in physical fitness and skills, week in week out.

Any player who did not feel inclined to make the many personal sarcrifices this spartan programme entailed had no business being among the new gladiatorial team.

Keating, toughened by the competitive commercial world of the oil industry, knew more than most that those from whom much is expected, who have to perform well under pressure, must be properly handled and treated well. He helped organise a vibrant supporters' organisation whose first task was to raise money to pay the expenses involved in a prolonged training programme. Food and hotel accommodation had to be first rate for men asked to forego some of their ties with family, friends and ordinary recreational pastimes. Amongst imaginative schemes to raise funds was the raffle of a racehorse!

The Tipperary team, all the time being reshaped, new players being given a chance, emerged out of the second division of the league to contest the quarter-final. They beat Limerick after a draw and extra-time replay. They met Clare in the semi-final and were beaten by a goal. With each game the side was developing a cohesiveness and team spirit, honing its skills, learning from experience. This was a case of the newcomer trying so hard to prepare for the big time in the championship.

Self-confident Cork

Cork had a much more relaxed and self-confident attitude towards the championship. They were well justified in feeling strong and composed. They had not taken the league very seriously, content to rest and regroup after their resounding All-Ireland victory of the previous year.

Their first game was the semi-final against Limerick. This match was in Thurles. The All-Ireland champions were expected to win but they were in for a shock. Limerick almost took the game and only in injury time did Cork manage to scrape a draw at 3–13 each.

Cork tightened up very considerably for the replay. Early goals by Kevin Hennessy and John Fitzgibbon set the trend. When the pressure came on later in the game, the goalkeeper Ger Cunningham played brilliantly and Pat Hartnett was a strong and dominant defender. The most memorable incident in that game was the once-in-a-lifetime goal, struck just above the ground from 40 metres out by John Fenton. This was a shot for which everything was right: player running, the hurley swung swiftly, the ball struck on the sweet spot of the boss and sent flying like a white bullet in excess of 90 miles an hour — too fast even for an experienced goalkeeper like Tommy Quaid.

Cork had once more qualified for the provincial final. They had an intimidating record. Since 1968, when they had been beaten by Tipperary, they had won twelve of the thirteen they had contested, with the sole exception of the 1980 game, when they lost to Limerick. They won five in a row between '75 and '79 and were now trying to set a record by going one further.

The teams as they lined out were:

CORK

Ger Cunningham
(St Finbarr's)

Denis Mulcahy
(Midleton)

Richard Browne
(Blackrock)

Johnny Crowley
(Bishopstown)

Dermot McCurtain
(Blackrock)

Pat Hartnett
(Midleton)

Denis Walsh
(St Catherine's)

John Fenton
(Midleton)

Jim Cashman
(Blackrock)

Teddy McCarthy
(Sarsfields)

Tomas Mulcahy
(Glen Rovers)

Tony O'Sullivan
(Na Piarsaig)

John Fitzgibbon
(Glen Rovers)

Kevin Hennessy, capt
(Midleton)

Kieran Kingston
(Tracton)

Substitutes: Michael Mullins (Na Piarsaigh); Paul O'Connor (Na Piarsaigh); Ger Fitzgerald (Midleton); Frank O'Sullivan (Glen Rovers); Sean O'Gorman (Milford); Tom Cashman (Blackrock); Sean McCarthy (Ballinhassig). *Coach*: Johnny Clifford (Glen Rovers). *Selectors/mentors*: Jimmy Brohan (Blackrock); Pat McDonnell (Inniscarra); Oliver O'Keefe (Midleton); Charlie McCarthy (St Finbarr's). *Team doctor*: Dr Con Murphy (UCC). *Masseur*: John 'Kid' Cronin (Glen Rovers).

TIPPERARY

Ken Hogan
(Lorrha)

John Heffernan
(Nenagh)

Conor O'Donovan
(Nenagh)

Seamus Gibson
(Kilruane)

Richard Stakelum, capt
(Borrisoleigh)

John Kennedy
(Clonoulty)

Paul Delaney
(Roscrea)

Joe Hayes
(Clonoulty)

Colm Bonnar
(Cashel)

John McGrath
(Borrisoleigh)

Donie O'Connell
(Killenaule)

Aidan Ryan
(Borrisoleigh)

Pat Fox
(Annacarthy)

Bobby Ryan
(Borrisoleigh)

Nicholas English
(Lattin-Cullen)

Substitutes: Liam Stokes (Kilsheelan); Philip Kenny (Borrisoleigh); Pat Fitzelle (Cashel); Michael Doyle (Holycross); Noel Sheehy (Silvermines); Gerry Stapleton (Borrisoleigh); Gerry Williams (Kilruane); Tony Sheppard (Kilruane). *Mentors*: Michael Keating; Donie Nealon; Theo English. *Medical officer*: Dr William Flannery. *Masseur*: Ossie Bennett.

The referee was Terence Murray of Limerick.

Eight of the team that had beaten Tipperary so sensationally in 1984 were still there — Cunningham, Denis and Tomas Mulcahy, Fenton, Hennessy, Hartnett, Johnny Crowley and McCurtain, who had been on the Cork side since 1977.

All of the side which had won the All-Ireland the previous year were there, with the exception of the retired Barry Murphy and Ger Fitzgerald, now among the subs. They were replaced by John Fitzgibbon and Kieran Kingston.

March Through Munster

Tipperary's march through Munster began in Killarney, where they easily overcame Kerry. They returned to the same venue to meet the side that had beaten them in the league semi-final. Clare came within an injury-time minute of beating them again but Tipperary managed to draw level in dramatic fashion.

In the replay Tipperary devasted Clare. Unlike the drawn game, they missed no chances and ran out winners by a massive 21 points.

The team mentors had done a good deal of chopping and changing over the previous months, seeking a strong, well-balanced side. They kept some experienced players but introduced many newcomers. Of the side that had contested the 1984 final only three remained — English, O'Connell and Bobby Ryan. These three along with Pat Fox were on the side that lost to Cork in 1986.

The stage was now set for the Munster final in Thurles. There was no doubt in any hurling follower's mind that this was going to be a battle of the giants. They could smell the whiff of gunpowder from far off and they came down from the glens of Antrim, from Dublin, over from the hurling areas of Galway, Roscommon and the small enclaves where the game was loved in Kerry, Mayo and Westmeath. A huge army of spectators came along the roads from the east — from Kilkenny and Wexford, from south Carlow and Wicklow. All the Munster strongholds poured forth a stream of people eager to watch the clash of two sides intent on besting one another.

The official attendance was 56,000. But before the game began frantic followers breached two gates and an estimated 3,000 gained admittance. Some 2,000 young persons were allowed in free so the final number of spectators crushed into Semple Stadium was over 60,000.

It was a humid, overcast day, one likely to tax the energies of even the fittest player. Tipp were to play into the town goal in the first half, with the aid of a slight breeze.

The rival mentors nodded to one another as the teams lined up for the national anthem. The Cork sideline men had much greater experience of the big occasion and seemed less tense than their counterparts.

'One of the problems that Donie and Theo and myself had to deal with was the fact that our fellows were brought up in an era where Cork were looked upon in awe, seen as unbeatable. We kept telling them that the Cork side were only another fifteen players, wearing red jerseys', recalls Michael Keating.

The atmosphere was electric as the referee threw in the ball to a great tribal roar from the crowd. The Tipperary players flung themselves into the game with everything they had. Without resorting to rough or tough tactics they set out to get the better of their more seasoned opponents, harrassing them, outrunning them, knocking them off their stride.

One thing was clear — their vigour was well controlled. Their eagerness was tempered with the astute conditioning they had received from the triumvirate in charge. These were no eager newcomers going to burn themselves out and run out of energy in the last ten minutes, as had happened in 1984.

Ger Cunningham, carrying a heavily bandaged leg, proved his fitness when he made a bold dash out to the 20-metre line to grab a hopping ball and clear it down the field. Not long afterwards one of Tipperary's new stars, Pat Fox, crossed the ball dangerously but Cunningham handled it well.

The Tipperary backs settled down very quickly, thanks to the competent performance and leadership of their captain, Stakelum. The tall, red-haired Borrisoleigh player handled the balls that came his way with an admirable calmness. More than that he began to help out his colleagues under pressure. In the centre of the Tipp line John Kennedy was also playing well, keeping the ball away from Tomas Mulcahy, who had devastated Galway the previous year with his ball-carrying forays towards goal.

Individual Duels

The two tough men of the sides, Hartnett and O'Connell, began a bruising battle of attrition, pulling hard, shouldering zealously. This was a physical encounter between two men who had starred in the final of 1984, when Hartnett came into his own in the last quarter and O'Connell played a powerful role, thundering down the centre. Now, in this game the moustached O'Connell began to get control, to win balls which he flicked out to the wings whenever he found his way blocked by the resolute Midleton man.

Denis Mulcahy was strong in the corner against English, using his weight legitimately to unbalance the finely-tuned skills of Tipperary's star performer. Just the same English got one of the first scores, racing out to the ball, a yard before his opponent, getting the ball, and sending it over the bar.

The fair haired Aidan Ryan, who was to be endlessly energetic for the game, got another point after the Tipperary players had swept the ball forward with great ground hurling that brought cheers from the crowd. His brother Bobby, normally a back, had been sent to the full forward line to try to give it the power it had lacked in the previous years. He found himself up against a sound marker in Richard Browne.

His Borrisoleigh team mate, John McGrath, also found it difficult to make headway against the strong Denis Walsh who had a great sense of positional play and began to clear much of the ball that came his way.

At midfield a player new to the hurling scene, Joe Hayes, was having a noticeable impact. He epitomised the spirit of Tipperary, vigorous and determined, tussling hard for every ball and hitting it hard into the forward lines. Fenton was playing well also, fast with the ground stroke, left or right. In the seventh minute he got hold of a ball. A quick, decisive swing, the ball bounded off his stick and went over the bar for his side's first score.

Cork Attacks

Playing with controlled fire Tipperary were four points ahead after 16 minutes before Cork began a series of attacks. From one of these a 65 was awarded. Fenton came up to take it. When he sent it over there was a feeling of relief among the Cork supporters. For Fenton not to be on song with placed balls from long or medium range would have spelt disaster for the Leesiders.

At this stage the tall hard-running Cork captain, Hennessy, looked the most dangerous of the forwards. When a free from Fenton came lobbing into the goal area there were roars of encouragement from the Cork followers as they saw the big full forward rise above the swinging sticks to grab hold of it. But Conor O'Donovan, another big man, shouldered him away and the ball was smothered and cleared.

In the next Cork attack Kieran Kingston got the ball but his tenacious marker, John Heffernan, harrassed him, blocking his way. The Tracton man managed to get a pass to Hennessy who in turn was bottled up. He let it go John Fitzgibbon. Here was a player who went for goal at every opportunity; his greatest asset was ability to whip the ball off the ground, left or right from the narrowest angle. He hesitated, while the Tipperary supporters held their collective breath, and Seamus Gibson put him off his shot.

Despite the sound play of the Tipperary backs, the burly Ken Hogan in the Tipperary goal had much more to do than his counterpart. He showed his alacrity and grit the way he faced the incoming balls and handled them. If Cork had an inspirational goalkeeper so also had Tipperary. He exuded an air of weighty confidence. With his missing front teeth he gave the impression of a battle-hardened veteran who knew all the tricks. Hogan was to make his name that year and remain one of the mainstays of the team.

Fenton's Free Taking

Midway through the half it was evident that Cork were finding it difficult to make headway in the forward line. Only the clockwork free-taking of Fenton was keeping them in the game. Teddy McCarthy, who gathered several good balls but was well marshalled by Paul Delaney, was switched with Tomas Mulcahy. The mentors also moved Hennessy out to the right wing. None of these moves made any real gain because their new markers were effectively curbing them.

It was in the 29th minute that the hard-pressed Cork side almost had a goal. Fitzgibbon gathered the ball and made a strong run towards goal, with the Leeside followers yelling at him to keep going. Shouldered heavily, he let the ball loose to Kingston, who could only get in a weak shot off the ground. There was a loud groan of disappointment from the Cork supporters concentrated under the scoreboard at the town end.

What was heartening for the Tipperary followers was the way their side was playing, using skilful first-time pulling from the half back line out, with Hayes sending it on from midfield. Aidan Ryan was using his speed to try to outrun the vastly experienced McCurtain and partly succeeding. McGrath was also beginning to win more ball from the very effective Denis Walsh. The left-handed Fox, low to the ground, was hard to counter when he got the ball and turned to run goalwards.

What made the game such a delight for hurling lovers was the way two tight marking sides still allowed one another to hurl. There was a minimum of fouling. This was a game where hurling artistry, honed and shaped over years of practice, came into its own despite the desperate races for the ball, the thunderous shoulder-charges, the fierce tussles.

English had come out to the right half forward position. He got the ball. Tightly marked, he used his foot-skills to kick a neat pass straight into the path of O'Connell who sent over from 65 metres out.

As half time approached Tipperary were leading by 11 points to 7. When the whistle went the huge crowd gave a prolonged ovation to the players as they trooped off. Many Cork followers were pleased that their men were still well in the game despite being outplayed for much of it. They knew from years of following their victorious side that there comes a time in every game when the experienced side gets a rhythm going, knows how to get crucial, demoralising scores against eager newcomers who seemed so dominant for so long.

The Tipperary supporters were elated. They were seeing winning hurling for the first time in years and years. All that bothered them was the feeling that they should have been much more ahead on the scoreboard.

Cork Attacks

Whatever was said to the Cork forwards in the dressing-room at half time, they came charging into the game from the resumption. They now had the breeze to their backs. Kingston showed how dangerous he could be when he clipped a lightning-fast shot towards the Tipp goal. Hogan brought off a save that generated a huge cheer of applause and which spurred his own side on. In another attack, the strong-running Hennessy moved in and had the goal in his sights. Only a last second shoulder from Stakelum made him fluff his effort. The dark-haired Fitzgibbon, finding it difficult to display his adroit stickwork for much of the game, had one good shot at goal. Again Hogan saved and cleared with sturdy confidence.

A battle of the mentors was taking place in parallel to that on the pitch. Tipperary shifted the forward line about, bringing English to full forward. This move was to have a vital bearing on the game.

The most significant move by the Cork sideline men was to take Jim Cashman from midfield, where he had only barely been holding his own, and put him in the faltering halfback line. This player, who had great anticipation and, like his brother Tom who was on the injury list, had a wristy style that made him difficult to hook. He made a difference to the Cork defence at a time when Tipperary seemed about to sow this game up. The tiring McCurtain was taken off and replaced by Paul O'Connor while Michael Mullins was sent in for Tomas Mulcahy, who could not get into his stride in this game.

Tipperary went four points up with a great point from Fox from 60 metres out. Then they got what seemed like a clinching goal. The ever-alert English raced behind as Joe Hayes passed a high ball over the head of Richard Browne. English collected it but Cork backs crashed into him. In the tussle English lost his hurley. The ball ran towards the goal with English chasing it. Cunningham dashed out to take it. This was when the Tipperary man's nimble footwork and skills stood to him. He tipped up the ball on the run and then kicked it swiftly and accurately past the outstretched goalkeeper and into the empty net.

It was the kind of unusual score that set him apart from other players; he could do unexpected things. It also ensured his being vigorously marked in game after game.

The huge cheer of delight from the Tipperary supporters signalled the fact that, after so many years in the wilderness, so long regarded as has-beens, the team in blue and gold were finally to take their place at the top. Tipperary were now seven points ahead and seemed destined to take the trophy.

But there was no way that this battle-hardened Cork outfit would succumb without a real fight. Their spirits were restored by a fine Fenton free. They thundered back into the game, with Mullins very effective and forceful. Tony O'Sullivan used all his guile and smooth skills to go for the ball, get it, slip away from tackles, side-stepping and weaving and send the ball goalwards. The powerful McCarthy kept hurling and hustling and got better as the game went on. Ger Fitzgerald, who came on for Fitzgibbon, was another vigorous runner and forager.

Five Points Without Reply

Some of the Cork energy was wasted in that they were trying to go for goals against a sound defence, with Kennedy and Stakelum playing inspirational hurling. Yet in a ten minute spell they put on five points without a reply from Tipperary — three frees from Fenton and one each from O'Sullivan and McCarthy. This team had been in many a tight corner before but had the tenacity and confidence to play its way out of them. The deficit was down to a mere two points.

This was a period of the game when Tipp lost the initiative, became defensive and let their skilful opponents take up the running. Yet it was a time also that Tipperary showed their fighting spirit. Back pedalling they might be but they had the confidence to come back and set up a series of attacks.

It was the indomitable fighting spirit of both sides, two strong person-alities battling it out with vigour, calling on all their skills and resolve, trying to best one another in every corner of the field that thrilled the huge crowd. Every tussle was a momentous event, a cameo of the fighting rivalry between the sides. The play moved quickly as the ball was clipped fast along the field. Sometimes long, soaring high balls came dropping into the goal areas, seemingly helped through the air by the powerful, roaring gust from the supporters. A sightless person could have guessed what was happening from the clamour — exuberant cheers when a back made a power-packed clearance, groans of disappointment when the ball went wide of the post and an immense ear-wracking uproar when a score was achieved.

There were huge groans from the Tipperary followers; Aidan Ryan and Pat Fox both missed reasonable chances of points which would have put the game out of Cork's reach. Then when Tipperary won a very scorable free Fox came up to take it. He had proved to be the outstanding forward that day, having scored three points from play and four from frees up to this point. Now, to the consternation of the Tipperary followers he sent the ball wide. Yet he made amends in the 65th minute when he sent a free over the bar to leave a goal between the sides. At this stage Liam Stokes had replaced the injured John McGrath.

With Tipperary now back on their game it seemed inevitable that Cork's second-half rally would come to nothing. Even the loss of the outstanding Joe Hayes with a thumb injury — replaced by Philip Kenny — was not seen as a serious setback because Colm Bonnar was playing very forcefully. The Tipperary followers were now daring to smile, to reassure one another as they looked at their watches, kept asking one another 'How long is there to go?'

But Cork came back. They attacked and Mullins was heavily tackled. Fenton took the free, lifting the ball forward perfectly, swinging grace-fully on it, hitting it on the dead centre of the sweet spot of the boss. It shot away decisively, sped inevitably between the uprights. Two points behind and four minutes plus injury time to play.

Last Minute Goal

To a swelling roar from the massed Cork followers the men in red went on a do-or-die attack. Teddy McCarthy leapt for a ball amid swinging hurleys, caught it, and sent it out to Jim Cashman who had run forward in support of the all-out assault. He in turn sent it to the captain, Hennessy, who managed to get it in to Mullins, 15 metres out from the Tipperary goal. Under desperate pressure from the unrelenting Tipp backs he swung and missed.

But the ball ran through and here was Kingston on hand with a powerful ground shot to blaze the ball past the helpless Hogan for a thunderous Cork goal.

The huge rumbling boom that went up from the Cork supporters was fueled by pride and joy. Their side had been behind for 67 minutes, often struggling under the vigour of their younger opponents. Yet here they were once again, using their skill and game-experience to snatch a goal at the most vital time completely against the overall balance of play.

The Tipperary followers were aghast. The dread spectre of the last-gasp defeat of their side by Cork in 1984 now seemed to hover over the jam-packed stadium. Their anguish was visible in the tense, strained faces. It was made all the worse in that they had been preparing to cheer, to rush onto the field, to celebrate their county's comeback to the pinnacle of the Munster scene after a long and dismal sixteen years.

This goal now put the champions into an astounding lead. Then with two and a half minutes remaining Denis Mulcahy came running out and passed the ball to Fenton at midfield. The Midleton man, who had already scored 11 points, now rifled one of the most valuable long-range points of his career between the uprights. Cork were two points ahead.

Desperate Forays

It was in this desperate plight that the character and tungsten-hard will of the young Tipperary side emerged. While their supporters clenched their fists and bit their knuckles the men in blue and gold went into the attack once again. They were awarded a free 50 metre out. Pat Fox cantered out to take it while the forwards ran into the square. This was a trial in composure for the small-sized Annacarthy man, who had fought so hard to overcome a badly damaged knee and take his place on the team.

Many expected that he would lob the ball into the square, hoping that a Tipp hurley could flick it into the net to win the game for Tipperary. Fox however sent it over the bar. Tipp were now only one point behind.

As the powerful puck out from Ger Cunningham sailed high in the air above the trembling stadium below the game went into injury time. Tipperary backs and midfielders fought tigerishly for the ball, got it in to the attack. There was a shout of desperate hope from the Tipperary supporters when English, so sharp to spot an opening, so quick to strike accurately, got the ball. As he tried to round Richard Browne for a run towards goal, he was fouled. The tension in Semple Stadium was almost visible, a collective shimmer of strained nerves, as Fox came over to take it. This had to be one of the last pucks of this momentous game. If the previous free had been crowded by pressure this one was doubly so. But the modest Fox was a man of calm temperament. He rose the ball left-handed and sent it over the bar, to a huge sigh of relief from Tipperary.

Cunningham's puck out was still in the air when Terence Murray blew a long, shrill note that tailed downscale at the end to mark the end of the game.

Reactions

The huge attendance was so stunned by the endless drama and the great climactic last five minutes that many shuffled away speechless. People in the stands and terraces began to stretch their shoulders, arch their backs, and rub their shoulder muscles to relieve some of the throbbing strain of it all.

The Tipperary team and its huge following felt a sense both of loss and of relief. After being so long in command they had been robbed of the title that had been almost theirs. Yet they had come back from the brink of what would have been a spectacular defeat. There was heartache there too. On his way out of the ground that evening, after he had written his report, the doyen of the hurling writers, Paddy Downey of the *Irish Times* overheard a downcast Tipperary man repeating to himself the phrase, 'God, what do we have to do to win?' It was the cry from the heart of those who have to try so hard to do what seems so easy for others.

The Cork dressing-room was a place of joy and jauntiness. Here they were, put to the pin of their collar to keep in the game for most of the time but yet they were still there and had come within an ace of pulling off what would have been a melodramatic win. They had dug deep into their traditional reserves of fortitude, spirit and skill to match a younger side and to make one of the best games ever seen in Munster or anywhere else.

Apart from Fenton the Cork scorers were O'Sullivan (0–4), Kingston (1–0), McCarthy and Hennessy (0–1) each. Apart from Fox the Tipperary scorers were English (1–1), O'Connell (0–4), Aidan Ryan (0 –2), Stakelum and McGrath (0–1) each.

It took several hours for the great gathering of people to disperse. Even before some left news came through that the replay was to be the following Sunday in Killarney. It was to be an all-ticket game, limited to 45,000 spectators. The scramble for tickets began that evening.

The rows of cars moved along all the roads out of Thurles. The excursion trains pulled in to the crowded platform of the railway station. One of these was bound for Dublin. It carried hurling lovers and rival supporters living in or near the capital. Many were middle-aged men, now drained of emotion and energy by the momentous event. By the time the train got to Templemore they were fast asleep. Some had to be shaken awake when the train eventually pulled in to Heuston Station, Dublin. One, blinking his eyes, said 'Jaysus, I was dreaming that I had got two tickets for the replay in Killarney.'

Changes for Replay

For the replay both sides made some changes. The broken thumb of Joe Hayes ruled him out and his place was taken by Pat Fitzelle of Cashel, one of the most experienced players on the Tipp panel. Gerry Williams was recalled to the team at right half forward, in place of John McGrath. Before the game began Bobby Ryan at full forward and Nicholas English in the right corner were to switch places.

Cork were boosted by the return of the taleted and game-wise Tom Cashman, who was to partner Fenton at centrefield, while his brother Jim went to right half back. Michael Mullins, who had been successfully introduced in the last three games, held his place and was at right half forward. Teddy McCarthy went to centre forward with O'Sullivan on his left. The full forward line read Kingston, in the right corner, Hennessy at full and Mulcahy. John Fitzgibbon was now among the subs.

Fitzgerald Stadium was filled to capacity on this overcast, heavy day, with a light breeze blowing into the town end. This was Tipperary's third game there and it was a venue with a good tradition for the county. They had won the 1937 All-Ireland there and had beaten Cork in the tempestuous provincial final of 1950. Terence Murray was again in charge.

When the game got under way, with Tipperary having the breeze behind them, there was a resumption of the battle that had ended a week before. Many individual duels were renewed. The same level of courage and skill was evident. From the start the spectators sensed that they were in for another epic encounter.

Different Pattern

There was, however, a striking contrast to the drawn game. Cork settled down almost immediately and took control. Any ball that came up the right side of the Tipperary attack was grabbed by Denis Walsh; he then sent low hard balls into the forwards. Tom Cashman got into his stride in midfield, reading the play perceptively, running onto the breaking ball, striking the ball quickly. McCarthy was troubling Kennedy with his powerful catching and running and O'Sullivan, sprightly and clever, was giving the Tipperary captain, Stakelum, a difficult time.

Fenton had Cork's first score, a point after 35 seconds. It was to herald another impressive performance, particularly from placed balls, during the game. Two minutes later, Tomas Mulcahy improved immeasurably from the drawn game, sent over another point.

After ten minutes of inspired hurling Cork had five fine points on the scoreboard. Not alone that but Fox, Tipperary's saviour in the Thurles game, sent three frees wide; and two long-range efforts by Stakelum went wide as well. Tipperary were going all out, contesting every ball, challenging and chasing but somehow could not get into a rhythm. For neutrals in the attendance it was a fascinating example of how the same two teams can make a different game each time they play.

Eleven minutes had gone by before Tipperary got their first score, a point from a free by Fox. Cork kept the initiative. The ball came blazing into the forward line in the 13th minute. Kingston pulled on it and sent it goalwards. It deflected off a hurley or body and hopped in front of Hogan, who grabbed it authoritively and made a huge clearance.

Not long after Hennessy sent a hard drive goalwards but the tenacious Gibson stood his ground and the ball bounced off his chest and away to safety. Hennessy turned the full back, O'Donovan, and raced for the goal but the Nenagh man baulked him and he fluffed his shot. From then on O'Donovan began to get the upper hand and became a dominant figure in front of goal. At this time of great pressure Hogan gave great confidence to his backs by his assured performance.

The Cork supporters had much to cheer about as their forwards kept coming in waves. It was a riveting display of skill and power. What made the game so exciting was to see the way the beleagured Tipperary defence threw everything into the effort to stop being overwhelmed.

'Hold on Tipperary till ye get going', shouted a grizzled Tipperary supporter, hoping that Cork's period of dominance would soon come to an end.

Goals

The men in blue and gold did get a badly needed boost in the 29th minute. O'Connell, renewing his battle of muscle and stickwork with Hartnett, rounded his opponent and came charging in with the ball. It was knocked away from him but went to Bobby Ryan out on right. He and O'Connell engaged in a great tussle with Browne and Crowley while the crowd roared them on. In the meanwhile, English had slipped his effective marker, Jim Cashman, and run in front of goal. Out of the desperate four-man scramble O'Connell kicked the ball straight across to English in front of goal. This adept stick-artist tipped up the moving ball and first-timed an unstoppable shot to the net in a piece of scoring artistry. It billowed the net, despite Cunningham's lunge.

This score visibly put heart into Tipperary. Their supporters were still cheering when Cork mounted another attack. The ball seemed to be going wide when Kingston, with great wristwork, flicked it back. Mulcahy got it on the edge of the square and from the narrowest of angles belted it goalwards. Hogan got his stick to it but it was going to hard and fast from too near and flew into the net.

This was a blow to the challengers to concede a goal so quickly but the English goal had a hopeful aura about it that was hard to dispel. Just the same when the half-time whistle went the score was 1–10 to 1–5 in favour of the champions. They would have the breeze at their backs in the second half. Their fast striking and pace had given them the upper hand, together with Fenton's machine-like scoring. It was hard to see them being beaten.

The Tipperary mentors had switched Kennedy and Delaney. The Nenagh man had begun to curtail the catching, running game of the bustling McCarthy and Kennedy was playing well on the wing. Gerry Williams, who had found it hard to find his form, was replaced by Martin McGrath who already was becoming a handful for the previously rampant Walsh.

During the interval several agitated Tipperary officials came rushing up to Keating and his colleagues, exhorting them to make drastic changes in order to save the game for Tipperary. The Tipperary mentors kept their cool.

'We knew the team as it stood was capable of coming into its own once it got going', says Keating. 'We decided to stick by our own convictions.'

Six Point Lead

When the game restarted Cork looked the more confident side. After points had been swapped Tomas Mulcahy almost had a goal but his kicked effort went into the side netting. Then Tony O'Sullivan flighted over a neat point to give his side a lead of six points. Despite the fiery play, the great surges of attack and defence by both sides which enthralled the spectators, Cork still seemed a sure bet to create a new record in consecutive provincial titles.

Then, slowly at first, Tipperary began to wrest control of the game from their opponents. When Cork went on the attack John Heffernan cleared the ball confidently; he had had a hard time trying to curb the in-form Tomas Mulcahy but he now began to command the corner. O'Donovan and Gibson became even more forceful in the full back line.

The Tipperary captain, Stakelum, who was marking the mercurial, nimble-footed O'Sullivan and finding it a difficult job, now got more into his game. In the middle Delaney and McCarthy effectively cancelled one another out as they went elbow-by-elbow for every ball, shouldering and pulling together, overhead and on the ground. The stinging clash of their hurleys could be heard above the rising uproar even on the highest tiers of the steep sloped terracing.

Often the ball broke to the left. When it did there was Kennedy to pick it up. He, who had had so difficult a time for much of the first half, now caught and cleared anything that came his way. He also ran forward with ball on stick and sent low balls into the forwards, by-passing the midfield. Mullins, his marker, was replaced by the tall, strong Ger Fitzgerald.

Fenton and Cashman, skilful and effective, still had the upper hand at midfield but Fitzelle and Bonnar, whose energetic running won more and more ball for the men in blue and gold, began to even the tally.

Changes

The Tipperary mentors then made changes to try to break the grip of the Cork backs and to give better expression to the scoring abilities in the forwards. Richard Browne was playing consistently well at full back, matching the resolute vigour of Bobby Ryan. Denis Walsh and Jim Cashman were both very strong on the wings, difficult for the Tipperary forwards to pass.

Bobby Ryan now went to left full forward and English took his place. Martin McGrath went in to the left corner where his style of play started to trouble the reliable Mulcahy.

In the right corner Johnny Crowley, drawing on his long experience and using his skill, had been well able for Pat Fox in the close exchanges. Now, again and again, the small, fast Tipperary man came racing out to the incoming balls with his weighty opponent pounding at his heels. With low balls Fox was lethal; he lifted them on the run, turned to his right and hit them towards the uprights off his strong left side.

Sixteen minutes into the half Tipperary had narrowed the gap to three points. They almost levelled when English got the ball, juggled with it to draw the backs and then got a neat pass out to Fox. The Annacarthy man shot goalwards as the followers of both sides gasped. But the ball hit the upright and bounced back out. Pat Fitzelle, running forward, caught it and sent a fine point between the uprights.

Not long afterwards Tipperary had another chance. O'Connell, getting away from Hartnett more and more, came running in with the ball. He passed to the agile, ingenious English who, with his back to the goal, hand-passed the ball goalwards under his legs. It was saved but it demonstrated the danger that English posed. Browne, playing exceptionally well, could not take his eyes off his unpredictable opponent for a minute.

Tipp Edge Forward

As Tipperary edged forward point by point there came a succession of massive roars from their supporters crowded on the slopes of the high embankment. The banners and flags waved again and again. It gave great sustenance to their heroes battling it out below with the reigning champions, striving to get the better of a side which had shown great courage, resolve and skill in beating the powerful Galway side in the All-Ireland of the previous year.

The biggest roar came when Tipperary, for the first time in the game, drew level in the 23rd minute of the half when Fox struck a typical point from play.

Cork suffered a grievous disappointment a few minutes later. Teddy McCarthy, breaking free of Delaney, sent in a hard centre. O'Sullivan, with great skill, tipped the fast-moving ball onwards and into the net, to a huge cheer from the Leeside followers. There were moans of dismay — and some shouts of anger — when the goal was disallowed for an infringement in the square that few had seen.

It was the beautiful striking style of the Na Piarsaigh player that came to Cork's aid shortly after when he put his side in the lead again with another point.

Level Pegging

Martin McGrath, who had only been in the Tipperary squad a week, then hit his second narrow-angle point to bring the sides level again. When the white-helmeted Fenton, giving an exhibition of free taking, sent over a 65 to regain the lead, McGrath again hit the ball over from the corner to level once more.

At that stage one of the great sportsmen of Cork hurling, Tom Cashman, limped off the field. He had starred consistently for Cork for ten years. Now he was hampered by old recurring injuries. He was replaced by Paul O'Connor. His departure was a serious blow to Cork at a time when Colm Bonnar was now going like a train, winning ball after ball in the centre.

Now as the game came into its last minutes the tension for spectators, even neutrals, became nerve-wracking. Every single puck of the ball, every break, every bounce, every tussle and scramble, every clean stroke, every block-down became vital. This titanic struggle now rested on a knife-edge.

Teddy McCarthy rose in the air for a ball and caught it. He was fouled. Fenton ran over to take it, straddling the ball, looking at the posts.

'When Fenton took a free he had the confidence that only comes when you have taken thousands of similar frees in practice', recalls Michael Keating. To Cork-accented shouts of 'Good man, Johnny boy' the Midleton player put it over the bar. Cork were ahead again. At that time John Fitzgibbon came on for Kieran Kingston.

There was a minute of frenzied play, with the crowd now at fever pitch, as the ball went from end to end. Hartnett, defending bravely, was forced over the end line. To the dismay of the Tipp supporters, Delaney's effort from the 65 was turned wide by the breeze near the end of its flight. Fenton got the ball from the puck out and hit it quickly, while a Tipperary player lunged at him. To the great relief of the Tipperary followers the ball went wide.

Crucial Point

Hogan took the puck out. He put all his weight into it, running forward with a full swing. The ball travelled over the midfield and the Cork half backs, landing almost 30 metres from the Cork goal — a prodigious feat against the breeze. English raced onto it, grabbed it and, dodging and jinking past opponents made for goal.

Everybody in Fitzgerald Stadium knew that the time was up and many in the stand rose spontaneously to see the final outcome of this thriller. Going like a hare, with Browne right behind him, English found himself with only Cunningham to beat from 15 metres out. In the split second it crossed many minds that he might hit a winning goal. But

English could not risk being hooked or the agile Cunningham making a game-winning save; he palmed the ball over the bar to bring the sides level once more at 1–17 each.

Extra Time

At the puck out Terence Murray blew the long whistle and indicated that two fifteen-minute periods of extra time were to be played. The level of endeavour on the field and excitement among the spectators had been so intense that there was something strangely unreal to see the players once again exchange ends and take up their positions.

'I don't care if we miss the excursion train home — we'll bed down out there on the pitch for the night when its all over', said one game-enthralled member of the hurling community.

All over the country listeners to RTE Radio 1 were captivated and invigorated by the unforgettably colourful and zesty description of the game by Micheal O Muircheartaigh. Several hundred miles away one of the thousands of hurling lovers listening in sat alone in his car in a lonesome place on high ground on a treeless plain in the far north of Scotland. On his car radio he followed the surges of this memorable contest. He was one of many, at home and abroad, who would have given anything to be in Killarney that day.

Even before the throw-in Jim Cashman was hobbling and he was substituted by Sean O'Gorman, who played with verve during his time on the field. Cork still looked the more composed side and they went into a two-point lead with points from Fenton and Fitzgerald. Yet Tipp kept up the all-out challenge and forced a 65. Delaney put it over the bar — the third such score by him. It was followed by a point by Pat Fox to level again.

Every Tipperary indiscretion was punished by the infallible Fenton. He sent two more points over the bar. However the sharpshooter began to limp sorely from cramp and the mentors sent him in corner forward and brought Hennessy out in his place. Michael Mullins rejoined the fray when he replaced John Fitzgibbon.

Then Aidan Ryan, whose energetic play was coming into its own at a time of tiring, cramping limbs now ran forward, leaving Cork backs in his wake and scored a point to add to the two others he had scored during the course of the game proper.

Another player immobilised by cramp was Delaney. The mentors had no alternative but to take him off. In doing so they made what was to prove the most significant move of the game: they brought in Michael Doyle at full forward and brought back Bobby Ryan to take over at centre-back.

Second Fifteen Minutes

After the first fifteen minutes of extra time Cork led by 1–21 to 1–20. As the teams wearily changed places and the emergent sun heated up the stadium it still seemed that Cork would win. Tipperary had caught up with them again and again but somehow found it impossible to go ahead. For many onlookers this indicated the shade of difference between the sides — the ability of the Cork side to bring their hard-won big game experience to the fore at crucial times.

Tipperary, however were relentless in their pursuit of the ball. It was becoming apparent that the overall youth of the side was no longer a disadvantage. They were leaving many of their opponents struggling along behind as they raced about. One who raced away was Pat Fox who scored another point to level the scores again.

Ahead For First Time

Then came one of the most momentous scores of the game. Donie O'Connell's tenacity and endless drive had at last worn down Pat Hartnett. The Killenaule man burst his way down the centre, rode several hard challenges and, to a tumultuous roar of applause, sent over the point that put Tipperary ahead for the first time in the entire game.

Another significant event followed. Cork were awarded a free 50 metres out, in front of the posts. Fenton came limping out to take it. For the first and only time in the game he sent it wide. It seemed to signal that something was going out of the Cork effort.

Tipp Goals

Now began an avalanche of scores that finally decided this marathon contest. Colm Bonnar, now unbeatable in midfield got the ball and came charging in. As the backs ran out he passed to O'Connell who had again come thundering forward. When Browne challenged, the Killenaule man swung hard and low. Browne got his hurley to it but the ball flew out to Doyle. With Cunningham already going the wrong way the big Holycross man simply tapped it into the empty net.

All round the ground the Tipperary supporters leaped to their feet, yelled their lungs out, waved their flags and banners in an ecstasy of joy. This was the break that Tipperary so badly needed.

The flag-waving supporters along the sideline had hardly settled down again when, just after Dermot McCurtain had replaced the injured Crowley, Tipperary mounted another attack. Browne got the ball and was breaking forward when he was dispossessed by Fitzelle, now playing at his best. The Cashel man sent a low delivery into the square. It was taken by Doyle. He was buffeted about but he was strong and fresh enough to ride the challenges and kept possession until he was able to handpass the ball over the head of the advancing Cunningham. It rolled into the empty net, hooshed along by the hoarse cries of the success-hungry Tipp followers.

The man who had been unfairly blamed for losing the 1984 provincial final through a misdirected handpass had now effectively put the game beyond the reach of the champions. They did make a last score, yet another point by Fenton, but by that stage the curtain was coming down on the great drama.

The Tipperary cheers were hushed however when, with six minutes to go, Hogan fouled the ball in the goalmouth and a penalty was awarded. Fenton didn't miss many penalties. He blazed low for goal but the Tipp backs got their hurleys to it and it was cleared away. Tipp tails were up and everything was now going right for them. Even the loss of the heroic O'Donovan near the end — replaced by Gerry Stapleton — was not really felt.

Final Goal

Then with three minutes to go Bonnar and Fox combined in another attack and in the ensuing scramble got the ball out to the unmarked O'Connell. He rounded off a great individual performance by palming the ball home for Tipperary's fourth goal.

Tipperary supporters were waving flags along the sideline, some encroaching on the field of play, as the last seconds of the game went by. When Terence Murray blew the final long whistle, a long three-deep line of flag-bearing supporters raced onto the field from both sides which someone vividly likened to the charge of the dervishes at the battle of Omdurman.

The scenes of jubilation in front of the stand were exceptional. There were torrents of emotion, of laughter and ecstasy, hugging and kissing between strangers. There were tears in the eyes of hard men who bore the knuckle scars of long-gone games. A proud county and people had regained something of a dearly-loved heritage.

When Stakelum went up to receive the cup, totally oblivious of the blood dripping from a wound over his eye, he shouted that the 16 year famine was over at last. Then he led the crowd in the singing of the Tipperary anthem, 'Slievenamon'.

Before that he had paid generous tribute to Cork. The men in red had lost nothing of their reputation for skill, courage and sportsmanship by this defeat. The final scoreline of 4–22 to 1–22 gave no indication of the neck and neck race that had taken place until the final ten minutes out of a total of 170 plus the injury time played in both games.

Cork went down like champions and were gracious in defeat. This game was to be the championship swansong of several of the veterans who had served the county so well and provided the hurling community with so much entertainment over the years — players like Fenton, Crowley and Tom Cashman.

Tipp Pride

These two games fully restored the pride of Tipperary in its hurling. They gave the game a great impetus. But the energy-sapping encounters and the joyous celebrations drained the players physically and emotionally. Though they came near it, they did not quite reproduce quite the same performance against the powerful and experienced Galway side they met in the semi-final; they were beaten by the Westerners then and in the All-Ireland of the following year.

But there was no stopping the revived Tipperary and they won the All-Irelands of 1989 and 1991 and reclaimed their place at the top of the hurling scene.

One of the great benefits to the hurling community of the two epics of 1987 was that they began a new era of Cork-Tipperary rivalry which produced some of the best games seen over the past thirty years. The Munster final of 1990, when Cork unexpectedly beat the reigning champions, was another great encounter. The drawn match in 1991 and the replay were acknowledged to be the among the best exhibitions of championship hurling ever seen at any time.

Christy Ring once said that the Munster championship always needed a strong challenge from Tipperary to give it colour and vibrancy. Tipperary's re-emergence has certainly given it that.

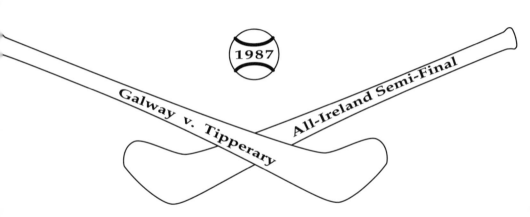

COLLISION OF THE HUNGRY ONES

What made this game between Galway and Tipperary one of the greatest All-Ireland semi-finals of the last twenty years? It was the first real, full-scale battle between two of the finest teams of the 1980s. It was an open game in which many talented and competitive players from both sides were allowed to display their skills and endurance. It was played at a searingly fast pace from start to finish. There was nothing between the sides in terms of ability or on the scoreboard until the last few minutes.

But what lent this game a fervour and frenzy rarely seen in any match was the great collision of ambitions, of hopes and of anxieties. On a warm, sunny, windless day a huge army of Tipperary followers, sporting flags, banners and colours, packed the stands and terraces. They easily out-numbered the maroon and white decked followers of the Galway team in a near-record crowd of 49,410.

Many of the younger followers of the Munster champions had never seen their county play in an All-Ireland semi-final or final before. They knew about Tipperary's years of hurling dominance and its traditions only by hearsay or reading old reports of the great days from browning newspapers or by seeing the memorabilia collected so lovingly by the hurling historian, Sam Melbourne.

First Since 1971

Tipperary had not been in a semi-final since 1971. That year they beat a Galway side languishing in a morass of self-doubt, poor organisation and half-hearted preparation. Tipperary were one of the giants of the game then. It would have been a sensation if Galway, long cast in the role of gallant or floundering losers, had beaten them. The Munster team, powered by great players like Michael Keating and Mick Roche, won in a canter and then went on to win one more All-Ireland — their 22nd — by overcoming a strong Kilkenny team in the final.

Nobody coming out of Croke Park that day could have imagined that Tipperary would not return there for a championship match for sixteen long years. Nor would they have found it easy to envisage that the perennial losers, Galway, would by 1987 be a major force on the hurling scene.

Yet the Galway team to contest the semi-final of 1987 were by no means favourites. They had lost two All-Irelands in a row. In 1985, having beaten the reigning champions, Cork, in torrential rain in the semi-final, they were favourites to beat Offaly on All-Ireland day. Instead, although they were in control for much of the game and looked like winners for a long time, a typically never-say-die, resourceful Offaly side got the scores that mattered.

Doubtful Mantle of Favourites

The following year Galway met Kilkenny in the semi-final in Thurles. They had not beaten the men in black-and-amber in the championship since 1953. The emergence of Galway as a hurling power in the 70s had been baulked by the Noresiders. Kilkenny had beaten them in the All-Irelands of 1975 and 1979; but that day in 1986 they pulled Kilkenny apart with an unorthodox ploy, using only two players in the full forward line while taking control of midfield with three players. After that very decisive victory they were installed as firm favourites against the team they had beaten in the previous year's semi-final, Cork.

But once again the doubtful mantle of favouritism did not sit well on the westerners' shoulders. An early goal by John Fenton of Midleton seemed to throw their well-honed hurling machine out of gear. Although both teams played well in a highly entertaining game, Galway never displayed their full force and went out to a skilful and determined Cork side.

'We don't want to be semi-final specialists and All-Ireland losers', said many of the Galway supporters who once again travelled in thousands from the west. They, like many neutral observers, now harboured doubts about a team of great drive and hurling ability which had failed the final test two years in a row.

'I hope this team hasn't gone off the boil, is on the way down rather than up', was often expressed from the faithful followers yearning for the success their team deserved.

Great Expectations

This doubt about Galway's quality was constantly voiced in Tipperary, where a great tidal wave of expectation and enthusiasm was beginning to build up for the game.

'Our fellows are hardened battlers by now — first match against Kerry, then the draw and replay against Clare, then the draw in Thurles against Cork and then the replay and extra time in Killarney. They're surely not going to go down to a Galway side that haven't had a serious game for ages and are after losing the last two All-Irelands.'

The celebrations in the villages and towns and countryside of Tipperary had gone on for days after the winning of the game in Killarney. The team and the cup had travelled the highways and byways, from crossroads beneath the Galtee mountains to the boglands about Littleton, to Keeper Hill in the north and the hilly country in the west, criss-crossing the rich plain drained by the river Suir. The streets echoed to cheers and paeons of praise for the men who had ended sixteen years of disappointment and frustration.

Tipperary had been so proud of its hurling prowess, the grit and courage of its menfolk, their skill with hurley and ball and their capacity to win big games. After sixteen years of failure and, sometimes, humiliation this deep pride was now fully re-awakened. To the flags that had followed the team round Munster were added a huge crop of new flags and streamers and car stickers which Tipperary folk intended to take with them to Dublin for the semi-final and final. Up to that time they had lost only one of the fourteen semi-finals in which they had participated — to Galway way back in 1924.

In all the recollections of days of dominance Tipperary had easily mastered Galway. They had met in the All-Ireland of 1958 when, due to an unwise administrative decision, the westerners were awarded a bye into the final. It was a one-sided affair. Many Tipperary followers did not even bother to go to it.

Micheal Keating, who had acted as advisor to the Galway team in 1979 and was now managing the Tipperary team, had no doubts about the western side's worth. He continually warned his charges not to listen to the endless babble about winning handily and going on to meet Kilkenny in the final.

'Don't forget they are league champions. They haven't come out of nowhere. They have experience of Croke Park on the big day — earned the hard way', Keating said. During his brief period as advisor to the Galway side he had stressed the need for the team to build up a strong self-belief and he was aware that the westerners under Cyril Farrell had done just that.

Pressures

Just the same the GAA correspondents of the national media, responsive to tradition, had begun to make the Munster champions favourites. This added to all the continuous pressure being put on the Tipperary players every day as they went about their daily lives.

'Everywhere fellows went — into a shop to buy a paper, at the job, everywhere they went — people came up and wished them well. You could not fail to see the longing in their faces that the team would beat

Galway and go on to win the All-Ireland', said Nicholas English, of whom so much was expected in terms of vital and inspirational scores.

The Galway team, training each evening in Athenry under the experienced eyes of team manager Cyril Farrell and selectors Phelim Murphy and Bernie O'Connor, knew of the predictions about the game being made outside the county.

'The reality was that Tipp could not have met us at a worse time, from their point of view. We were very aggressive, stung by the defeats of the two previous All-Irelands. We knew our way about Croke Park, knew what the atmosphere was like on the big occasion and knew how to handle it. Most important, we had a settled team — the six backs, the midfield and at least four of the forwards were part of a well-oiled unit', says Peter Finnerty, the All-Star right half back whose strong play was one of the features of the Galway side. He and Gerry McInerney, who had been working in the Bronx district of New York, flew home some weeks before to join their colleagues in training and give an immense boost to the side. This epitomised the kind of mobility that had become a feature of the travel-wise younger generation of hurlers.

The barometer of interest in a county team is the number who make their way to the training fields in the evenings to watch the players go through their paces, play backs and forwards or hone their hurling skills. In Athenry there was a now-traditional gathering along the sideline and the embankment. In Semple Stadium, Thurles the crowds were as big as at many a county game in the very near past. The years of failure had undoubtedly diminished the interest in the game in Tipperary. Now it was renewed with a vengeance.

When the teams were named a few days before the game there was intense discussion among the followers and in the county and national media.

They were picked from panels of dedicated players, all of whom made a contribution to the team and the game. Galway had players of the calibre of Noel Lane, P.J. Molloy and Pat Malone in the subs. Tipperary had on call players whose ability was as good as those named on the team, such as John McGrath and Michael Doyle.

Galway's Running Game

A lot of the pre-match discussion centred round individual duels between key players and also the clash of styles. Galway had been the principal proponents of what was referred to as the 'running game'. Only the full back line made long, sweeping pucks down the field in the 'running game'. Other players who got possession tried to keep the ball, run forward with it, wait until challenged and then pass to an unmarked colleague. It was a passing game, using hand or stick and it needed a lot of practice and team cohesion to make it work. It had worked for Galway in the defeats of Cork and Kilkenny in the semi-finals of 1985 and 1986. It was vulnerable to fast

Aidan Ryan and Colm Bonnar of Tipperary challenge Dermot McCurtain of Cork.

Munster final of 1987: The final whistle! Nicky English celebrates Tipperary's return.

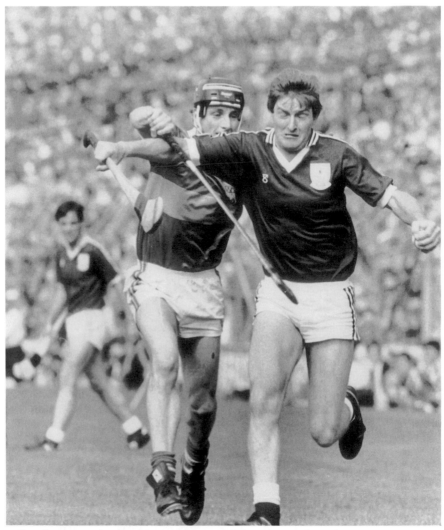

All-Ireland semi-final 1987: Noel Lane of Galway bursts through.

All-Ireland semi-final 1987: Nicholas English of Tipperary and Conor Hayes of Galway in hot pursuit.

The Galway team that defeated Tipperary in the All-Ireland semi-final of 1987 and went on to win the county's third title. Front row (*left to right*): Joe Cooney, Michael McGrath, Tony Kilkenny, Anthony Cunningham, Conor Hayes, Gerry McInerney, Sylvie Linnane, Eanna Ryan. Back row (*left to right*): Peter Finnerty, Steve Mahon, Brendan Lynskey, John Commins, Tony Keady, Martin Naughton, Ollie Kilkenny.

All-Ireland final 1990: Dermot Fahy of Galway and John Fitzgibbon of Cork.

The Cork team that beat Galway in the All-Ireland final of 1990. Front row (*left to right*): Tony O'Sullivan, Brendan O'Sullivan, Kieran McGuckin, Tomas Mulcahy, Kevin Hennessy, Sean McCarthy, Ger Fitzgerald, John Considine. Back row (*left to right*): Teddy McCarthy, John Fitzgibbon, Sean O'Gorman, Jim Cashman, Mark Foley, Ger Cunningham, Denis Walsh.

All-Ireland final 1990: Noel Lane of Galway and Denis Walsh of Cork.

All-Ireland final 1990: Sean Treacy of Galway and Kevin Hennessy of Cork locked in a strange embrace.

The Antrim team beaten by Kilkenny in the All-Ireland semi-final of 1991. Front row (*left to right*): Dessie Donnelly, Ciaran Barr, Dominic McKinley, Declan McKillop, Gary O'Kane, Donal Armstrong, Aidan McCarry. Back row (*left to right*): Terence McNaughton, Ger Rogan, James McNaughton, Pat Gallagher, Paul Jennings, Paul McKillen, James Close, John Carson.

The Kilkenny team that beat Antrim in the All-Ireland semi-final of 1991. Front row (*left to right*): Eddie O'Connor, D.J. Carey, Liam Walsh, Christy Heffernan, Michael Walsh, Bill Hennessy, Adrian Ronan, Liam McCarthy. Back row (*left to right*): Richie Power, Pat Dwyer, Michael Phelan, John Power, Liam Simpson, Eamon Morrissey, John Henderson.

All-Ireland semi-final 1991: Dominic McKinley of Antrim, Christy Heffernan of Kilkenny and Patrick Gallagher of Antrim.

All-Ireland semi-final 1991: Bill Hennessy of Kilkenny and Des Donnelly of Antrim.

This was the Tipperary team selected by Michael Keating, Donie Nealon and Theo English.

TIPPERARY

Ken Hogan
(Lorrha)

John Heffernan	Conor O'Donovan	Seamus Gibson
(Nenagh)	(Nenagh)	(Kilruane)
Richard Stakelum, capt	John Kennedy	Paul Delaney
(Borrisoleigh)	(Clonoulty-Rossmore)	(Roscrea)

Colm Bonnar   Joe Hayes
(Cashel)   (Clonoulty-Rossmore)

Martin McGrath	Donie O'Connell	Aidan Ryan
(Knockavilla)	(Killenaule)	(Borrisoleigh)
Pat Fox	Nicholas English	Bobby Ryan
(Annacarty)	(Lattin-Cullen)	(Borrisoleigh)

Substitutes: John McGrath (Borrisoleigh); Michael Doyle (Holycross); Pat Fitzelle (Cashel); Tony Sheppard (Kilruane); Gerry Williams (Kilruane); Noel Sheehy (Silvermines); Gerry Stapleton (Borrisoleigh). *Team manager*: Michael Keating. *Mentors*: Donie Nealon; Theo English. *Physiotherapist*: Emma Delahunty. *Masseur*: Ossie Bennett. *Medical officer*: Dr William Flannery.

The Galway trio of Farrell, Murphy and O'Connor named the following Galway team.

GALWAY

John Commins
(Gort)

Sylvie Linnane	Conor Hayes, capt	Ollie Kilkenny
(Gort)	(Kiltormer)	(Kiltormer)
Peter Finnerty	Tony Keady	Gerry McInerney
(Mullagh)	(Killimordaly)	(Kinvara)

Steve Mahon   Tony Kilkenny
(Beagh)   (Kiltormer)

Michael McGrath	Joe Cooney	Martin Naughton
(Sarsfields)	(Sarsfields)	(Turloughmore)
Eanna Ryan	Brendan Lynskey	Anthony Cunningham
(Killimordaly)	(Meelick-Eyrecourt)	(St Thomas)

Substitutes: Pat Malone (Oranmore-Maree); Noel Lane (Ballinderreen); P.J. Molloy (Athenry); Peter Murphy (Loughrea); Michael Earls (Killimordaly); Pearse Piggot (Gort); Pat Nolan (Castlegar). *Manager/coach*: Cyril Farrell (Tommy Larkins). *Selectors/mentors*: Phelim Murphy (Turloughmore); Bernie O'Connor (Oranmore-Maree); Tom Callanan (Kilconieron). *Team doctor*: Dr Michael McGloin. *Masseur*: Colm Flynn.

The referee was Gerry Kirwan of Offaly.

interception or to the ball being knocked off the stick of the player carrying it forward.

Tipperary's style was to let the ball do the work most of the time. They, too, could pass to one another and carry the ball but they favoured the crisp puck to send it quickly forward, especially into the full forward line where players of the talents of English and Fox were fast to the ball flying in.

'Will Conor Hayes be able to hold Nicholas English? Will Richard Stakelum continue to play an inspirational role? How will Galway's new-comer to the championship scene, Eanna Ryan, perform in his first game? Will Keady be able for the bustling ball-carrying style of O'Connell? How will Conor O'Donovan handle the aggressive strong man of the Galway side, Brendan Lynskey? Is corner forward the right position for Bobby Ryan?'

These questions were being asked in the days coming up to the game. They were part of the buzz of excitement in Croke Park as the packed spectators waited for the teams to emerge.

Emotional Scene

One of the loudest cheers ever heard in Croke Park greeted the men in blue and gold of Tipperary as they ran out onto the pitch from the corner of the Hogan Stand. It was an emotional moment for Tipperary hurling lovers to see their men swinging their hurleys, doing warm up exercises and hitting balls to one another to try to get the feel of scene that was new to all of them.

The cheer that greeted the familiar players of the Galway team was more subdued. Their followers had a hidden fear that this fine group of players might somehow let the game slip from them on the big occasion.

As referee Gerry Kirwan of Offaly prepared to start the game the atmos-phere was crackling with tension and excitement. Few actual finals could match it for colour and noise.

The smack of hurleys and a great exultant roar saw both sides go racing into the fray. Almost immediately a Tipperary hurley sent the ball in towards the full forward line. English came fleet-footed out to meet it, with the brown-helmeted Hayes pounding after him, determined not to let this dangerous artist take a run at goal. English controlled the ball beautifully and struck it neatly over the bar to a resounding roar from the Tipperary followers.

Blistering Goal

Tipp elation was not to last long. Almost from the puck out the workhorse of the Galway forwards, Lynskey, shouldered his way beneath the ball and made a brave catch. The Tipperary backs converged on this player, whose heavy build make it difficult to knock him off the ball or knock him over. Lynskey, who had great vision, waited until Stakelum, the tall red-haired

Tipperary captain, was beside him and then deftly handpassed the ball out to the man Stakelum was marking, Martin Naughton. The Turloughmore player, 25 metres out sent in a blistering shot that went to the left of Ken Hogan and into the net.

This score and the manner in which it came about was a blow to Tipperary so early in the game. 'Mark your men, for God's sake — don't all go jumping on top of Lynskey if he gets the ball', shouted an angry Tipp fan from the stands.

'A more selfish player than Stakelum would have marked his own man. Instead of that he went to the aid of a colleague in trouble', said Michael Keating, whose admiration for the Tipperary captain is undiminished.

If the goal was a bad start for Tipperary it seemed to act as a signal for the speedy, skilful Galway attack to go into action. On their left wing, the goal scorer, the fast running Naughton, outpaced the Tipperary captain, whose long legs had suffered a succession of injuries which slowed him down. But it was the right wing of the Galway attack that was most lethal. Michael McGrath gathered and ran and struck with style, often sending the ball neatly ahead to Eanna Ryan. Showing no sign of nerves, the newcomer to the Galway team gave such an exhibition of controlled stickwork, keen positional play, astute linking with colleagues and accurate striking that people began to ask why he had not been on the team the previous two years.

It was the speed of the attack which the Tipperary backs found so difficult to handle. Cunningham, in the opposite corner to Ryan, gathered and ran with determination. Joe Cooney was getting the better of John Kennedy, who was slow to settle down. Conor O'Donovan kept Lynskey under some control but all in all this was an exhibition of attacking play rarely seen in any game. After seven minutes Galway were 1–4 to a point ahead.

There was no question that this spirited Tipperary team, who were used to fighting their way back into games, were going to be swept away. They were not in the least overawed by the occasion, nor did they freeze under the pressure. They matched Galway in fire and vigour and skill.

Duels Around The Field

At centrefield Colm Bonnar and Joe Hayes stuck to their task with great determination. There was a battle royal with the Galway duo of Mahon and Kilkenny. There was little between them but Bonnar chased and struck a lot of ball while Mahon, the big man from Beagh, used all his experience to win enough ball for Galway.

Donie O'Connell was proving a handful for Tony Keady. The Killimordaly player, one of the great centre halfs of modern times, was accustomed to commanding the ball, bursting out of defence with shoulder power and sending long attacking clearances down into the opponents' goalmouth or, on occasion, over the bar. In this game his work was cut out trying to baulk O'Connell, who grabbed many balls and rounded his man, heading for goal.

McInerney held his end up against Martin McGrath but the Tipperary man was dangerous, he had scored many good points in previous games. McInerney's characteristic incursions into the half-forward line were effectively curbed.

However, the star of the Galway defence proved to be Peter Finnerty who played a storming game, using skill and weight, in control of his patch of ground from start to finish of the game.

His prowess was to prove invaluable as Tipperary grew in strength and put scores on the board.

Almost A Goal

The man who was doing most to keep Tipperary fully in the game was Nicholas English. The close marking of a full back of the calibre of Hayes showed just how good a player the Lattin-Cullen schoolteacher was. He was forced to run far out from goal to collect incoming balls. But he hit them with cool accuracy, left and right, under great pressure and each of them raised a great cheer from the Tipperary followers.

In one nerve-wracking incident he cleverly blocked down a clearance by Commins, who had run out of goal. The ball came back to him and he struck it along the ground. The redoubtable Finnerty, knowing the goalmouth was unguarded behind him, dropped quickly onto his knees to block the dangerously wobbling ball and scooped it over the endline for a 65.

Fighting hard to come on terms, Tipperary began a series of attacks. Martin McGrath scored two points and Aidan Ryan, for once eluding the attentions of Finnerty, scored another. Eanna Ryan and Anthony Cunningham scored two for Galway. After 26 minutes Galway were seven points clear.

Then came a crucial penalty for Tipperary. It arose because Galway knew well that a goal scored by English would have an immense bearing on the game. It was the reason Hayes stayed behind him at all times even when it meant a point for Tipperary. On this occasion the ball came in to English in the form of a pass from Donie O'Connell. He was crowded out by the Galway backs, who gave him no room to move. The referee judged that he had been fouled in the square. Pat Fox, who was getting little leeway from Ollie Kilkenny in the corner came forward to take the penalty.

Fox's Penalty

Peter Finnerty, who faced the powerful left-hander describes the shot. 'It was a very good penalty. He hit it hard, bouncing it off the ground ten metres out. The ground was hard as a road and the ball flew up — a very difficult type of ball to deal with. It went off John Commins's hurley into the roof of the net.'

Just on the 35 minutes Steve Mahon sent a soaring long-range point over from centrefield. It was to be a sign that he would play a thundering second half and score two more vital points. When the half-time whistle blew the score stood at Galway 1–13 to Tipperary's 1–9.

The Munster champions were not at all displeased with their performance after the bad start and the quality of their opponents' hurling. They had had to do a lot of hurling to stay in the game but it was unlikely that the Galway forward machine could operate so effectively in the second half.

The Tipp mentors had taken off Seamus Gibson, who found the scintillating Eanna Ryan more than a speedy, tricky handful. They brought back the reliable Bobby Ryan from the forward line to mark his namesake and brought on John McGrath to take his place in the forwards. Though he had been playing well, Tony Kilkenny was replaced by Pat Malone of Oranmore-Maree.

There was a great babble of sound round the ground. The spectators were exhilarated by the end-to-end play, the duels, the goalmouth incidents, and the marvellous show of skills from so many players. Nobody could say how the game might go for the second 35 minutes. In the heart-stopping replay of the Munster final in Killarney, Tipperary had also got off to a bad start but were within striking distance at half time and eventually won the marathon tie. 'We're used to being behind at half time — it's nothing new', said one happy supporter.

Tipperary Power

Tipperary started the second half with a great surge of determination and power. Donie O'Connell rounded Keady and sent over a point. Aidan Ryan added another. Now the Tipperary forwards were beginning to come into their own. Pat Fox had come out to the wing and although he was now being marked by Gerry McInerney he was revelling in the greater freedom. Tipperary pressure resulted in a 65. Paul Delaney, playing a good game despite his difficulties with Michael McGrath, struck it with great precision and sent it over the bar.

The score now stood at 1–13 to 1–12 and the Tipperary followers were creating great waves of sound to encourage their men. Two Galway wides by Mahon and McGrath from scorable positions made the western contingent frustrated and uneasy. They hated to think that the old squandermania might return. But Eanna Ryan then struck a beautiful ball from out on the sideline. It floated accurately between the posts for a score as worthy as any of English's.

Tipperary were carrying the game to Galway. But now came one of the key misses of the game. Martin McGrath took advantage of a rare miscalculation by Sylvie Linnane who was playing a sound game in the corner. The Tipperary forward came racing goalwards but lost control of the ball and had no option but to pull on it as it bounced. Just the same he nearly scored what would have been a crucial goal. His shot hit the upright and bounced outfield and was cleared away. Michael Doyle replaced him shortly afterwards.

The other McGrath on the Tipp team, John, had the agony of seeing two good efforts at points swing away from the posts. And another Donie O'Connell raid ended in a half-hit shot going straight into the very safe hands of Commins. Joe Hayes however, with a fine long-distance effort, reduced the Galway lead to a single point.

Some Tipperary followers felt that their side was throwing the game away with these misses at the very time when they were on top in many parts of the field. But the game was so fast that there was hardly time to think, to swing the stick. On the dry sod the ball whizzed about. The bodily clashes were bone-crunching. Perspiration darkened the jerseys of the players. And no player got more than a few seconds to get sight of the goal before a marker was crunching in to him. Moreover, the Galway backs, especially Finnerty, were able to reduce the effectiveness of the flying Tipp forwards. Their All-Ireland experience was standing well to the westerners. They kept their composure under the growing pressure. They added two points, including another long-range effort from Mahon.

Fox Goal

For all that it seemed only a matter of time before the brilliantly playing Tipp side would take the lead. It happened in the 21st minute when Pat Fox gathered the ball, rounded Gerry McInerney and went galloping goalwards. McInerney recovered and chased after him, hurley held out to make the hook. But Fox's unorthodox swing, close to the body, was never easy to hook. He let fly and the ball zipped into the net.

When the umpire raised the green flag and the scoreboard changed to show Tipperary now gone ahead for the first time since the first minute the stands and terraces bloomed with blue and gold flags. The starved Tipperary followers sensed now that their battle-hardened team could take the match. The score now stood at 2–14 to 1–16 in favour of the Munstermen.

By this time both sides had made strategic switches and counter-switches to try to get the better of their opponents as well as to replace injury-hit players. Michael Doyle, saviour of Tipp in the Killarney replay, had come on in place of Martin McGrath. A really significant substitution for Galway was that of Noel Lane, the vastly experienced Ballinderreen player, for the injured Michael McGrath.

After Tipperary's great goal the puck out was returned to the Galway half. There English, now operating on the wing, got it in his hand and scored the finest and most telling of the six gems he scored that day.

Galway Grit

This was when Galway's grit and burning determination was put to the test. They looked a little uneasy but they put all they had into the great fray. Even neutrals in the crowd, who had come to see a good game, were caught up in the second by second thrills and spills. The followers of both sides were going into states of hoarse, voiceless exhaustion.

One of the key factors in Tipperary's resurgence was the way John Kennedy at centre back took control and began to outplay Joe Cooney. Despite the fact that he was on one of the most incisive stick-artists in the game, he caught and cleared balls with great style, putting Tipp on the attack several times.

At this juncture the Galway mentors made a crucial switch. Cooney and Lynskey changed places. Lynskey was the most aggressive challenger for the dropping ball and Kennedy's freedom of movement would now be severely curtailed.

Galway, giving their utmost, came back into the game. They attacked again and forced a free. Joe Cooney pointed it. Then Steve Mahon, who was always good for several points from the centre of the field, flighted one over the bar to bring the sides level again.

Turning Point

What many observers and most Tipperary followers saw as the turning point of the game came shortly afterwards, in the 61st minute. The ball came into the Galway goalmouth and was caught safely by Commins, who had dispelled all doubts about his ability during the course of the game. He cleared it out but the ever vigilant English snapped it up. Even as he swung to send it over for another point the whistle sounded. John McGrath of Tipperary had come running in on Commins and made a somewhat innocuous lunge at the Galway goalkeeper well after he had cleared the ball. Referee Kirwan saw it as a late tackle and awarded a free out, to the dismay of the Tipperary followers who had been cheering for English's disallowed point.

Conor Hayes came over to take the free. A big heavy man, he had one of the longest pucks in the game. He lifted the ball perfectly, swung powerfully on it, and hit it with the sweet spot on the boss of his hurley. The ball took off into the sky, soaring high and travelling far and fast. Fifty thousand pairs of eyes watched it reach its highest point, well into the Tipperary half and then drop down towards the 40-metre area. There, waiting, the jostling, hurley-brandishing bunch of players began to compete for the ball while it was still falling. Lynskey and Kennedy were amongst them, shouldering one another.

Amidst flailing, finger-breaking hurleys Lynskey put up his large right hand and caught the ball as it came down. He absorbed shoulder charges and elbows. He turned and saw Eanna Ryan running parallel to him. Ryan took Lynskey's pass and as Ken Hogan came out to challenge, hand-passed the ball into the net.

This was a turning point in the game. Instead of leading by a point, as might have been the case, Tipperary found themselves a goal behind.

Then Anthony Cunningham managed to escape the vigilant attentions of the sound John Heffernan, raced along near the end line and sent over a point for Galway. It looked like Galway's game.

But Tipperary were far from finished. The unstoppable English once again got possession and hit the ball sweetly for a point. O'Connell, playing very well, got through also and scored another point to leave just two points between the sides as the final whistle neared.

Tipperary swept back for another attack and the ball went narrowly wide of the posts as Tipperary supporters cheered for what they thought was a point. With nerves of players and spectators strung taut, the Tipperary players hurled the ball up the field again. This time the Galway backs cleared the ball back down into the Tipperary half.

P.J. Molloy, the Athenry veteran, who had come on in place of the injured Martin Naughton, combined with Cunningham and then Ryan to send the ball towards Noel Lane. The lithe Ballinderreen man whipped the ball past Ken Hogan for a clinching goal.

It was a cruel twist of fate for Tipperary who had seemed to be on the brink of winning the game. Joe Cooney closed the scoring with a point just before the final whistle.

It had been a tough but sporting game and the players shook hands, congratulated and commiserated. The Galway team knew all about losing as well as winning. This fine match ended with the scoreline at 3–20 for Galway to 2–17 for Tipperary. It did not reflect the closeness of the game or how near Tipperary had been to taking it.

This was a game in which all the players gave of their best and in which many hurled very well, including substitutes and those who had been substituted. Competitive as it was, good players were allowed enough leeway to express their abilities and energies on the field of play. There was a good feeling about this game among the players, though it took some days for the Tipp team to accept just how much they had contributed to this memorable occasion.

There was great disappointment among the exhausted Tipperary throng that their side had come to the end of a great crusade to capture the All-Ireland after such a long lapse. But, as Michael Keating said in the dressing-room, 'All-Irelands do not come in the post.'

On reflection, many of the Tipperary players and followers saw that their side had given the game of hurling a tremendous boost during the year, recapturing the Munster crown after two truly enthralling matches with Cork. They had lost to Galway but their pride had been restored. They were not going to go away or go out tamely in the years ahead.

'The two games against Cork — and the extra time in the replay — drained that team', says Michael Keating. 'When we resumed training after the Munster final, with little time to get ready for the Galway game I said to Donie Nealon and Theo English "This team is stone dead with all the effort." If I had the courage and confidence then that I have now I would have taken them all to a remote hotel for the weekend, let them unwind in the swimming pool or the golf course, away from all the hype.'

The Galway side, relieved to be over this dangerous encounter, were hugely encouraged by this victory. They knew they had met and mastered a great side which had some outstanding players and was very astutely managed.

From that game they went on to their third All-Ireland appearance in a row. This time, after a dour and bruising battle with Kilkenny, they took the crown they so richly deserved. They were to meet and again beat Tipperary in the final of the following year and a great rivalry developed between them.

The year after that again, 1989, it was Tipperary's turn to beat the westerners in the semi-final and go on to meet and beat Antrim in the final and win their first crown in seventeen years.

Of all the matches between these two great sides over a period of four years the semi-final of 1987 was hard to match for excitement, endeavour, great skill and a nail-biting finish.

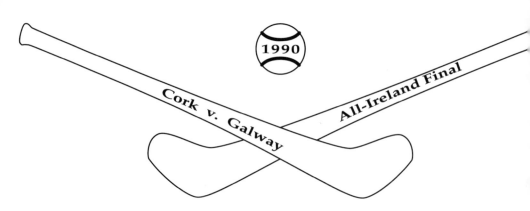
1990
Cork v. Galway
All-Ireland Final

THE RIP-ROARING FINAL OF 1990

As the huge mass of people dispersed along the streets and roadways leading away from Croke Park on that hot September evening the noise was like that of a myriad swarm of bees. One of the most exciting, incident-lively finals over a twenty-year period had taken place. It could justifiably be compared with the great finals of 1972 and 1976, in which Cork had also competed.

The animated conversations along the streets, in the crowded, sweating bars, in cars and buses and trains on the way out of the city reflected the differing emotions aroused by a thrilling encounter between Cork and Galway.

This game had so many facets, provided so much to discuss and argue about afterwards. It had everything. It had a total of 7 goals and 36 points, some of them of exceptional quality, some bizarre, many unexpected. It had some extraordinary misses as well, heart-stopping for the supporters. There were displays of truly great hurling, of courage and of stamina. The most memorable thing about this final was the astonishing comeback by Cork in the last quarter of the game, after they had been outplayed for most of the game and seemed about to be well beaten.

It was not alone a battle between two teams with game-hardened players as well as newcomers to the All-Ireland scene, but between the managers and mentors from both sides. Then there were controversial incidents, some of them affecting what might have been crucial scores.

Cork were a side that seemed to come from nowhere that year. They had been written-off at the start of the championship. They proved that year that the county has such a rich store of hurlers that, with good organisation and astute management, a team can always be put together that is capable of winning an All-Ireland.

For Galway this game marked the end of an era of great endeavour. Many of the team had contested four All-Irelands in a row in the 1980s, losing two and winning two, being narrowly beaten in 1989 in the semi-final and now making a great effort to avenge the All-Ireland defeat of 1986 by Cork and to begin the new decade on the same high note that had marked the start of the '80s.

This was an extraordinary game of mixed fortunes. At one stage Cork seemed only to be hanging on, on the brink of a crushing defeat. Yet they powered back into the game in an astonishing reversal of strength. There were heroic displays by players on both sides, memorable performances. In the first half the Galway captain, Joe Cooney, gave an exhibition of forceful centre-forward play. In the second half the massive puck outs of the Cork goalkeeper, Ger Cunningham, were crucial to the eventual victory of his side.

Celebration and Regret

There were exuberant celebrations in the Cork camp and among the supporters when this game ended. The joy and emotion was all the more because it seemed that the game was well out of reach for much of the time. It was a triumph of spirit and skill over adversity.

For Galway the aftermath was a time of agonising at what might have been, of soul searching. This was a game that could have been won and that wasn't. It was a match where the westerners were on top for so long yet ended up losing. There were recriminations. Some players were blamed for their performances. The sideline mentors were blamed also for not reading the signs quickly enough and not taking decisive action.

The speed of the play and the controversial incidents raised again the point whether one man, one referee, can be expected to do justice to the game, to the players and to himself when the ball is flying within seconds from one end of the field to another.

When the referee, John Moore from Waterford, blew the final whistle the Cork supporters were radiant and proud. The Galway supporters were frustrated and angry, not in the least consoled that they had seen one of the best finals in twenty years. Those waving the red and white banners were fired by a fierce pride in a county that never lacked skilful hurlers and an indomitable spirit of combat, most especially when they were cast in the role of underdogs by the commentators.

Among the Galway followers there was a numb feeling of bitter disappointment. Despite being the leading hurling team of the past decade they had not shaken off a bad habit of losing games that seemed there for the taking.

Outsiders and Favourites

Cork started the campaign as outsiders. From 1982 until 1986 they had dominated Munster hurling. Then came the resurgence of Tipperary in

1987 after a long absence in the hurling wilderness. They had beaten Cork after two tremendous games to wrest the Munster title from a team going for its sixth provincial crown in a row.

The following year Tipperary met Cork in another Munster final and beat them well. In 1989 Cork were beaten by a very moderate Waterford in the first round of the championship. There was a feeling that the Leesiders might be in for a protracted period of playing second fiddle to a great Tipperary side and that it might be a fair number of years before they could expect to make it to the final in Croke Park.

Even if they got to a final there was one other team that they would find very hard to beat — Galway. The westerners possessed a team of many talents and much experience, one that had shown tremendous grit and resilience to come back from the devastation to losing two finals in a row to contesting and winning the next two very convincingly. In 1989, deprived of their outstanding centre back, Tony Keady, because of his suspension and down to thirteen men in the closing stages of the semi-final against Tipperary, they gave a display of the kind of resourceful hurling that only comes from vast experience and time-hardened resolve; only the width of the cross bar stopped them winning in the last few minutes. After that game the westerners were determined to power their way to another All-Ireland and win it.

McCarthy and O'Brien

One of the most important factors for the Cork side was the selection as coach, in late 1989, of a tough-minded man who understood all the facets of motivation and encouragement, Father Michael O'Brien, parish priest of Carrigaline. He had much experience of training teams and of the game itself. He had trained Farranferris college to four Harty Cup wins and Blackrock to a county championship. He saw his appointment as a challenge to ensure that the county would put forward its best team.

This white-haired middle-aged man was determined that the team would be fully fit physically and mentally. More than many team managers he made it his business to develop a keen understanding of human nature, of character and personality. He knew players give their all when they are in the right frame of mind, coming from a team environment where their strengths are appreciated and their vulnerabilities understood. He was determined to get to know the players well and to bring out the best in each of them. He knew when to be kind and when to stamp his authority in no uncertain manner.

Another key person, who had charge of team training, was Gerald McCarthy. He was an astute judge of a hurler's skills and temperament, a great reader of the ebb and flow of a game, a man who could see quickly where a game was being lost and won. He had several years experience as trainer with the Cork senior team. More than that he could draw on his own long career as one of the outstanding players of the era, captain of the 1966 team, winning more All-Ireland medals in 1970, '76, '77, '78. McCarthy, so fiercely competitive on the field, with his thick hair, aggressive moustache and glistening blue eyes, was full of good nature and good humour off it. He played a key role in setting the tone in which the team of 1990 was to train and plan and play.

O'Brien and McCarthy were well supported by game-wise selectors in Denis Hurley, Martin Coleman, goalkeeper on the the three-in-a row 1970s side, Frank Murphy, the county secretary, and Liam Ó Tuama.

At the end of 1989 and the start of 1990 these men set out to select and mould a side that would give a good account of themselves in the championship. None of them made any claims that the side would win the Munster championship, let alone take the All-Ireland title.

Galway Angry at '89

A rather different mood prevailed in the Galway camp at the start of the year. The semi-final defeat by Tipperary had been a searing experience. This had been so because in the previous two years Galway had finally proved that they were far and away the best team in the country by, for the first time, winning two finals back to back. It was no more than a great team deserved. Under the inspirational leadership of their manager, Cyril Farrell, they had overcome all the mental and emotional scars of losing two in a row and gone on to beat Kilkenny in 1987 and Tipperary the following year. They had to overcome great pressures to make this kind of comeback.

Having proved their point that team had badly wanted to put Galway hurling into the record books by keeping their title in 1989.

Not long before the semi-final with Tipperary the county was hit by a bombshell. Tony Keady, their star centre back, was suspended for playing illegally in the US. This caused consternation in the county and the team, for the Killimordaly man, so competent and solid, had been the sheet anchor of the back division in the two All-Ireland campaigns.

All the appeals to the GAA authorities, fueled by a feeling that Keady was being victimised for being merely foolish rather than wantonly disregarding the rules, only served to engender a corrosive bitterness among hurling followers in the county. Some of this spread to the training camp, affecting the mental attitude of the players and mentors. It proved to have a disruptive influence on the training programme.

This came to the surface in the semi-final of 1989. Galway had beaten Tipperary the previous two years, had been the barrier between the new Munster champions and their dream of taking the county's first All-Ireland since 1971. The rivalry between the two teams had been tuned up to an intense pitch, with a certain acrimony now not far beneath the surface. The Keady affair did not help Galway to approach the game in a calmly resolute state of mind.

Another factor added to the tension. In the first match of the double-header that Sunday the Ulster champions, Antrim, had scored a well-merited but unexpected victory over the Leinster champions, Offaly. Despite the obvious quality of the northern side many in the crowd of over 60,000 felt that the winners of the Galway-Tipperary game had the All-Ireland there for the taking.

Most Galway followers and many neutral observers felt that the referee, John Denton of Wexford, had been unduly harsh in sending off Sylvie Linnane and Michael McGrath. Denton maintained that he had to be very firm in order to keep a tension-crackling and sometimes bad-tempered game from boiling over. It was a sad end to the inter-county career of one of the most skilful, hard-tackling characters in the game, Linnane. The controversy and the cascade of criticism also effectively ended Denton's chances of refereeing an All-Ireland final, something this decent man would dearly love to have done.

After that defeat the Galway side hurled indifferently. They seemed to have lost heart. They played badly in the league, lost game after game and were relegated to the second division at the end of it all.

Revival of Spirits

It was only when the league was over that Cyril Farrell and his colleagues Phelim Murphy and Bernie O'Connor began to motivate the team to make a resounding impact on the championship once again. The ardent love of hurling in the county engendered a feeling that there was another All-Ireland in this fine team and that they should go for it.

They got down to training after the league was over and a spirit of grim resolve began to take hold of the side. They were missing two of the great performers of the past, Sylvie Linnane and Steve Mahon, one of the most under-rated midfielders who had battled valiantly for years against the serious knee injury which eventually hastened his retirement. There were two other players from the immediate past who were no longer on the first fifteen but were on the panel — Conor Hayes and Brendan Lynskey — and even at an early stage there was much comment in Galway about whether players of their proven calibre should be relegated to the subs.

A very vigorous programme of physical training began under the supervision of Cyril Farrell, one of the influential personalities to emerge on the hurling scene in Galway. He had an aura of success about him, had been one of those who had set about breaking the losing tradition in the western county. He had coached the All-Ireland winning under-21 team in 1978. Then with Bernie O'Connor and M.J. Flaherty he had steered the senior team to its first victory in 57 years in the final of 1980 against Limerick.

Some of the power potential of the Galway side, full of All-Ireland medalists, was seen on 22 July when, in the quarter-final they met a London side at Ballinasloe. Gone were the days when the westerners were in danger of being beaten by London, as indeed they had been on one inglorious occasion in the early '70s. They won on a scoreline of 1– 23 to 2–11.

The real test of their worth was to come a fortnight later when, in the semi-final they met their old bogey team, Offaly. Their midland adversaries still had men who had beaten them in 1985 in the All-Ireland. So before that game there were many who said that Offaly, now with a reputation of tremendous spirit, might well beat their neighbours from across the Shannon.

However, this Galway side played strong hurling that Sunday. They were brisk and efficient in everything they did. Their half-back line, one of the best ever to adorn any team — Peter Finnerty, Tony Keady and Gerry McInerney — were hard to pass. A newcomer to the senior team, Dermot Fahy from Ardrahan, played well in his first semi-final. The forwards, led by the captain, Joe Cooney, showed verve and control in getting decisive scores. The westerners were far better than their six point victory might indicate. The final score was Galway 1–16 to 2–7 for Offaly. In the other semi-final Cork had to contend with a sturdy Antrim side that played the ball well along the ground. Cork got the better of the northerners in the last quarter and won by seven points. But they were not anything as impressive as Galway. That evening the westerners were already being installed as favourites — an ominous sign for a team that had never done well in that role.

Shaky Start to Year

Under its new coach the Cork team had shaped itself into an effective team. It was a blend of experienced players, several from the last All-Ireland winning side, many who had come up through the successful minor and under-21 county teams. From the start of the year each game seemed to see some improvement in the way they set about playing. It was no surprise that they reached the semi-final of the National League where their opponents were Wexford. An unspectacular game suddenly came to life near the end when both sides raced to the finishing line. It ended in a draw.

The replay proved to be a dismal affair for this Cork team. They were well beaten by a Wexford side that was anything but impressive. Only one of their forwards, a tall newcomer called Mark Foley, managed to get a score that day.

That league defeat seemed to many to indicate that this team had a long way to go before it would make any real impression on the championship scene. When the championship began Cork were regarded as outsiders.

Good Championship Campaign

Their first championship encounter was when they took on Kerry in the semi-final. The Kerry side, picked mostly from the small enclave of hurling on the good farmlands of the northern plain, were not up to the standard of skill and game-wisdom of the Cork team and were beaten by seven points. The most heartening aspect of this Cork side was the performance of players who were either new to the side or had been round the fringes in the past: Sean O'Gorman, a 30-year-old school principal from Miltown; Brendan O'Sullivan from an almost unknown club, Valley Rovers; and Kieran McGuckin of Glen Rovers.

Something of the new vibrancy of this Cork side and its well organised teamsmanship was seen in the next round when they met their conquerers of the previous year, Waterford. They won very convincingly on a score-line of 4–15 to 1–8. Yet, as the prospect of another clash with Tipperary approached, Cork were not really given much chance.

For the first time in years — since 1965 in fact — Tipperary were contesting the Munster final as the reigning All-Ireland champions. They were a star-studded outfit with players like Nicky English, Pat Fox, John Leahy and Paul Delaney in their ranks. They had had to strive hard over the past three years. Having at last won out in Munster in 1987 they had to haul themselves back after being beaten by Galway in one of the great semi-finals of modern times. They were back again in 1988 only to meet their arch rivals from the west in the final and again be beaten by them. Only in 1989 did they finally take the All-Ireland title after an absence of 18 years. Everybody knew they would not easily be beaten and many felt they would win rather easily.

Great Munster Surprise

That Sunday of the Munster final there were many Tipperary followers seated comfortably and confidently in the stands, looking forward to seeing their side winning rather than wanting to watch an exciting neck and neck contest. There was a certain air of relaxation about that occasion as distinct from the high-strung tension of 1984 and 1987.

Yet, as soon as the ball was thrown in, it became apparent that here was a Cork team full of fire and the most extraordinary vigour. They contested each ball as if their lives depended on the outcome. Their half backs — McCarthy, Cashman and McGuckin — pulled with great skill and confidence on every ball, clearing them away quickly. Their forwards, including the tall Foley, whom many had not seen in action before, and Tony O'Sullivan began to look very dangerous. The roar of the crowd got louder and louder as the spectators realised that this pell-mell game belonged among the best provincial finals of the previous twenty-five years.

Cork's zest and skill gave them an unexpected upper hand in the opening quarter. After eleven minutes they were ahead by three points to one, with forwards like Fitzgibbon and Fitzgerald creating real problems for the experienced Tipp rearguard.

In the second quarter Tipperary began to get a grip on the game. In the 27th minute Michael Cleary of Nenagh hit a fine shot to the net. A minute later John Leahy put Tipperary in front for the first time with a point. Not long after, English pulled deftly overhead on a ball in front of goal and sent it whistling to the net. Almost on the call of full time the champions looked well in control, almost against the run of the intensity of Cork's play, on a scoreline of 2–5 to 6 points.

Then Cork were awarded a sideline ball on the left of their attack, facing into the Tipp goal at the Killinan end of Semple Stadium. Kieran McGuckin took it, cleaving down and under the ball, sending it into a long, soaring trajectory. As it came down just outside the square, the tall Mark Foley made a great overhead pull, higher by feet than the nearest Tipp hurley. He met the ball perfectly and it sped into the goal. This was a crucial score. Just when the game seemed to be going away from them despite all their efforts Cork were back in, only two points behind as the half time whistle blew. As the teams left the field there was a great buzz of excitement and exhilaration from the big crowd.

In the second half Cork got off to a great start with two great points from Tony O'Sullivan, a player of elegant, elusive footwork and finely-tuned striking ability. The intensity of their challenging was a thrilling spectacle as they went hell for leather after the champions. John Fitzgibbon, who was to come to the fore that year as a goal-getter of exceptional ability, helped to put the challengers ahead with a fastly whipped goal.

Cork were ahead by six points with twenty minutes to go. However, Tipperary brought on Colm Bonnar at midfield and the champions began to haul themselves back into the game with a great effort which had the crowd cheering continuously. With eight minutes to go Cork were hanging on tenaciously to a one point lead. Then Foley scored a point, followed by a goal. Tipperary, seeing their crown now definitely slipping, made desperate efforts to get the better of their high-flying opponents. However, the Cork rearguard held out very effectively and the game ended when Fitzgibbon got the ball, took it on his stick, went racing goalward and hit a fine goal just as he was being challenged.

When the final whistle went, a great cheer of exhilaration went up from the Cork supporters and indeed some of the players. Zest and spirit, allied to skill and organisation, had won the day for them against all the betting. The pitch, the streets, the pubs, the roadways home were full of fast-spoken Cork accents, recounting all the incidents of a truly exciting game. Cork pride was flowering at its fullest.

Still Unfancied

Why the Leesiders should not have been made favourites to win the All-Ireland there and then is hard to understand. Perhaps it was that in the semi-final against Antrim they were well held until the third quarter. The traditonalists of the game decreed that Antrim must always be beaten by a huge score, beaten without any one of the big guns of the hurling armoury having to go into the 'continuous firing' mode. When Cork were unable to be totally dominant over a hardened, hard-tackling northern side, some people felt that they might have played their major game against Tipperary. Another reason may have been the fact that they seemed to have come from nowhere that year with quite a few players new to the championship pressures.

Galway displayed their great power and experience in the other semi-final against their old adversaries, Offaly. They showed why they were considered the great team of the 1980s — fast forward play, an outstanding half back line, and Michael Coleman at midfield emerging as one of the strongest players on the scene. Commentators said they would have won much more easily were it not for hesitancy in the full back line, where the experience of Linnane and Hayes was missed. Yet overall this was a strong display and for that reason the westerners were made favourites to take the title from Cork.

Galway were anything but comfortable with the title of favourites. Against Cork in the final of 1986 they had run out onto the field as odds-on winners. Everyone expected them to win, with their experience and their talent and drive. The same atmosphere had prevailed in 1981 when they were All-Ireland champions and Offaly were given little hope against them. On each occasion they were beaten.

Score to Settle

The survivors of the 1986 debacle, the mentors and followers felt that there was a score to settle with Cork. This Galway side had beaten Tipperary and Kilkenny in All-Ireland finals but never Cork. There was a feeling that they would have to do so if they were to be properly acclaimed as the team of the decade.

There was also the nagging feeling that the team could have made it three-in-a-row were it not for the suspension of Tony Keady the previous year. Keady was now back, hurling with his customary command and the great understanding he had developed with McInerney and Finnerty.

'In past years when the ball was heavier and had bigger rims, the puck outs did not go much further than midfield', explained Donie Nealon, the former Tipperary star and latter-day mentor. 'Then there was a lot of play at midfield and the quality of the midfielders was very important. But with the new, lighter ball the puck outs usually go into the half-back line and there are crucial duels there. No team will get anywhere today without a good half back line. '

Cork Backs

When the followers and commentators began to assess the strengths and merits of the two sides they acknowledged the great vigour and competence of the Cork backs.

The Cork full back line had performed well in the championship. John Considine, who had made his senior debut on the team that year, had been assigned the very difficult task of marking one of the most skilful, clever opportunists of all time, Nicky English, in the Munster final. The Sarsfields man had performed very well despite the tension, the noise of the vast crowd, the thousands of pairs of eyes scrutinising every puck of the ball as it flew about.

At full back was one of the most outstanding athletes on the Cork team, Denis Walsh. He had been on the side which beat Galway in 1986. Equally talented as a footballer, he had won a football All-Ireland medal in 1989 and was in the Cork squad contesting the 1990 final against Meath later in September. In the other corner was the tall, slim Sean O'Gorman who had come to the fore several years before but had been on the periphery of the senior side until this year. He had showed a great sense of positional play, tremendous skill and verve in all the games of the 1990 champioship that Cork followers regretted that he had come so late on to the senior team, playing in his first All-Ireland at the age of 30.

At right wing back was the left-hander Sean McCarthy, a stocky, forceful player from one of the lesser-known clubs, Ballinhassig. He was a player who had had to work and to train hard to get a place on the Cork side, training alone over the previous winter months, going to a gymnasium three or four nights a week. This kind of disciplined determination showed in his game — crisp ground strokes, fast to the ball, and every now and then long, long clearances off his left side, some of which went all the way over the bar.

In the centre was Jim Cashman of Blackrock, tall, fair-haired and one of the most accomplished players on the side. He seemed to gain possession easily, then hit the ball quickly, close to his body in the manner of his brother Tom, who had also manned this pivotal position.

On the left wing was Kieran McGuckin. This was his first year on the team and his first All-Ireland but, like several of his colleagues he had won minor and under-21 All-Ireland medals and he was unlikely to be overwhelmed by the occasion. In the Munster final his tigerish marking and lightning sharp reflexes had done a good deal to frustrate Tipperary attacks.

Centrefield and Attack

At centrefield Cork had two very strong players, who challenged with great vigour for every ball, Teddy McCarthy and Brendan O'Sullivan. McCarthy was also on the senior football side, a muscular player who used some of his footballing skills on the hurling field. He knew how to use his weight. His most spectacular feat was the way he ran forward, rose into the air, reached up and caught the dropping ball. His colleague at midfield, O'Sullivan, was a sturdy workhorse who covered a lot of ground and was able to gain regular possession and burst away from opponents to send the ball into the forwards.

In the centre of the Cork attack was a player who had come into his own in his first Munster final, Mark Foley. He was 6 ft 5 ins and 14 stone in weight; a commanding figure not easily knocked off the ball, a man good on the overhead pull. With 2–7 scored against Tipperary he was considered one of the trump cards of the side, someone who would give Galway's Tony Keady a difficult time.

At right half forward was the tall, rangy Ger Fitzgerald. He was one of the key players who powered his club, Midleton, to success in the fiercely competitive Cork championship. He had been one of the best forwards on Cork teams since he won his All-Ireland medal in 1986. Fitzgerald was a very astute reader of the game, a great opportunist who made sudden darts with the ball, was always moving dangerously around the goal area when the ball came into the square. On the other wing was one of the great stick artists of the Cork side, Tony O'Sullivan of Na Piarsaigh.

'Tony had a great ability to use his skill in taking the ball out of a tussle of players, using his footwork to weave and feint past opponents', said Gerald McCarthy. 'He had a lovely side-step that avoided the shoulders of opponents — like a ballet dancer — and he had tremendous skill with the ball in taking points from all distances and every angle.'

In the right corner was the captain of the side, Tomas Mulcahy. This player had scored one of the goals which had really killed off Galway when the sides met in 1986. It was typical of his style of play — to gather the ball, turn on an astonishing burst of speed for a big man as he went for goal with hurley on ball. It took great courage and composure to hit the ball on the run into the farthest corner of the net while dodging the tackles of opponents. He was one of the inspirational players on the side, a man for the big occasion.

At full forward the tall red-haired Midleton player, Kevin Hennessy, would bring a lot of experience with him. He had been playing a long time, had scored many memorable opportunist goals. His height made him difficult to beat in the air. He was strong and speedy for someone of his size. He had another quality which was an asset to any team going into an All-Ireland — an impish sense of humour and a wit which helped lighten tension as players travelled to games in buses or trains or as they laced up their boots in the dressing-room.

The number 15 jersey was worn by a dark-haired unobtrusive player who was proving to be one of the sharpest goal-getters the team had had for a long time, John Fitzgibbon. From the merest half chance, left or right, he was able to whip the ball across the goal and into the net. He had the skill to run with the ball and to go for narrow-angle goals without hesitation.

Cool Cunningham

At the far end of the field was the tall figure in his striped red and white jersey, Ger Cunningham. This was one of the best goalkeepers of the era.

He had the indomitable self-confidence that every goalkeeper needs along with a cool temperament. He worked endlessly at his game, practising ball control, taking shots from every angle, stopping penalties, pucking the ball out so that it would land exactly where he wanted it to go. And he was one of the great long hitters of the ball — eighty, ninety, one hundred metres and over. He had been unbeatable up along the Cooley mountains in the annual Puc Fada competition.

Galway Side

The Galway team were just as experienced as their rivals. Most of them were hardened All-Ireland battlers. The goalkeeper, John Commins, had played heroically in the two All-Ireland finals Galway had won. Against both Kilkenny and Tipperary he had made crucial saves when the outcome hung on a knife-edge. These saves were inspirational and when, after his puck out, Galway went into the attack they did so with renewed vigour.

Even the Galway followers were doubtful about the full back line. They felt that Dermot Fahy, who had played very well against Offaly and was being hailed as an upcoming star, was essentially a full back. It would be his first final.

It was difficult for Sean Treacy to shake off the constant comparison with his commanding predecessor, Conor Hayes. Treacy was big and strong and had plenty of grit and determination. He had established himself on the team by a good display in the tough semi-final of the previous year.

In the other corner was one of the most experienced and astute corner backs in the business, Ollie Kilkenny of Kiltormer. He knew what it was like to lose finals and to win finals, having played in four to date. He had marked well the best corner forwards and he was exceptionally speedy for a corner back and was not easy to pass.

Galway Half Backs

The Galway half back line of Finnerty, Keady and McInerney was the sheet anchor of the team and had been so since the semi-final of 1985 when, in torrential rain, an emergent Galway had beaten Cork. These three, who had developed a great understanding between them, had been the bulwark against which some of the most feared forward lines had crumbled. They snuffed out attacks and sent their own forwards into action.

Finnerty was strong and determined. He had great confidence in his own ability and was a gritty competitor, who was fast to the breaking ball and could cover off whenever Keady was under pressure. Keady himself had a great sense of positional play, commanding the centre very well. He challenged very cleverly for every ball and every now and then came bursting out to sent a long delivery down the field. He had a very accurate stroke on the ball and had scored many long distance frees and 65s for his side.

McInerney had first come to the attention of the hurling followers as a tenacious, tireless wing back on the first Galway minor team ever to win the All-Ireland crown in 1983. He was fast to the ball, very hard to dispossess as he came flying along the wing and raised great cheers from the supporters for the way he cleared the ball, despite using the unorthodox grip on the hurley. Both he and Finnerty often came forward into the midfield area and sent in low balls for the forwards to chase.

Galway had one of the strongest, most competitive midfielders in Michael Coleman from Abbeyknockmoy. It was an area that had little hurling tradition but Coleman proved a great asset in 1988 when he replaced Steve Mahon. Beside him was an experienced midfielder, Pat Malone of Oranmore-Maree, who won two All-Ireland medals at midfield. He was an unobtrusive kind of player but he had come into his own on the big days in the past and Galway expected him to do the same this time.

Galway had a style of forward play based on speed, the ability to run with the ball and to pass it accurately with the hand. They had perfected the art of the hand-pass to a better placed colleague, having drawn the defence. Martin Naughton of Turloughmore epitomised this type of play, collecting the ball and thundering along towards goal, with Joe Cooney running parallel to him some distance away, waiting for a pass or the rebound if Naughton's shot should be saved by the goalkeeper. The Turloughmore man had fought a long, grinding and lonely battle to overcome the disadvantage of a serious knee injury but was now back to his old self.

Centre of the forward line was the Galway captain, a farmer from Bullaun, Joe Cooney. He held the hurley in the right-hand-under grip but it never hindered his scoring capacity, or his skilful first touch on the ball or his ability to take close-in frees. He was an industrious ball juggler who was also an unselfish player; his ability invariably attracted the full attention of the backs and when that happened he flicked the ball or handpassed it to a waiting team-mate.

On the other wing was another forward who liked to run with the ball, Anthony Cunningham. This tactic had served him well in the past especially when he led the minor team to their first All-Ireland in 1983. His game was predictable, as was Naughton's, and they sometimes found themselves bottled up at the end of long runs down the wing.

Galway had three talented players in the full forward line. In the left right corner was the red-helmeted Michael McGrath who had great speed and could lift the ball deftly on the run. He often rounded his man and raced goalwards but he could put points over from out near the sideline. At full forward was a man who had been part of the great surge of Galway hurling in the latter half of the 1970s, Noel Lane of Ballinderreen. He was the veteran of the side, had played in the finals of '79, '80 and '81 and was still there when Galway came back to the fore in 1985. He played in the final that year and was captain of the side beaten

The teams as they lined out were:

Cork

Ger Cunningham
(St Finbarr's)

John Considine	Denis Walsh	Sean O'Gorman
(Sarsfields)	(St Catherine's)	(Milford)

Sean McCarthy	Jim Cashman	Kieran McGuckin
(Ballinhassig)	(Blackrock)	(Glen Rovers)

Brendan O'Sullivan   Teddy McCarthy
(Valley Rovers)   (Sarsfields)

Ger Fitzgerald	Mark Foley	Tony O'Sullivan
(Midleton)	(Argideen Rangers)	(Na Piarsaigh)

Tomas Mulcahy, capt	Kevin Hennessy	John Fitzgibbon
(Glen Rovers)	(Midleton)	(Glen Rovers)

Substitutes: David Quirke (Midleton); Cathal Casey (St Catherine's); Tom Kingston (Tracton); Christy Connery (Na Piarsaigh); Pat Buckley (Milford); Michael Mullins (Na Piarsaigh); Anthony O'Sullivan (Bishopstown). *Coach*: Fr Michael O'Brien (Carraigaline). *Trainer*: Gerald McCarthy (St Finbarr's). *Mentors/selectors*: Frank Murphy (Blackrock); Martin Coleman (Ballinhassig); Liam O Tuama (Glen Rovers); Denis Hurley (Sarsfields). *Team doctor*: Dr Con Murphy (UCC). *Masseur*: John 'Kid' Cronin (Glen Rovers).

Galway

John Commins
(Gort)

Dermot Fahy	Sean Treacy	Ollie Kilkenny
(Ardrahan)	(Portumna)	(Kiltormer)

Peter Finnerty	Tony Keady	Gerry McInerney
(Mullagh)	(Killimordaly)	(Kinvara)

Michael Coleman   Pat Malone
(Abbeyknockmoy)   (Oranmore-Maree)

Anthony Cunningham	Joe Cooney	Martin Naughton
(St Thomas)	(Sarsfields)	(Turloughmore)

Michael McGrath	Noel Lane	Eanna Ryan
(Sarsfields)	(Ballinderreen)	(Killimordaly)

Substitutes/panel: Tom Monaghan (Killimordaly); Brendan Lynskey (Meelick-Eyrecourt); Richard Burke (Oranmore-Maree); Conor Hayes (Kiltormer); Pat Higgins (Athenry); Jerry Burke (Turloughmore); Peter Murphy (Loughrea); Noel Morrissey (Sarsfields); Joe Rabbitte (Athenry). *Manager/coach*: Cyril Farrell (Tommy Larkins). *Selectors/mentors*: Phelim Murphy (Turloughmore); Bernie O'Connor (Oranmore-Maree); Tom Callanan (Kilconieron). *Team doctor*: Dr Michael McGloin. *Masseur*: Colm Flynn.

The referee was John Moore of Waterford.

the following year by Cork. After that he had been relegated to the subs, partly because he had to contend with injury and partly because he was considered too old. He had proved his worth in the finals of '87 and '88 when he came on in the second half of both games, scoring a crucial match-winning goal on both occastions. Now the selectors felt that this 36-year- old should be on from the start.

In the other corner was a player of great skill and ball control, Eanna Ryan. He had a neat first touch, used his hurley to send pinpoint passes, was a fleet footed opportunist and had scored some memorable goals off the ground at narrow angles.

These then were the teams and their supportive panels of substitutes which lined out at Croke Park that first Sunday in September 1990. This was an exceptionally hot day for the time of the year. But it was anything but calm. A warm wind blew down the pitch from the Canal end ruffling the sideline flags. This wind was to play an important part in the destination of the Liam McCarthy cup that afternoon.

First-Minute Goal

Cooney and Mulcahy walked towards the centre spot to meet and shake hands with one another and with the referee, John Moore of Waterford. Cork lost the toss and Cooney elected to play with the wind into the Railway end.

To a great cheer from the 63,954 spectators the ball was thrown in and there was a great flurry of hurleys as the four midfielders shouldered for possession. With only forty second gone the ball sped towards the Galway end line in a quick Cork attack. John Fitzgibbon on the left tried to get it but was bowled over. The Galway backs were uncertain in those vital first seconds and the old red fox, Hennessy, got the ball under control in front of the posts and pulled hard. The ball went along the ground and to the astonishment of all went into the net for a rousing first score for the Leesiders. It was a great start for the outsiders and had to have a somewhat dampening effect on the Galway men.

Almost from the puck out Joe Cooney, in the kind of inspirational gesture that a captain can provide, battled for the ball on the right and made space to hit it over the bar.

Players from both sides were sizing one another up at this stage and it was clear that the midfield would be brought into play through puck outs from the Railway end. Even the long puck champion Cunningham could not get the ball much further than midfield against the good breeze. Teddy McCarthy, compact in build, with strong shoulders, burst out from a ruck of players to swing hard on the ball and send it over the bar.

The danger posed by the superb agility of John Fitzgibbon was demonstrated two minutes later. He sped out to gather an incoming ball, spun around and tore goalwards. He slipped as he tried to avoid a tackle but deftly sent the ball over the bar as he went down.

Cork had taken the initiative and as the game surged from one end to the other they fought tooth and nail to hold on to it. Their wing backs, McGuckin and McCarthy both began to play well, pulling quickly on the ball, keeping it away from Cunningham and Naughton. Sean O'Gorman cleared with great style and composure when the ball flew into the right corner of the Galway attack.

Cooney Starring

However it was soon apparent that Cooney was playing the game of his life. He went for ball after ball, catching them amid smacking hurleys, scooping them off the ground in front of his opponents. He began to play great hurling and even a player of the calibre of Cashman couldn't keep him in check. In the eighth minute Cooney hit a beautiful point that brought a great cheer of delight from the attendance. A minute later he raced over to the right hand side, way out of his centre forward domain, and swung his hurley delicately to send a point over the bar from a narrow angle. His trusty hurley did not survive that score as the stick of one of the Cork defenders smashed into it and he had to get another.

If Cooney was getting the better of Cashman then Tony Keady began to dominate the centre back area. He kept the ball away from the dangerous Mark Foley, darting back and forward across his line, well supported by McInerney and Finnerty. Keady made a characteristic move in the tenth minute, leaving his man behind as he went up the field and sent over a rousing point from 50 metres out.

Hennessy, constantly moving about in front of the Galway goal, was proving something of a trial for Treacy. The full forward was deceptively fast and athletic and he had no intention of matching weight and pulling power with his marker. In the battle to keep the initiative he played another role — taker of frees from close in. He had the temperament for the big occasion and sent the first of these over in the eleventh minute. Two minutes later he restored Cork's one-goal lead with another free from 30 metres. His opposite number, Lane, at the far end showed all his wiliness and ball control in front of goal. Despite his veteran status he was fast to the ball, could hold it on his hurley, send out a pass or spin round to take a shot himself. He sent a hard shot just over the crossbar in the 15th minute from a very narrow angle. Only a player of his confidence would have attempted this kind of shot.

Denis Walsh found the Galwaymen's style of play hard to handle but neither he nor Cashman deliberately fouled their men. This was a game where, despite hard knocks and desperate tackles, sportsmanship prevailed in large measure. Apart from that the Cork mentors, especially Fr O'Brien, had impressed their charges that no easy frees were to be given for Cooney to send over the bar.

Lane and Cooney were proving to be the spearhead of the Galway attack but their colleagues were being well marked and in the corners

Considine and particularly O'Gorman, playing in their first All-Ireland, were giving Ryan and McGrath little room to move or make scores.

Ger Cunningham was composed in goal as he controlled and cleared the first balls that came into him. He was the kind of player who lent confidence to his backs.

'Great Stuff'

'This is great stuff, great stuff', shouted one of the commentators as play swung from end to end and two talented and determined teams tore into every tackle with abandon, fought for every ball.

The lanky, ever moving Hennessy scored a point from play to keep Cork ahead. Two minutes later Ger Fitzgerald managed to elude the close tackling of Gerry McInerney and sent over a fine point from 40 metres out. Cork were now four points ahead again despite the efforts of Galway to wrest the initiative from them.

Then the Galway engine went into a high-pitched effort, as if the team were being assailed by a fear that if they did not now reduce the lead it might never be done. Martin Naughton for once rounded Sean McCarthy and racing goalwards sent a good point over the bar.

Teddy McCarthy and Brendan O'Sullivan had held their own against Pat Malone and Michael Coleman for the opening quarter but now Coleman began to play power hurling. Tall and strong, he used his weight to hold his ground under high balls, sending long sweeping shots at head height into the forwards.

Galway Level and Lead

Cooney, playing a captain's part, raced into the goal area, jumping over legs and hurleys, weaving past opponents, sliding away from tackles. From close in he shot for goal. The alert Cunningham managed to parry it but Cooney gathered the rebound and, harassed on both sides, still managed to kick the ball into the net. The sides were level at last. A huge cheer of applause and delight went up.

Now Galway, playing as if their lives depended on the outcome, took a firmer grip on the game. Eanna Ryan, who had got little change from O'Gorman, gathered the ball and clipped it neatly over the bar.

'That's it, lads — now you have them', roared a Galway accented voice from one of the stands. Galway had gone into the lead for the first time. A minute later Cooney again made an heroic effort to trap and control a ball at full speed, hampered by hurleys and arms and legs. From 50 metres out he sent a great point over the bar to give Galway a two-point lead.

At this stage the Galway backs were well in control, with Dermot Fahy having settled down to marking the dangerous Fitzgibbon and the half backs allowing little in to the Cork full forward line. Keady had established some mastery over the tall Foley, who was not getting the kind of high ball on which he could show his advantage. Tomas Mulcahy and Tony O'Sullivan were getting little change from Ollie Kilkenny and Peter Finnerty in great competitive battles and began to rove about in search of better ball.

In another attack by the westerners Lane took a pass from the right and doubled on it confidently, sending it sizzling just over the bar. This was one of his hard-hit shots that might as well have been put into the net as over the bar. However, under great pressure, the Cork backs were defending desperately, trying all they knew to tie up the other Galway forwards and limit the damage being done by Cooney and Lane.

Crucial Disallowed Goal

Then came one of the crucial moments of this final. Cooney, slim and mercurial, able to ride the tackles, was twisting and turning through a net of harassing hurleys to the left of the goal and, despite being fouled, managed to winkle the ball out to Eanna Ryan. This was the kind of shot that the quick-striking Killimordaly man rarely missed and he billowed the net with his shot.

However, the referee, who had been a fair distance away, had failed to spot the advantage which Galway had created and he had whistled back play for a free. Cooney converted this but a goal would have been a tremendous boost for the westerners and a blow to the Cork side at this stage. Galway needed a goal to reflect their superiority at this stage of the game.

A few minutes later came a miss that was to add to the frustration of the Galway team and followers. Lane, running rampant at this stage, got in behind the defence and raced onto an incoming ball from Paschal Ryan. Only Cunningham stood between him and an open goal but Lane's foot accidently pushed the ball too far ahead and Cunningham lunged forward to rescue what seemed like a very damaging situation for the Leesiders.

These were lost opportunities for the Galway side. They were going through a period of control, had the momentum of the game going their way. This was the time to have won the game.

'In any championship game you can have the initiative for part of the time but not for all of the time — the advantage can move from one team to another, even from one player to another', observed Peter Finnerty of that game.

Some advantage was going to be lost as soon as the Cork mentors decided to move Sean O'Gorman from the corner to the full back berth, where he was just as fast and nimble as Lane and reduced the Ballinderreen man's effectiveness.

In the 27th minute the burly Teddy McCarthy, playing well on a struggling Pat Malone, took a full swing on the ball from 70 metres out. It took off like a missile, began to slow down against the wind but had gone far enough to drop down behind the uprights for a heartening Cork point.

But Galway returned to the attack. Once again Lane rifled the ball just over the bar from a narrow angle. One of the most significant factors at this stage was that, despite the ball and the forwards sweeping in time after time, the Cork rearguard gave away few frees.

Not long after Naughton, coming more and more into the game, shook off the tenacious Sean McCarthy to get free 50 metres out when he sent over a fine point. It left the score 1–12 to 1–7.

All this time Joe Cooney was giving one of the greatest individual displays ever seen in an All-Ireland. He went for balls that only someone of his speed and agility could attempt. He showed great courage in grabbing or rising the ball in a welter of flailing hurleys. And he usually got it and ran clear either to score or to give a pass. He got his last score of the half when he ran out to the left and sent a ball that went on a curving trajectory and drifted over the bar to a great round of applause from all the spectators.

Just before half time the sequence of Galway scores was broken when a sideline puck was awarded to Cork within striking distance of the Galway goal. Kieran McGuckin came up and cut it beautifully so that it took off and sailed againt the breeze over the bar.

Soon afterwards came the sound of the referee's whistle which brought an action-packed, incident-filled first half to a close with the score 1–13 to 1–8 in Galway's favour.

'We were praying for him to blow the whistle', recalled Gerald McCarthy. 'We thought it would never come and we felt very lucky that we were only five points behind. We needed the break to get our breath and to see how we would organise ourselves for the second half.'

For all that they had been outhurled for much of the time, Cork had shown great spirit in adversity, playing away, hoping for a break in the rhythm of dominance that had been established by the westerners. But they could easily have been ten or twelve points down instead of five.

There was a buzz of excitement as the spectators discussed what they had seen and what they might expect in the second half. The seasoned Galway side had shown their power and resilience to come back into the game after a bad start. How much of their energies this effort had consumed was something only the second half could tell.

There was no abatement of the warm wind during the game and it was still flapping and stretching the flags atop the stands as the teams emerged for the second half.

Second Half Begins

As if to emphasise their determination to set about reducing the deficit, the Cork side went into the attack almost immediately. The ball came in quickly to the full forward line and Fitzgibbon was only foiled by sturdy defending by Fahy. Half a minute later the ball came in again and Ger Fitzgerald was just baulked enough to miss his shot. John Commins' puck out was returned shortly afterwards and he had to make a save right on the line.

The large Cork contingent in the crowd, especially the great mass of supporters on Hill 16, sporting red and white banners, began to give great roars of encouragement to their men, who had seemed almost out of the game for good during the second part of the first half. An indication of their impish, irreverent attitude was the way they adopted the flags of other causes and used them for their own ends — Confederate crossed banners, the Rising Sun of the Japanese empire, and the white crescent on green of Islam.

The Galway followers heaved great collective sighs of relief at these misses by Cork. They felt a great sense of delight when Michael McGrath, coming out from the corner where his talents had been severely restricted, gathered the ball 50 metres out and struck a fine ball which soared over the bar to put the westerners six points ahead.

Coleman was lord of the midfield area and joining in an attack he got a hand-pass out to Anthony Cunningham, who lashed the ball over the bar. Right then it looked as if Cork's hopes of getting back into the game were snuffed out.

However, Tomas Mulcahy, effectively curbed by Ollie Kilkenny, was coming out more and more and from 50 metres out he struck a fine point for the Leesiders. Yet it was quickly responded to by Coleman, who was showing great strength and thrust and who sent a hard ball over the bar, against the breeze, from a distance of 65 metres.

The game was at its most exciting as the two sides fought for mastery and the ball went up and down the field. There were great exhibitions of astute play by players like Keady and O'Gorman, great ball-juggling skills by Ryan and Fitzgibbon and attacking flair by Tony O'Sullivan and Joe Cooney. There were stirring man-to-man clashes all over the wide spaces of Croke Park as duels were fought, sportingly but relentlessly.

Telling Move

One of the most telling tactics adopted by the Cork selectors was to move the hard-running Mulcahy out to the 40 where Foley had been greatly subdued by Keady. Mulcahy was a different style of player, darting here and there to seek opportunities and being capable of running hard with the ball whenever he got it. On one of his forays he was fouled and Hennessy put the point over the bar.

Galway struck back when Martin Naughton, showing all his speed and dash, collected the ball and whirled about then raced goalwards along the left wing to score a point and restore his team's seven-point lead.

At this stage many Galway supporters had a comfortable feeling that their side could always step-up a gear if called upon to do so, could score at will in response to their opponents' efforts. Here was another knife-edge period of the game when a small push could have sent Cork down for good. But then the ball-pucking ability of Ger Cunningham began to play a key role in the whole contest. Every time Galway attacked and the ball went wide or over the bar the tall goalkeeper went back behind the goal, took a run forward, threw the ball forward and swung powerfully on it. Cunningham's puck outs were starting to land in a line between the Galway half back and full back line.

From such a puck out the ball ran fast and Mulcahy, eluding Keady, took it and ran with it goalwards. His speed and weight and power carried him into the goal area and despite being challenged he pulled on the ball on the ground from the right to score a smashing goal. This goal raised a tremendous cheer from the Cork fans. It was a great boost for the beleagured team that had only been hanging on for long periods.

'This was a typical Mulcahy goal — running with the ball and letting fly on the run', said Gerald McCarthy. 'He makes it look easy but it is far from easy in an All-Ireland.'

In the 1986 final the Glen Rovers man had scored a very similar goal at the end of a powerful sprint, with Galway backs in hot pursuit.

Brave Save

Yet almost from the puck out Galway had a great chance of wiping out the advantage Cork had gained. Peter Finnerty cleared the ball well down the field and Martin Naughton swooped on it, going at full speed, leaving his markers trailing. He raced towards goal and had only Ger Cunningham to beat. The Galway followers raised a great roar as he swung his hurley to send the ball to the net. But Cunningham made one of the bravest efforts seen in Croke Park — he flung his body towards where he thought the ball might go. His courage paid off for he saved a certain goal. This was done at the cost of a large red weal on his forehead for the ball, going at some 90 miles an hour, struck his face and ricocheted out over the end line.

Cunningham's save evoked a long round of applause from spectators from every county including Galway. But the westerners' disappointment was further compounded when the umpire inexplicably signalled a wide instead of raising his arm for a 65. It was another frustrating incident for the Galway players. And yet another was to follow.

Not long afterwards Mulcahy's marker, Tony Keady, was bursting his way out of a ruck of players when he was tripped. It should have been a free but the referee, having to run more than any single player to try to keep up with such a fast, exciting game, did not notice. As Keady fell to the ground he tried to hand-pass the ball to a colleague. Instead the man with the most elusive footwork on the field, Tony O'Sullivan, snapped it up and with controlled and long-practised accuracy, sent it over the bar.

Referees' Burden

This was an important point for Cork, strengthening the belief that they were capable of coming back into the game. It was a frustrating point for Galway. It raised the question of whether one man should be given the responsibility for ensuring fair play on so important an occasion, with the ball zipping from one end of the field to the other at great speed, leaving the referee yards behind in its wake.

'In any game you get a number of decisions that go your way and some that go against you', said Gerald McCarthy. 'On this occasion Galway lost out.'

Foley looked more effective when moved from the centre forward position to the corner but he roamed out to where he thought the ball might break. Not long after O'Sullivan's point he used height and weight to get the ball near the right sideline and sent over a fine point. Cork were now only two points behind.

Croke Park was a welter of excitement as these two teams battled for supremacy. The ball flew in the air or along the ground at great speed, men went shoulder to shoulder for it, tussled hard. Whenever there was a clean stroke, a good clearance it aroused a cheer of admiration because these were not easy to come by in the tight marking.

At this stage Galway no longer dominated. Joe Cooney, who had played so well in the first half, got less of the ball in the second.

'In the first half he went for — and got — balls that weren't really his. He gave a great performance but it used up a lot of energy', said Peter Finnerty. 'In the second half he was going for the same kind of ball but being just that crucial few inches away from getting and controlling it.'

Cashman to Fore

There was another factor. Jim Cashman was now coming more and more into the game. 'At half time we wondered if we should shift him but decided to persist with him and it paid off', said Gerald McCarthy. 'A player of his character is going to keep trying no matter how badly things are going and very often will begin to win out at some stage.' Peter Finnerty was in accord. 'You might get the better of a player of his calibre for 30 or 40 minutes but not for the whole 70 because he will have his time of dominance too before the game is over.'

McGrath and Ryan were no longer getting much ball and Anthony Cunningham made some dashing runs along the sideline or the middle without getting value for his efforts by getting in a good pass or a score. His marker, Kieran McGuckin, had played well but began to tire and was replaced by David Quirke, who proved to be a good substitute. Cork's midfield battler, Brendan O'Sullivan, had played himself into the ground in the fierce midfield exchanges. O'Sullivan was replaced by Cathal Casey who was an experienced player in the position.

Galway too decided to substitute at midfield. Pat Malone had had a difficult time against Teddy McCarthy. Against all odds, however, he had started to hurl his way back into the game when he was taken off. Because Cunningham's mighty puck outs were putting great pressure on the six backs Malone had moved back a little from his midfield position on the left, helping the beleaguered defence. His substitute, Tom Monaghan, stayed on the mid-line or even played a more forward game at a time of steadily growing pressure on the back line.

Huge Puck Outs

One of the most important factors in putting the Galway backs on the grill was the length of Ger Cunningham's puck outs from his goal line.

'It wasn't just that they were landing twenty or thirty yards from the Galway goal. He hit them into the right corner, the left corner, in front of goals, varying them all the time', explained Gerald McCarthy. 'We had learned our lesson from the All-Ireland of 1983 against Kilkenny when a strong wind also blew down the field. Ger took great pucks of the ball but they all landed in the same spot behind the half back line. If you had put a bucket down on the pitch they would all have gone into it. Kilkenny read the play well, the backs bunched under the ball to shut our forwards out while Frank Cummins came from midfield round behind and collected ball after ball and cleared them away. So our plan was to keep the backs guessing about where the next puck out might land. Indeed on one or two occasions, Ger deliberately hit short ones that landed in midfield in order to bring the Galway backs out again.'

Ironically it was the determination of Galway to give as good as they got that led to these massive puck outs, for the westerners attacked with equal fervour if less success. Denis Walsh had moved back into the full back position and seemed to be able to better manage Noel Lane but this was an experienced Galway attack and Cunningham had balls to deal with and balls to puck out.

From one of these Hennessy, whose height was a help in aerial warfare, sent a pass to Mark Foley. The big man took it. As he spun about to face the goal he hit a great shot on the turn. It rocketed into the net for the best goal of the game. Cork had gone ahead and were now taking the initiative from the westerners.

Yet Galway struck back again. The ball once more went up the field and the stick-artist Ryan got it and sent it over to level the scores and keep western morale alive.

Scores Exchanged

Cork took the lead again when the burly Teddy McCarthy, who had jumped for some great hand catches during the game, shot another point to put his side in front again. This was answered by Noel Lane when he got the ball on the right in another Galway attack. For a second the crowd rose in the expectation that a goal was on but the Ballinderreen man sent it over the bar to bring the scores level once again.

Eight mintues to go and the teams were level. This reflected the swaying fortunes of the sides, the individual battles around the field when both players in a particular duel had times of advantage and dominance. This was the time of the game when a puck of the ball could decide the issue.

If the Cork backs had been under fierce pressure in the first half now, as the game neared the end, with the winning post in sight the Galway backs were subjected to an endless series of attacks by their opponents.

'All Ger Cunningham's puck outs were sailing over our heads in the half back line, falling near the goal. Our full back line had a nightmare time. The ball was coming in to them, they had their own men to mark, the half backs were backing into the goal area and Cork's half forwards running in as well', said Peter Finnerty. 'There was chaos in the goal area. And when there is chaos it generally favours the forward because the ball will break some way and he has a great chance of sending it over the bar or into the net.'

Two Decisive Scores

In the 62nd minute of play came a decisive score. A centre from Foley looked as if it could easily be handled by the Galway backs but the master of the half-chance, Fitzgibbon, swung on the ball on the ground and sent it inside the far upright for an opportunist goal which stunned the Galway followers.

While Galway were trying to recover from this blow the ball again soared into their square. The gangling Hennessy got hold of it in a great clash of hurleys and bodies and passed it out to the dark-haired Fitzgibbon who was running goalwards. He was challenged but he kept going. Scrutineers of the video of the TV coverage argued that he took more than four steps with the ball in hand. The referee let him go on. One of the Galway full backs charged at him but he shimmied past and lashed the ball to the corner of the net. Cork had gone a totally unexpected six points ahead with time running out fast.

Their followers, some of whom had given up on the team for much of the game, were ecstatic that the grit and skill of their side had not alone brought them back into the game but now made them look like winners.

However, Galway too were not lacking in spirit and determination. They attacked desperately. The broad-shouldered veteran, Brendan Lynskey, who had come on for the tiring Anthony Cunningham, made an impact as soon as he arrived on the scene. He broke up the play, disrupted the rhythm of the Cork backs, blocked down clearances. 'Did Galway make a mistake in not bringing him on earlier?', asked one of the commentators. The answer seemed to be yes because in a Galway attack he moved onto a pass from Eanna Ryan to belt the ball to the net. This served to silence some of the celebrations of the huge Cork contingent.

Galway, with all their big game experience and now only a goal behind, were capable of getting an equaliser. Yet it was the Cork captain, Mulcahy, now playing an inspirational game and troubling Keady a good deal, who got the next score. It was from a pass from Fitzgibbon, now being marked by Finnerty. This seemed like the insurance point for the Cork side as the seconds ticked away.

The Galway side battled back, setting up several attacks. Once again the lion-hearted Lynskey caught a ball amid flailing hurleys and, when bottled up himself made use of his exceptional side-vision to send a pass out to Naughton who was running in. The Turloughmore man's way was blocked and he could do no more than send it over the bar to keep a goal between the sides.

Yet in these last few minutes, with only the puck of a ball between the sides, many of the Galway players were visibly wilting. In the angry post-mortems of the following week voices were raised against what was seen as an excessive amount of physical training the team members had to undergo. 'They were fit but were they fresh?' was an oft-repeated question.

Peter Finnerty has a different explanation. 'Cork got off to such a flying start that we found we had to hurl out of our skins to catch up with them, to burn so much energy to get back into the game, to keep them at bay and to get ahead while we had the wind at our backs. Then we faced the wind in the second half and in the last quarter we lost the momentum. When you are going well you don't think about tiredness, you seem to have an unlimited amount of energy. But when things begin to go badly, when you miss a few balls then everything is uphill and nothing is easy. That is what happened to us. Cork came good at the right time in the game. I would say that if we had met them again the following day we might have won because there was really little between us.'

From Cunningham's long puck out after Naughton's point Tony O'Sullivan of the elusive footwork and beautiful stroke sent a point over the bar to put the southerners 1–1 ahead.

It seemed apt that the last score of this great game should go to the inspirational captain of the losing side, Joe Cooney, who had played himself into the ground. The power and drive of his first half play was one of the outstanding features of the game. When Galway were awarded a free on the right he came over to take it. There was some expectation that he might try for a goal but the ball went low over the bar.

Almost from the puck out, with Cork very much in the ascendant on the field of play, the referee blew the long whistle. The final score was Cork 5–15 to Galway's 2–21.

This game marked a renaissance for the Cork side. They had showed that with the kind of top organisation and motivation provided by O'Brien and McCarthy they could match the best. Though they fell to Tipperary the following year they were back again in 1992 in the All-

Ireland final. There they went down to old rivals and bogeymen, Kilkenny, but they were there, fighting for the top prize.

The game marked the end of the great Galway side of the mid-'80s. While some of the key players remained on, others retired or were relegated by age or injury to the substitutes bench. The team that took the field the following year was a pale shadow of the team that contested the final of 1990. However the under-21 side came out on top in 1991 and by 1992 the best of these were melding with the experienced players to begin to present another challenge for top honours in the 1990s.

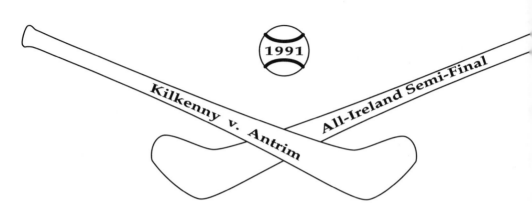

LAYING THE FOUNDATIONS

The biggest cheer of the day from the crowd of 61,000 was for the team in silk-sheened saffron jerseys. The Antrim team had come within an ace of pulling off what would have been a sensational result — beating a well-prepared and highly-motivated Kilkenny team in the All-Ireland semi-final at Croke Park.

Not alone that but this had been a tremendous game, full of whole-hearted hurling. There was something deeply satisfying about the full-blooded way both teams set about the match. It had been embellished with the characteristic hurling skills and that ingrained sense of astute movement and timing of Kilkenny matched with marvellous first-time pulling along the ground and flamboyant speed and power from Antrim.

It had been a battle of wits between the two managers, Jim Nelson of Antrim and Ollie Walsh of Kilkenny. Both tried hard to make best use of their teams' strengths and to probe what they saw as the weak points in their opponents.

This game had got off to an electric start, when one of the fastest, most opportunistic forwards on the Kilkenny side, Eamon Morrissey raced in from the wing to score a goal almost before the Antrim players had got a grip of their hurleys. It had ended in a fever of excitement as Kilkenny, outclassed and out-weighed for most of the game, made a great comeback which in turn engendered another surge of resilience from the Glensmen.

As the players left the field the packed stands and terraces gave them a grateful ovation that lasted five minutes. Much if not most of the accolades were directed towards the losers, Antrim, who had given such a show of skill and style.

Antrim were not in the least content to be gallant losers, pleased to have contributed to one of the most enthralling games of the year. 'We could have won and we should have won', said Terence 'Sambo' McNaughton, battle-scarred face grim with frustration and annoyance. He had been the outstanding player on the side, dominating midfield and ensuring a good supply of ball to the hard running forwards.

Nelson, the manager, consoled the players as they sat in the dressing-room, chests still heaving with exertion. Some had nothing at all to say, jaws tight with disappointment after coming so near to winning, after all the hours of training and all the ergs of effort. Others just shook their heads and muttered a few words in sharp northern accents.

'We played for 66 minutes out of 70', said Nelson emphatically. 'Our concentration wasn't there in the first minute when we conceded a stupid goal. We lost concentration under pressure in the last five minutes when we lost the game. In fairness it has to be said that Kilkenny showed tremendous character in hanging in there with us all the way. We had our chance and we lost it.'

Nelson had prepared his team well for this contest. He knew that to give Kilkenny players time to rise and handle the ball, or to tip it deftly to better placed opponents, to feint this way and that with the ball in their grasp would spell disaster for the Antrim side. So he spent a lot of time training the team in first-time pulling, in keeping the ball moving, not giving the men in black and amber the chance or the time to settle on the ball and settle on their game.

'It's not just a question of pulling on the ball, but hitting it accurately as well, sending it in fast to one of your players waiting for it, giving him an advantage over his opponent', said Ciaran Barr, one of the stars of that game and captain of the Antrim side that contested the All-Ireland final against Tipperary in 1989.

The Antrim team were generally bigger and heavier than their opponents and were well prepared to use their strength legitimately. As well as that most of the players had been part of the great resurgence in All-Ireland championship hurling that began in the middle of the 1980s and that still continues today.

Impatient Kilkenny Followers

The Kilkenny side had a hard edge to its play, bred by hunger for success not alone among the players but from all the followers as well. The Noreside hurling public was used to triumph. It never liked to be out of the honours list for very long. Winning was part of their tradition, as was clever ball play and an innate craftiness in deceiving opponents and striking telling scores at vital moments. Now, however, Kilkenny had not won an All-Ireland since 1983. This seemed like an awful long time to many.

Ollie Walsh, the former great goalkeeper, was in charge of the team. His prowess and that of the players was being carefully watched by the game-wise followers. Some of the commentary was highly critical and even unfair. But the philosophical Walsh was keeping his nerve, making his own decisions. This was not easy to do. The county was enveloped in a mood of frustration and hope. Eddie Keher, who himself managed Kilkenny sides as well as being one of the great forwards of the game, explains.

'What happens is that followers and indeed the officials get impatient. They become panicky for success. They are aware of the criticism of many who feel that the county team should be doing far better.

'The mentors can get very uneasy under public pressure and scrutiny. They begin to change players from game to game, to play men out of position. This is a common reality not just in Kilkenny but in counties used to winning. They don't give a team time to settle down. People get afraid of being blamed for not succeeding. All this begins to affect the performance of the players as well. They can become tense and tentative, play well below their best', Keher says.

Victory Over Wexford

This kind of pressure on the Kilkenny side was intensified by the fact that all except the most partisan supporter said that they were extremely lucky to be in the semi-final at all. In the first round they were pitched against their greatest rivals, Wexford. The Wexford side was one of the best for several years and were being tipped at least to reach the final, if not actually win it.

The match at Croke Park on 30 June was a rip-roaring encounter with fortunes swaying from side to side as the ball went from one end of the field to the other. Wexford looked the stronger side and they had the support and sympathy of all except the Kilkenny followers. Kilkenny, however, had that great characteristic of making the most of limited chances, holding off the opposition.

'You have to be twice as good as Kilkenny to beat them in a tight finish — there's no use being just a bit better than them', is a well-used adage which more often than not is proved right.

In a thundering finish Wexford went ahead and their faithful followers massed on the terraces and in the stands were cheering themselves hoarse and whistling for the referee to call full time. They were two points to the good and went on another last minute attack. But the attack broke up and one of the Kilkenny backs clipped the ball hard off the ground and sent it whizzing fast into the Wexford half. There it was gathered nimbly by the lithe, elusive D.J. Carey, the most accomplished of the Kilkenny forwards. A light but very fast player he side-stepped a few challenges and went fleet-footed goalwards.

Near the end of his run he was being bottled up but he kept going, ball in hand, and from five yards out kicked the ball. It went in under the hurley of the Wexford goalkeeper, David 'Stoney' Burke, and into the net.

There were protests from the Wexford players that Carey had carried the ball for at least six steps. But the referee stuck to his decision to allow the goal. While the ball was still in the air from the puck out he blew the whistle.

Antrim Beat Down

That same day, in Casement Park, Belfast, Antrim had met Down to see who would represent the province at the semi-final stage. For many outside the province it was taken as a foregone conclusion that Antrim would win rather easily. They were always the strongest team in a province where hurling had been confined to relatively small areas in both counties.

This was, however, a very significant game in terms of the spread and the strength of hurling in Ulster. Antrim had always been the dominant side in the province because of the long tradition of the game over the centuries in certain of the glens in the north-eastern part of the county. They were being seriously challenged by a Down side drawn from three teams from the end of the Ards peninsula, a small hurling territory embracing Portaferry, Ballygalget and Ballycran and surrounded by sea, with Strangford Lough to the west and the North Channel to the east.

The Down men would have been the first to say that their progress and determination in senior hurling had been inspired by the way Antrim had pushed their way onto the national hurling scene over the previous five years.

Antrim Hurling Tradition

There had been versions of hurling played in Antrim for centuries. Since early Celtic times, when Antrim was part of the kingdom of Dalriada, there were close links across the sea of Moyle with fellow Celts in Scotland. In both parts a game played with wooden ball and bent sticks has been known. It was played by people in the Glens usually on the strands and flat green lands along the coastal strip. The game, an older version of the shinty now played in Scotland, was not confined to the Glens but also played as far south as Carrickfergus, where there was an annual game being played on the strand each Christmas Day in the 1830s.

Shinty was played beside Cushendall beach on Christmas Day up until the early part of the 1900s. The most famous hurling match under GAA rules was played on the strand at Red Bay, in Glenariff in 1904 as part of Feis na nGleann. The game was between Carey Faughs and Glanarm Shauns with Roger Casement as one of the umpires. The superb 'Shield of the Heroes' which Carey won that day now hangs in the team's local hall near Ballycastle.

Teams from Cushendall, Cushendun, Glenariff, Loughgile, Dunloy and Armoy began to compete under GAA rules and a county championship as well as regular challenge games ensured the strengthening of the modern hurling tradition in the area as well as in the nationalist areas of Belfast.

The Antrim County Board was founded in 1901 with Laurence O'Neill as chairman and Bulmer Hobson, one of the stalwarts of the independence movement, as secretary. Belfast clubs began to play in the county championship and a tradition of great rivalry developed among the city clubs and between the city and country teams.

Antrim suffered badly from lack of competition with the strong hurling areas. Their only opposition in Ulster was from Down and Donegal. They were usually trounced whenever they met teams from Cork, Kilkenny or Tipperary even at junior level. These beatings at national level did nothing to diminish the love of the game in the county nor the determination to strengthen it.

In the 1940s, during the bleak and deprived years of the war, the county hurling team made a breakthrough. In the quarter-final they beat Galway at Corrigan Park, Belfast. The next game was the semi-final against a Kilkenny side that had many All-Ireland stars — players like Jack Mulcahy, Jimmy Langton, Terry Leahy and Paddy Grace. Perhaps it was knowing they had nothing to lose the team opened their shoulders and hurled with abandon.

Despite desperate efforts by Kilkenny to retrieve the game Antrim ran out winners on a scoreline of 3–3 to 1–6. A star of that Antrim victory was the most famous GAA star the county had produced up to then — Kevin Armstrong from the now-defunct Belfast city side, O'Connell's.

It was an unusual pairing in the All-Ireland final of 1943 — Cork , the reigning champions of the previous two years against a team of unknowns from one of the 'weaker' counties. It turned out to be a nightmare for the newcomers. Despite the travel difficulties a crowd of almost 49,000 turned up. Several of the Antrim men who had played with such freedom of movement in the two qualifying games seemed to freeze on the big occasion.

'We were far better than the scoreline of 5–16 to 0–4 might suggest', said Kevin Armstrong, recalling the one-sided match many years later. 'But Cork were a super side, one of the best ever to play for the county — after all they went on to win another All-Ireland the following year to make it four-in-a-row', he said.

Resurgence of the '80s

One of the factors which propelled Antrim on to the senior championship stage at the start of the '80s was the emergence of strong teams from the western side of Belfast city. From the endless labyrinth of houses in the Andersonstown area, with a population of some 80,000, emerged teams like O'Donovan Rossa, St John's and St Paul's. There developed a keen rivalry between these teams from neighbouring areas in the crowded streets in the shadow of Cave Hill. They took on the teams from the Glens in games of fierce intensity. Some of the county championship matches were rough and tough and those who endured and survived were hardened battlers, not afraid to take the leap into the All-Ireland club series.

Ballycastle reached the final of 1980 to be beaten by Castlegar of Galway at the end of a great game of hurling. Two years later Loughiel Shamrocks captured the club title when they beat the leading Offaly club, St Rynagh's.

There was a feeling abroad that Antrim was growing in skill and in strength and would no longer be ritually dismissed in games by ridiculous scorelines.

In 1986 Antrim gave Cork a hard game in the semi-final, losing by five points to the side that went on to win the All-Ireland. The following year Antrim met Kilkenny in the semi-final. The venue was a setting unusual for hurling — the Dowdallshill pitch at Dundalk, with the legendary Slieve Gullion and the brooding mountains of the Cooley peninsula as backdrop.

'It was a new, strange venue for us', said John Henderson, the Johnstown Fenians player who was one of the linchpins of the Kilkenny side. 'We did not know much about Antrim either. We were taken aback by their power and determination and their level of skill', he recalls.

The scores were tied at 2–11 each with seven minutes to go and many in the crowd sensed that a sensational result might be in the offing. Then the Noresiders clicked into gear, with Harry Ryan spearheading the attack, and finished with a scoreline of 2–18 to 2–11.

Two years in the first division of the league seasoned the team and in August 1989 they met Offaly in the first of the All-Ireland semi-finals before a crowd of 64,127 at Croke Park.

Offaly had players who had won All-Ireland medals in 1981 and 1985. The county had contested every Leinster final since they first won the provincial title in 1980. They were firm favourites. But in one of the great upsets of the decade Antrim powered to a three-goal win to the thunderous applause of the many hurling lovers who loved to see the underdog come out on top.

The northerners brought great colour and zest to the All-Ireland final against Tipperary. In the first twenty minutes they missed the kind of vital scores, some of them easy points, that any team needs to give it a boost and get it going in a tense encounter. In the second half, when Tipperary got the scores that enabled them to open their shoulders, the game gradually went away from Antrim. Tipperary won their first All-Ireland since 1971 on a scoreline of 4–24 to 3–9.

'Game-cuteness is what Antrim lack. They have just about everything else at this stage', was a comment now heard regularly.

The following year Antrim went under to Cork in the semi-final, having stayed with the Munster champions for three-quarters of the game but they had not the hurling guile and match experience of the Cork side. However one of the best goals seen in Croke Park for a long time was scored in the second half by Ciaran Barr. He caught the dropping ball and went thundering through down the middle, shouldering aside several challenges. Then, from 25 metres out he swung powerfully on the ball while running at full speed. Even a goalkeeper of the calibre of Ger Cunningham could not stop this 100-mile-an-hour bullet.

Now, in 1991, the Antrim side retained their Ulster title with a polished display against Down. They went on to beat Westmeath by an impressive 18 points in the quarter and qualified to meet Kilkenny in the semi-final.

Kilkenny Prepared

Meanwhile Kilkenny had recovered from their injury-time escape against Wexford and beat Dublin in the provincial final. It was only to be expected that they found themselves firm favourites going into the semi-final against Antrim. Yet the players themselves were well aware of the quality of their opponents.

'We were well prepared for Antrim. We did not take them lightly. Most of us had played against them in 1987 and knew how tough they were likely to be', said John Henderson, who was to wear the number 3 jersey that day. 'They were no longer a team of no-hopers. But they were coming into the game as total outsiders and the media gave them little chance. You just can't ignore the media and a feeling creeps into your mind that you are expected to win. This can put pressure on you. On the other hand it can induce a feeling of inferiority in the other team.'

Kilkenny were favourites with most hurling followers because in the league they had played well and reached the final as well as showing a great Kilkenny tradition in being able to win games in the last vital five minutes of closely-fought encounters.

Michael Walsh in goal was sharp and alert. He never took his eye off the ball and he had extremely good footwork around the goal area. He had made some vital saves in the previous two games. He was sound without any of the entertaining flamboyance of his father, Ollie, who had been a goalkeeping legend twenty five years before.

Right corner back was Eddie O'Connor of Glenmore, a small, light player whose greatest attribute was the speed that allowed him to get to the incoming ball before his opponent and a sure first touch to get the ball under control and clear it.

Full back was one of the most experienced, battle hardened of the Kilkenny side, John Henderson. He was tall and lithe and had a great pair of hands. Over the years he had developed a great capacity to flick the ball off an opponent's hurley, tip it deftly away, wielding his light hurley like a magician's wand.

Liam Simpson was a big strong player who tackled hard for possession and stopped his opponent scoring. He could shoulder forwards out of the way and get in long clearances down the field, as he had done very effectively during the year.

The three full backs had developed a good understanding among themselves and with the goalkeeper.

The outer line of defence was manned by three very sound players Liam Walsh on the right, Pat Dwyer in the centre and Bill Hennessy on the left. Walsh was a very experienced and accomplished player who won an under-21 medal in 1984 and played in the All-Irelands of 1987 and '91. His career had been dogged by injury but he was now back to himself.

In the centre was a tall, bone-hard farmer from Carrickshock, Pat Dwyer. He had a great sense of positional play and could strike the ball rapidly, left or right, close to his body so that he was hard to hook. He was fast and nippy for a centre back. On the other wing was the first player from the famous Tullaroan club to hold down a permanent place on the county team since Sean Clohosey retired in 1963, Bill Hennessy. He was a reliable player who marked his man very closely and had a good positional sense.

At centrefield Kilkenny had two very good performers in Richie Power and Michael Phelan. Power was the veteran of the side at 36. He had two All-Ireland medals and had played in two other finals. He was renowned for his dedication to the game. The Carrickshock man was very athletic, could run all during a game, played in a very vigorous inspirational way that aroused his colleagues and the Kilkenny followers. Beside him was a man 13 years his junior, one of the emergent strong players from the Glenmore club. He was muscular enough to make room for himself in the close exchanges, to get free for a good stroke of the ball left or right.

Right half forward was the star of the Leinster final, the versatile Adrian Ronan who had actually come on as a sub in the Wexford game to take over in goals from the injured Micheal Walsh. He had All-Ireland minor and under-21 medals, had a very good first touch on the ball and an aggressive style of forward play. In the centre was the fair-haired, lithe John Power. He played with endless energy and vigour, always foraging for the ball and able to tear away with speed when he got it.

On the other side was one of the most talented forwards in the game, D.J. Carey. He looked deceptively light and even frail but he could turn on a six-pence and was one of the speediest players about. Most of all he had great skill, could control the ball unerringly, hit it left or right to land on the nose of a colleague or into a corner of the goal. Carey gave the lie to those who said that you had to be big and strong and wield a heavy hurley if you were going to hit the ball really hard. The slim Carey had a fine wristy swing, he hit the ball with the dead centre of the hurley and it shot away at speed.

In the right corner was one of the most forceful and skilled of the Kilkenny forwards, Eamon Morrissey. Solidly built, he was very fast from a standing start, could run with the ball and he had a neat, controlled way of slotting the ball over the bar from narrow angles.

Full forward and captain of the team was one of the gentle giants of the game, Christy Heffernan of Glenmore. An All-Ireland winner in '82 and '83 he was great to catch a high ball and he had a powerful overhead pull which had resulted in some spectacular goals in his long career. The most unselfish of players, he attracted the hard attentions of backs and then was big enough and weighty enough to make room for a neat pass to an unmarked colleague. In the other corner was a stocky workhorse from Piltown, Liam McCarthy. He was a player of quiet skills who was very hard to knock off the ball and backs got few clean clearances when he was about. His career had been plagued by injuries, sometimes incurred by the courageous way he went for the ball, but he had persisted and was now back on the side.

This was the Kilkenny side, full of Croke Park experience, full of winners of medals in various grades — colleges, club, minor and under-21 as well as those who had won in '82 and '83 and played in the final of 1987. It was little wonder that they were installed as firm favourites.

Antrim Players

The Antrim side were of a different background. Many were virtually unknown on the hurling scene. This was to be goalkeeper Patrick Gallagher's first experience of the big occasion. But he had the jaunty self-confidence that every goalkeeper needs. Both Gary O'Kane at right corner back and Ger Rogan in the other corner were ball-playing sticksmen rather than the kind of tough tight-markers that might give away easy frees. O'Kane had played in the '89 final, on Nicholas English, but he was still, at 23 one of the youngest on the side. Rogan was essentially untested for the kind of concentration needed from start to finish for a game at this level.

In the centre was Dominic McKinley, reminiscent of the old-time hard pulling full back. His job was to match Christy Heffernan, pound for pound, to prevent him getting any kind of a clean stroke at the ball or catching it with his hand. He had the strength and the weight to do it.

One of Declan McKillop's hurling attributes was fair but robust tackling. He was strong and hardy. Nobody expected the right half back to quite match for speed the man he would be marking, D.J. Carey, but the Kilkenny man might find himself being shouldered off the ball when it came between them.

The centre back was the resilient and greatly experienced James McNaughton of Cushendall. He had come back onto the team after a serious knee injury and had not regained all his speed but he was a solid hurler, had a very good ground stroke, left or right. On the left was Paul Jennings, another newcomer to the team and the big event. He had played minor for Antrim and then gone to Chicago. When he returned several years later he honed his skills and worked diligently at getting physically fit. The other players were impressed with this returnee and his determined approach to the game.

Paul McKillen would have the very difficult task of marking the ever-moving Richie Power. He himself was one of the fittest men on the side, with great stamina, who covered acres of ground during games. He was not a spectacular kind of player but he would be able to keep in step with his opponent. His partner was one of the big strong men of the side, a man with an indomitable will to win the ball and well able to hit it left or right, Terence McNaughton. When he was at the peak of fitness he was very hard to subdue.

Right half forward was John Carson, another player getting his first taste of playing before 60,000 people. He had been given the key task of taking frees. He had performed that task calmly and with quiet efficiency in the Ulster final. There was no doubting his skill but he could not expect to get any easy ball in the game about to begin.

In the centre was Ciaran Barr who would be picked on any senior county team in the championship. He was the first Antrim player to be picked by the Bank of Ireland All-Star panel in 1988. Big and strong and courageous, this man was extremely hard to beat for the ball, was a fine reader of the game, had an intelligent approach to all that he did and was the kind of inspirational player that all teams need. On his left was the stocky, nippy son of Kevin Armstrong. From the O'Donovan Rossa club, Donal Armstrong played a lot of football and had good footwork to swerve and side-step past an opponent.

Right corner forward was Dessie Donnelly, who was a strong, bustling player. He held the hurley in the unorthodox grip but he had one of the hardest strokes on the Antrim team. At full forward was a man who normally played at centre-forward, Aidan McCarry. He was a strong runner. He pulled on the ball much of the time and was very dangerous with ground balls within goal range.

Jim Close, the left corner forward, was very fast. Like Armstrong, he had football-derived skills, jinking and dodging when in possession. This was his first game in the intimidating atmosphere of Croke Park on semi-final day.

People were still streaming into Croke Park as the teams pucked about and limbered up. The Galway v. Tipperary game, the second on the bill, was considered the real match of the afternoon. In reality it turned out to be a dour, dull game which Tipperary won with some ease near the end.

The referee, Willie Horgan of Cork, called the captains together for the toss. Kilkenny won and chose to play against the breeze which blew from the Canal end.

A huge contingent of Antrim followers peopled the stands and terraces, waving flags, shouting words of encouragement in sharp, combative northern accents as the referee looked at his watch. The Kilkenny colours were not anything as visible and the *Kilkenny People* was to take the followers to task for not supporting the team. The feeling among many followers was not alone that their side was going to win but that it was unlikely to be a good game to watch.

The teams as they lined out were:

KILKENNY

Michael Walsh
(Dicksboro)

Eddie O'Connor	John Henderson	Liam Simpson
(Glenmore)	(Fenians)	(Bennettsbridge)

Liam Walsh	Pat Dwyer	Bill Hennessy
(Glenmore)	(Carrickshock)	(Tullaroan)

Richie Power	Michael Phelan
(Carrickshock)	(Glenmore)

Adrian Ronan	John Power	D.J. Carey
(Graigue-Ballycallan)	(John Locke's)	(Young Ireland's)

Eamon Morrissey	Christy Heffernan, capt	Liam McCarthy
(St Martin's)	(Glenmore)	(Piltown)

Substitutes: Patsy Brophy (Erin's Own); Liam Fennelly (Shamrocks); Tommy Fogarty (James Stephens); Pat Ryan (Emeralds); Tom Murphy (Mooncoin); Ray Heffernan (Glenmore); Lester Ryan (Clara); Michael Cleere (O'Loughlin Gaels); Jamsie Brennan (Erin's Own). *Coach*: Ollie Walsh. *Trainer*: Mick O'Flynn. *Selectors*: Nicky Brennan (Conahy); Wattie Long (Glenmore); Ger Henderson (Fenians); Gerry Nolan (Clara). *Team doctor*: Dr Bill Cuddihy. *Physiotherapist*: Sean Kelly.

ANTRIM

Patrick Gallagher
(St John's)

Gary O'Kane	Dominic McKinley, capt	Ger Rogan
(Cuchulains, Dunloy)	(Loughgiel Shamrocks)	(O'Donovan Rossa)

Declan McKillop	James McNaughton	Paul Jennings
(Loughgiel Shamrocks)	(Ruairi Og, Cushendall)	(Ballycastle)

Paul McKillen	Terence McNaughton
(Ballycastle)	(Cushendall)

John Carson	Ciaran Barr	Donal Armstrong
(Cushendall)	(St Vincent's Dublin)	(O'Donovan Rossa)

Des Donnelly	Aidan McCarry	Jim Close
(Ballycastle)	(Loughgiel)	(O'Donovan Rossa)

Substitutes: Niall Patterson (Loughgiel Shamrocks); Michael Dennis (Carey Faughs, Belfast); Sean McKillop (Loughgiel Shamrocks); Gregory O'Kane (Cuchulains, Dunloy); Allister McGuile (Ruairi Og); Danny McKinley (Loughgiel Shamrocks); Fergal Collins (St John's); Ronan Heenan (St John's); Brendan McGibbon (St John's). *Manager/coach*: Jim Nelson. *Team assistant*: Henry McCabe. *Mentors*: Brendan McGarry; John Crossey. *Team physician*: Dr Alasdair McDonnell. *Physiotherapist*: Dan Turley. *Secretary of hurling board*: Anthony Mulvenna.

The referee was Willie Horgan of Cork.

Stunning Goal

This prediction of a one-sided match seemed ominously true within 24 seconds of the ball being thrown in. There was a fierce flurry of hurleys at midfield as the four players tusseled to take the initiative. The ball shot out into the Kilkenny half but the alert Liam Walsh raced to it and sent a long ball towards the left of his own half forward line on the Cusack stand side of the field.

Suddenly Eamon Morrissey erupted out of his right corner, leaving Ger Rogan in his wake, gathered the ball with his first touch and raced goal-wards. The Antrim backs were taken aback by this sudden attack. As Morrissey neared the goal the saffron shirts converged on him. He then had the choice of passing the ball into the unmarked Liam McCarthy in front of goal or trying for a score himself. Antrim hurleys were glued to his own just in front of goal but he managed to drop the ball onto his swinging boot and sent it into the net. Gallagher had no chance to save it.

This brought a cheer of delight from the small Kilkenny contingent. The big northern following was voiceless with dismay at such a disastrous start on such a big occasion before a crowd of over 60,000. Many spectators, waiting for the second game, were afraid Antrim would crumble and that a dreary one-sided affair might be in the offing.

Antrim Respond

From the very puck out it became apparent that Antrim had no intention of succumbing to the apparent superiority of the men in black and amber. They tore into the game with vigour. They used their weight and physique to advantage. More than anything else they hurled with great style, keeping the ball on the ground, pulling on it first time to prevent the Kilkenny players getting it into their hands, sending it on towards colleagues with admirable accuracy. All the spectators, including the hurling fans from Kilkenny, loved to see this entertaining, rousing style of play and each time an Antrim player sent the ball forward it was accompanied by a great roar from the huge crowd.

Antrim went on several attacks, looking dangerous and vigorous. From one of these a free resulted. The calm John Carson, who had been sending frees over the bar with aplomb in the league and the two previous championship games, took it and put it between the uprights.

The midfield battle for supremacy was under way. Two weighty men, Phelan and McNaughton, crashed into one another often but the bald headed Antrim man had a capacity to grab the ball out of nowhere and send long balls into the forwards. Barr won the first clash between himself and Dwyer and was to give the Carrickshock farmer a hard outing that day. But Dwyer raised a cheer when he trotted over to take an 80-metre free. He had a quick sharp way of striking the ball and, even against the breeze, it went over the bar. This is the kind of score that every team needs to take and more importantly have players capable of doing so.

Kilkenny needed this kind of indication of capability because now Antrim began to dominate the game. They were winning many of the man-to-man battles, so evident in the wide open spaces of Croke Park. Most of the northerners were not easily knocked off the ball and some of them seemed to be winning the physical challenges easily. There were races for the ball which were effectively ended with a stout Antrim shoulder knocking the man in black and amber to one side.

The midfielder McKillen, who was doing very well against the more experienced Power, caught hold of a ball, twisted about with great style and sent over a great point from far out. Not long afterwards Antrim were given a sideline cut from 40 yards out. McNaughton, now the most visible player on the field, came over to take it. A big strong man, he thunked his hurley under the ball and sent it soaring between the uprights, to the delight of the spectators.

It was now clear that Antrim were on top at centre back and centre forward and that John Henderson had his deft hands full with Aidan McCarry. In the tenth minute the Antrim full forward clipped over a point to put his side into the lead — a most unexpected turn of events for many onlookers.

The flow of play was mostly one way, with Declan McKillop and Paul Jennings curbing D.J. Carey and Adrian Ronan and very little good ball going into the Kilkenny forward line. But plenty of low dangerous ball was being whipped into the Kilkenny goal area. In one of these lightning raids McCarry pulled hard on the ball and it went acrosss the goal and barely wide. Only a few seconds later Barr sent in another low fast ball and McCarry whipped it goalwards. Michael Walsh made a great save at this vital time. There was a murmur of disappointment from the Antrim supporters — their team needed to convert supremacy into scores.

This happened a minute later. Dessie Donnelly chased a ball out the left of the goal, almost on the end line, lifted it and turning about to his strong right side, belted a rocket that sped across the goalmouth — the kind of shot that goalkeepers hate — and hit the netting on the far side.

An exultant roar went up, not only from the Antrim followers but from the many who loved to see the spirit and resolve of the underdogs being rewarded on the scoreboard.

Hanging On

At this stage Kilkenny were hanging on for dear life. Richie Power managed to send a few balls goalward but most of the time they were cleared out with great efficiency. McKinley, the Antrim full back and captain, was gaining the upper hand over Christy Heffernan and was dominant in front of goal.

In this period Kilkenny had to largely rely on the odd free for scores. Some of the vigorous Antrim tackles, wearing for those receiving them, were deemed to be fouls by the referee. Carey, getting so little out of play, was deadly accurate with these frees. He always approached each free with the utmost care, stood over the ball, lined his stance with the uprights. He placed his left hand well down the hurley, in the manner of Eddie Keher, and lifted the ball with great precision and control. He always took a full swing and hit the ball on the up, with great power. It was his accurate free taking that kept the score a respectable 1–10 to 1–6 in favour of Antrim at half time.

Even the two fine corner men, Morrissey and McCarthy, had had to live off scraps. But they both had dangerous touches about them and much was expected of them after the change of ends.

Liam Walsh, plagued by injury for so much of his career, was having a very sound game on the wing and were it not for his efforts Antrim might have been even more dominant. He was suffering great pain from all his old injuries and had to push himself to keep going and it was remarkable that he played so well. Few spectators realised this; one voice was heard to roar loudly on one occasion when the tearaway Donal Armstrong got the better of him, 'Come on Walsh, get the lead out.'

Henderson Goes Off

Another injury-plagued man, the veteran Henderson aggravated an old hamstring injury in his efforts to keep the shackles on his man. There was no alternative but to go off. His departure resulted in some confusion in the Kilkenny back line; he was one of these highly effective but visually unobtrusive players whose contribution is often under-rated.

Henderson now had to undergo another form of stress and aggravation — watching his team under severe pressure from the sideline but not being able to play his part, despite all the training and effort he had made. Patsy Brophy of Erin's Own went on in his stead.

'We were dying for the half-time whistle to blow, to give the team time to draw breath', said Henderson, an astute reader of the balance of a game. 'Half-time can change the trend of a game — and if the flow of a game is against you, then, you are holding out for all you are worth waiting for the clock to help you', he said.

Half-Time

When that whistle came there was a great cheer of applause for both teams but most especially the northerners. There was some unease among their followers. To be so dominant in one half and yet to only be four points ahead did not make for ease of mind.

'A great contest, with the ball flying from end to end, is more than a spectacle or a form of entertainment', said Ciaran Barr, discussing this game in retrospect some years later. 'It strikes chords in people. They identify with great effort, with courage, even with disappointment. They are roused by the fiece competitiveness, the rivalry. They revel in the man-to-man clashes.

'Spectators can throw their whole beings into a game like this, be touched deeply by it. They can be ecstatic after it, adulatory of players. But they can be bitterly disappointed and very critical of players whom they think have let them down', he says.

At half time in the dressing-rooms the rival managers and mentors were taking stock while the players, chests heaving, nursed wounds or retied their bootlaces.

Advice from Coaches

Ollie Walsh knew that his men must get back into the game, get into some kind of rhythm, break the dominant pattern which had been established by the opposition.

Jim Nelson's injunction to his men was to continue the pattern of control — but to make more of it in terms of scores. No use being on top if you are not getting the scores, he said. He knew also that no team in a real championship encounter can maintain control all the time. The rhythm of a game changes as some players tire or get injured or other players begin to flower, to regain lost confidence and lost initiative.

The teams came out for the second half with the huge attendance fascinated at the prospect of the battle of skill, will and tactics ahead. Nobody now imagined that either of these sides was going to give in without a mighty battle. There was a feeling that an upset might be on the cards.

When the ball was thrown in this feeling was strengthened as Antrim resumed control. Kilkenny had to concede another free when the northerners attacked and once again Carson sent it over the bar. Not long afterwards Ciaran Barr, playing one of the best games of his career, got free of Pat Dwyer to send over a superbly graceful point. Rogan and O'Kane in the corners were still keeping a good watch on McCarthy and Morrissey, who were not getting the kind of good low ball that they needed.

Astute Move

It was at this point that Liam Fennelly went in as substitute for Adrian Ronan, who had found it difficult to make headway against a rampant Paul Jennings. The Shamrocks man went in at full forward while Heffernan went out to the left corner where he fared a bit better.

This was one of the most astute moves made by Ollie Walsh. Heffernan had stayed on the edge of the square, hoping to win the odd high ball coming in or to lay off ground balls to his corner men. This did not happen because McKinley was faster to the ball and cleared it out the field with increasing confidence.

Fennelly was a different kind of player. He was a thin, quick-silver man who darted here and there, had a great first touch and great ball control and could whip the ball fast off the ground, left or right, in front of the goal.

His effect on the game was soon apparent. He broke up the play in front of the goal and left big spaces there as McKinley tried to keep step with him as he raced in and out, back and forward.

Yet the reality was that for twenty minutes of the second half Antrim were in control. They were six points up soon after the restart. And on the odd occasions when Kilkenny went for goals they found Gallagher in inspired mood.

The Time to Win

'This was when we should have put Kilkenny away. We were six points ahead at one stage and we could and should have been twelve. We had this momentum going for us and it should have been reflected on the scoreboard. As often happens with any team in a hard championship game, we lost the momentum, lost control', says Barr. 'There can be all kinds of reasons — guys are playing out of their skins and then they get tired or they take a blow which knocks them back. Or they find themselves up against a different kind of opponent whom they can't handle.'

One change that Kilkenny made that had some significance on the outcome was the switch between John Power and Michael Phelan. The John Locke's man gave his namesake Richie Power strong support and though McKillen and especially McNaughton continued to play well, their grip on the centre was weakened. More ball began to flow in to the hitherto frustrated Kilkenny forwards and Carey sent a free over the bar.

Yet Antrim were still going well and the score went to 1–13 to 1–7 when Jim Close, who had a hard time getting away from Eddie O'Connor, managed to boot the ball over the bar after a run in from the corner.

Richie Power won a good ball at midfield and sent a hard low shot straight into the path of the red-helmeted Morrissey who sent it straight over the bar. Shortly afterwards, with Kilkenny followers cheering as they saw their men getting into the game, the tousle-haired John Power got the ball from the puck out. He passed it out to Carey, who had managed to elude his tenacious marker, Declan McKillop. Carey was 70 yards from the Antrim goal but he hit a marvellous point which lifted his own side's morale. All was not lost while Kilkenny could score such long-distance points.

Now there were four points between the sides, with Kilkenny on the upsurge and Antrim having to try very hard to defend their lead. Morrissey was coming into his own at this stage, racing out on sturdy legs, side-stepping neatly, controlling the ball well, hitting it neatly and accurately. He now scored a point. Such scores were keeping Kilkenny in the game. Then Liam McCarthy scored another to leave only two points between the sides: 1–13 to 1–11.

Many spectators now expected Kilkenny to take full control. Instead, Antrim battled back. Aidan McCarry scored another fine point. The crowd cheered whenever McNaughton challenged for the ball. He invariably won it, using his weight, adept at grabbing it from under an opponent's nose. He risked hands and head with great courage and took a few hard belts. But it did not stop him getting within range and sending over a point which put the northerners four points up.

Morrissey kept up the effort and gathering a ball sent in a very hard shot goalwards. It was blocked out by Patrick Gallagher, who was keeping a very good goal. Not long after that he stopped another rasper from Heffernan. The play was flowing from end to end as the two teams fought for supremacy. Liam McCarthy got his third point of the game and McCarry scored for Antrim.

Once again Morrissey inspired his side when he raced onto a ball and sent it over from near the sideline. Several of his scores that day were real morale boosters, hit with great skill and style from difficult angles with his opponent Rogan breathing down his neck.

Although quite clearly Kilkenny were now beginning to get on top they had two chances of points, one from long distance by Pat Dwyer and a closer effort from Liam McCarthy which went narrowly wide. These were agonising misses for the Kilkenny followers and some of them felt that the game was lost. There was now only nine minutes to go and the Antrim team was holding out grimly, with James McNaughton, Jennings and McKillop doing their utmost to stop good balls going into the full forward line.

Crucial Score

Then came the most crucial score of the game. Liam Walsh, who was battling it out with Donal Armstrong for every ball and every half ball that came near them, sent a long hard shot flying towards the Antrim goal. Liam Fennelly, reading the play very well as he moved in and out, over and across, managed to get hold of it. With Antrim backs shouldering him he was able to get a neat, carefully weighted pass out to the unmarked Heffernan. The big man went running through with the ball on his hurley. His low drive was stopped by Gallagher. But a powerful shot like this was not easy to control. The ball actually hit the handle of the hurley he was holding across his chest and shot into the air. As it came down, right on the goal line, Eamon Morrissey's red helmet was to the fore as he deftly tipped the descending ball into the net.

The small Kilkenny contingent roared with delight as the numbers on the scoreboard turned to read Kilkenny 2–13 ; Antrim 1–16. The teams were level. Now the Noresiders very definitely took the initiative. Kilkenny had been chasing for 48 minutes since losing the lead to Des Donnelly's goal. The northerners' dominance was over.

Within 60 seconds Kilkenny had gone ahead. When the ball came towards the Antrim goal Fennelly won it again. He left his marker behind and there was a possibility of a clinching goal but the Ballyhale player took the sound option and sent over a point.

Now it was all Kilkenny. They swept down the field again and forced a 65. The unerring D.J. Carey bent carefully over the ball, rose it well and hit it hard to send it over the bar. Most of the spectators in the 61,000 crowd thought Antrim were finished with only a few minutes to go.

Key Incidents

'There are always small incidents that seem like nothing to spectators but which are crucial in terms of raising spirits and injecting encouragement into a team under pressure', recalls Ciaran Barr. 'I got the ball and decided to run with it. When a back came out to meet me I passed it to Donal Armstrong. I kept on running and he passed it back to me. I had time to steady up but I hit it on the run. After all that effort the ball went about two yards wide of the left upright.

'This kind of wasted energy can be a bit deflating. I knew that I should have struck it first time without passing it to Donal or he should have gone for a point or I should have slowed down to give me a better chance', he said.

He recalled another similar incident from play which can help change the complexion of a game, give a boost to the opposition and take something from the morale of one's own team.

'This was a relatively small moment in a game full of incident. When we were under pressure in the last quarter, Terence McNaughton, who was the star of our side that day and playing marvellously well, tried to lift and strike in one movement. He could have picked it and carried it, although he was under severe harassment. Eamon Morrissey came and blocked down his stroke, gathered the ball and scored a great point at a crucial time in the game', he said.

For all that, Antrim were far from finished. They attacked and a Kilkenny back gave away a free. John Carson, cool under the great pressure, with noise of the crowd so great that none of the players could hear the calls of their colleagues, lifted the ball and sent it over the bar. Then McNaughton, who had hurled his heart out from the throw in, got the ball in his large hand and sent over a mighty point to level the scores.

This is when the great determination and resourcefulness of Kilkenny came to the fore. It was the character, the self-belief that ensured they were going to put their all into a game-winning last effort.

Kilkenny Experience

'We never panicked. We were too experienced for that', said John Henderson, who watched from the dug-out the great struggle from which his injury excluded him. 'Some of our scores were inspirational for the whole team, especially the one struck from under the Cusack stand by Eamon Morrissey. When we drew level and went ahead this put pressure on Antrim — the prospect of defeat was before them. It must have affected their game, no matter how hard they tried to shut it out of their minds. In the last minutes our experience and skill gave us the advantage. I believe that if the game had gone on another ten minutes we would have gone further ahead', he says.

The 35 minutes were almost up when Kilkenny were awarded a sideline cut. Carey came up to take it. Under pressure to send it far towards the Antrim goal, he mis-hit it. Heffernan, however, ran across and sent a beautiful pass to Morrissey, who had an uncanny ability to run into the open spaces. The Muckalee man struck a lovely point to a resounding cheer.

The Antrim players shouted encouragement to one another and positioned themselves as Michael Walsh ran forward to take the puck out. It was nearly half a minute after full time. There might have been time to strike over a point and make it the draw that most spectators thought the northerners deserved.

Carey had also run into the centrefield area as the ball dropped to fierce overhead pulling and great jostling. He read the play very well, was in position to get the ball. It was over 80 metres from the Antrim goal and several shoulders lunged at him but he struck the ball beautifully. It took off and soared and soared until it only began to drop as it went between the uprights. As the reporter from the *Kilkenny People* wrote: this 'knocked the last breath out of brave, sporting and deadly dangerous opponents'. He also went on to remark that 'Houdini's spirit embraces the black and amber', after yet another last minute escape. The referee's whistle sounded.

After all this escapism Kilkenny were seen as outsiders in the All-Ireland final against traditional opponents Tipperary in the final. The Munster side had played in two of the greatest hurling matches of the decade — a draw and replay against Cork in the Munster final. Yet Kilkenny answered their detractors by playing with great grit and skill in a close-marking game where every score was hard earned.

They were in the match with a 50/50 chance until the Tipperary marksman, Michael Cleary, stood over the ball to send a free over the bar from about 35 yards out well into the neck and neck second half. He mis-hit it. The ball flew towards the goal only a hurley length over head height. A back, in an automatic reaction, raised his hurley and the ball deflected off it into the net.

There was a certain irony and indeed, as some said, a certain poetic justice that the great escapees should in the end be beaten by such a score. But this team proved its mettle by again fighting its way out of Leinster in 1992 and then confounding all the commentators by beating the hot favourites Cork with great style and vigour.

As for Antrim, everybody expected them to return to the fray the following year and make another bold attempt to take the top honours. But all the signs had been there that Down were each year creeping up in terms of skill and experience. Still it was a surprise for most that Antrim were beaten. From now on it seemed that an almost automatic emergence from the northern province was at an end.

'Victory in sport is not always reflected in the scoreline', says Ciaran Barr reflectively. 'It can be a victory just to get to a final or semi-final and to play well in it. It may take a few more years before Antrim wins an All-Ireland. A few years and a lot of work, especially at minor level. I believe that the appearance of Antrim in the second half of the 1980s and into the 1990s has laid the foundations for future victories. In retrospect it will be seen as significant', he concluded.

INDEX

(p) indicates that the subject appears in a photograph in this book.